T0195855

Fifth World Medicine

A Spiritual-Physical Journey to the Next World

BOOK I

Dr. John C. Hughes

BALBOA.PRESS
A DIVISION OF HAY HOUSE

Balboa Press books may be ordered through booksellers or by contacting:

Balboa Press
A Division of Hay House
1663 Liberty Drive
Bloomington, IN 47403
www.balboapress.com
844-682-1282

Because of the dynamic nature of the Internet, any web addresses or links contained in this book may have changed since publication and may no longer be valid. The views expressed in this work are solely those of the author and do not necessarily reflect the views of the publisher, and the publisher hereby disclaims any responsibility for them.

The author of this book does not dispense medical advice or prescribe the use of any technique as a form of treatment for physical, emotional, or medical problems without the advice of a physician, either directly or indirectly. The intent of the author is only to offer information of a general nature to help you in your quest for emotional and spiritual well-being. In the event you use any of the information in this book for yourself, which is your constitutional right, the author and the publisher assume no responsibility for your actions.

Print information available on the last page.

ISBN: 979-8-7652-2832-6 (sc)
ISBN: 979-8-7652-2833-3 (hc)
ISBN: 979-8-7652-2831-9 (e)

Library of Congress Control Number: 2022908330

Balboa Press rev. date: 10/07/2022

I am deeply enjoying *Fifth World Medicine*.... As I am reading, rabbit holes appear and lead me into other interesting areas. The book lends itself well to almost a daily meditation, where after a chapter, the desire to digest and explore the concepts overcomes the temptation to rush onwards. In particular, engaging me with the physical world... It's beautiful.

Ben Germann, RN

Fifth World Medicine is a highly thought-provoking, enlightening and powerful book that forces readers to step outside of their narrow "Fourth World" thinking to begin dreaming of a world where dreams can actually thrive. I will be happily recommending this book to all of my family, friends and colleagues, as "The Book They Must Read in 2022!"

Arlene Seegerts

Grandmother, Teacher and Author *of THE FOUR COMMITMENTS FOR TEENAGERS: How to Create & Live the Life of Your Dreams - GUARANTEED!*

In his brilliant book, *Fifth World Medicine,* Dr. John C. Hughes invites us to prepare to enter the world-healing, transformational experience of the Fifth World. Dr. Hughes qualifies himself as our ideal spiritual mentor and guide by sharing his many-layered journey to healing and wisdom. He invites us to examine and prepare ourselves for embarking on and living the sacred path to peace and love in his next book, *Fifth World Medicine: The Science of Healing People and Their Planet. Fifth World Medicine Books I and II* are extraordinary and timely guidebooks for all who hunger for wholeness, yearn to be one with the Divine and are committed to healing others and our sacred planet.

Martha Susan Horton, Ph.D.
Director, The Amate Institute, Pensacola, Florida
Developer of the Amate Growth Work method for achieving emotional maturity in adulthood.

Author, *The Seashell People: Growing Up in Adulthood* in softcover, *Growing up in Adulthood: The Journey to Emotional Maturity,* M. Evans & Co., Inc. (1990, 1992).

Dr Hughes' book *Fifth World Medicine* is a great vision on the future of medicine and culture. Only by restoring our humanity to the field of medicine and returning to right relation to our larger ecosystem will we be able to heal as a humanity and truly thrive. All healthcare practitioners who share a vision of a sustainable future would do well to listen and consider these deep teachings.

Dan Engle, MD
Author of *A Dose of Hope.* Founder of Full Spectrum Medicine and Thank You Life.

Through his own personal journey, Dr. John Hughes shows us what is possible. In a world full of chaos, he helps us find our authentic truth through conscious awareness. With grounded contemplative practice we can begin to move towards a more natural state of being and start the process of regaining not only our own health but the health of our planet through Fifth World medicine.

Jodie Rooks, RN

Only those
who have learned to live on the land
where the waters run pure
will find sanctuary. ...
You must go to where the Eagles fly,
to where the Wolf roams,
to where the Bear lives.
Here you will find life
because they will always go to where the water is pure
and the air can be breathed.
Live where the trees are old.
They are the lungs of this Earth,
and they purify the air. ...
They can change it by breathing and they give clean air back to you.
Where the snow falls,
you will find protection from the plagues and viruses.
The snow is a great purifier.
Go to where the Mother's blanket heals your body
as well as your emotions,
where she will give you new dreams of the emerging world.
If you learn to live in these places,
you will live through these times. ...

The Fifth World is the one we are about to enter.
In this new world,
we will learn to balance our spiritual and physical natures.[1]

—Prophecy given to Ghost Wolf, a Lakota pipe carrier

CONTENTS

Preface xi

Chapter 1   Hunger Pains.. 1

Chapter 2   Hopi Peaks, Spirits, People, and Messages....................15

Chapter 3   Osteopathic Coyote Medicine................................. 29

Chapter 4   Wolf Medicine 49

Chapter 5   Exodus.. 79

Chapter 6   God, Philosophy, and Medicine................................ 95

Chapter 7   Spirituality and Medicine: Silence Is Power.................. 107

Chapter 8   Love: The Medicine of Enlightenment......................... 129

Chapter 9   Healing Ceremonies: Spiritual–Physical Medicine.........145

Chapter 10   Womb Spaces 155

Chapter 11   A Grand Canyon Vision Quest.................................169

Chapter 12   Sexual Power and Healing 189

Chapter 13   The Vision: A Fifth World.................................... 207

Chapter 14   The Hero's Journey: A Return to Darkness................... 221

Epilogue.. 243

Appendix 245

Notes 261

Index... 285

About the Author 291

PREFACE

"Hunger," or longing for someone or something, can drive us insane or inspire great works of art or acts of valor. Hunger fans the flames of identity, courage, and love in all heroes of ancient and present eras. Hunger inspires the singer to create a first radio hit and the lover to ask for a first date. However, for hunger to transform us, our works, or our planet, one essential element must prevail—an element only a few are bold enough to voluntarily choose.

The essential element behind this transformation is an *open heart to the quest necessary to fulfill our hunger.* If worthwhile, a hunger-inspired quest requires that we open our hearts or fail. Maria Coffey, in her book *Explorers of the Infinite: The Secret Spiritual Lives of Extreme Athletes,* describes the quest as one in which our bodies and souls gain full exposure to this world and beyond. Coffey quotes Sir Thomas Moore: "We must live in the freefall of Infinity; standing at the edge, the heart opens."[1]

What does Coffey's phrase mean? She comments:

> It is often the hardest, most challenging experiences of our lives that crack us open. For some people, these experiences are chosen, or accepted as consequence of risk-taking. For others—for most of us—they come without warning. Unlikely gifts that rip away our layers of insulation, allowing us glimpses of the mysterious, the ineffable—the infinite realms of human consciousness.[2]

To sum this up, to have an open-hearted pursuit of our hunger, we must be vulnerable enough to put at risk our core understandings of life, even our temporal identity as only physical beings, to find fulfillment. Carlos Castaneda sums up this truth in *The Teachings of Don Juan*: "The end result which shamans like Don Juan sought for their disciples was a realization which, by its simplicity, is so difficult to attain: that we are beings that are going to die ... We must voluntarily acquiesce to infinity ... Our lives originate in infinity, and they end up wherever they originated: infinity."[3]

Ultimately, our hungers and their resulting quests for fulfillment stretch beyond our imagination or desire into an exploration of the infinite. Following this hunger—with an open heart—toward an ineffable, infinite destination can lead to great transformation of our beings. Perhaps our hunger, all hunger, exists as a collective hunger, a primal hunger that all humans (or even all beings) have as an innate part of current existence. Some observers describe this "collective and even individual hunger" as "desperation." Henry David Thoreau supports this line of thinking when he writes, "The mass of men live lives of quiet desperation."[4] "Desperation" is a strong word. It literally means, "at the end of one's rope or tether; at the end of one's endurance or resources, out of options; exasperated, frustrated."[5]

Are we really all that hungry inside, at the ends of our ropes, unable to get any more fulfillment or any more sustenance in what the Hopi people call the Fourth World? Has our hunger reached the point of desperation, or is it merely the ache of an unfulfilling life? And if we admit to this hunger, are we open to the point of risking our hearts and all our beliefs to seek full satisfaction beyond our current world? And what exactly is it that we are truly desperate for in this next world: companionship, food, comfort, or something more? And will pursuing our hunger's fulfillment really lead us on a journey of great transformation to a better world—a Fifth World, perhaps? What are we, as fellow two-legged travelers on a whirling planet in this time and space, longing for right now?

CHAPTER 1

Hunger Pains

I n the spring of 2007, the asphalt streets of the water-hoarding megalopolis of Phoenix, Arizona, cooked with the heat from extended days of the soon-to-be relentless desert summer sunlight. After finishing my shift at the medical clinic, I crept along the hot streets in my air-conditioned Prius to the suburban house my roommate owned in the outskirts of Phoenix in the metro town known as Glendale. No one was home. I fixed a meal but was overcome by loneliness mixed with hunger for something else.

I longed for something more than the standard fare of suburban life. I had just over a month left of osteopathic medical school and was glad to be almost finished. I'd passed all my medical exams and received confirmation of my residency. My life was cruising along like the convection currents that swirled above the baking Phoenix streets. But on that day, April 22, 2007, none of my medical education mattered. Something else beckoned me from beyond the city streets and the eight-to-five, doc-in-a-box clinic life. I craved raw, unplanned, natural terrain that was not gridlocked or surrounded by walls, not governed by stop signs and photo-radar, unaffected by modern civilization. That evening I wanted a piece of natural freedom—freedom from being told how to fit in, how to think, and what to say as an aspiring medical doctor. That kind of freedom necessitates natural space and solitude.

I packed up a red Dagger Ace kayak, paddle, and other boating gear in my Prius and drove north. Water, cold water, called to me. I steered the Prius toward Highway 101 then turned up Cave Creek Highway. As I passed through the town of Cave Creek, Arizona, the world began to

1

open up. The saguaro, creosote, cholla, and mesquite foliage took over the evening landscape as the city drifted into the distance. The air felt cooler, even at eighty-eight degrees, and the Prius windows fell away to reveal a wild, dark desert landscape. I reached the turnoff for Bartlett Lake and headed east. Just before reaching the lake, I steered onto a dark, bumpy washboard road and carefully guided the Prius down to the Verde River.

After parking on a beach of river stones, I stepped out of the car and looked up. Stars previously obscured by the yellow glare of the city jumped out at me. The river spoke with a rustling voice of changing overtones but constant volume. Her appeal ushered me into movement. I grabbed the kayak and then put on the skirt, life jacket, and helmet. Darkness surrounded me as I paddled upstream into the gently rippling waters on the dark Verde River.

I paddled several hundred yards until I reached some flat pools. I was about seventy-five yards below the Bartlett Dam. The water was cold. The stars glistened in the sky above and deep in the water below. Everything felt still and full of motion at the same time. It was timeless. It was surreal. It was dark. It was Earth Day. It was my birthday. I was alone, and it felt perfect.

While spinning in quiet circles on the dark river, words of a poem drifted to the surface of my mind.

River Stargazer

Shimmering ripples
Reflect tiny twinklings.
Far, far above,
These lights gaze
Perpetually
Into liquid depths.

The paddler's pupils
Open wide,
Peering at moving stillness
Of light and dark.

Patterns of dippers,
Of clusters, galaxies,
Nearby planets, and nebulae
Are all smoothly shifting
With water and sky.

Dynamic stillness
Permeates the scene.
The river,
She takes the heat,
The silence, the motion, the light
And transforms them.

Employing her rapids
And her pools,
She juxtaposes "fast" and "still,"
Bringing paddlers
And planets together.

"Gaze far, far above;
Gaze deep into your soul.
Feel the whispering
Breaths of air;
Feel watery torrents
In between, beside,
And all around.

Embrace all speeds,
All temperatures,
Even the coldness
In your core.
It is your destiny
To die.

Welcome the
End of life
As a gift
Of eternity.

As the heavens shift
In green water currents,
Bubbling up and down,
So does thy cycle.

As poles wobble,
Earth revolves
And rotates into day.
So will death
Come to an end
Again and again."

So on the face
Of a planet's river,
Listen, speak, float,
Live, breathe, die,
And paddle …
At once …
Forever.

Rereading the poem now, it is interesting how the themes of death and the end of life come up, particularly on my birthday! Yet thinking back, I'd had an eerie feeling of resonance and somberness on that dark river. What did these words mean? Had I really authored the poem, or was it dictated by some higher heavenly force—perhaps the Verde River herself?

These questions persisted as my medical school days ended. A few weeks later, in May 2007, I found myself wandering through the public library in Tempe, Arizona, where I stumbled upon a book called *2012: The Return of the Quetzalcoatl* by Daniel Pinchbeck. I usually steer clear of such new age books, but the words resonated with me at that time. What stood out initially was this passage:

> According to Buckminster Fuller, evolution takes place through 'precession.' ... 'Precession' might best be defined as polar 'wobble,' akin to that of a spinning top, or a gyroscope on a table as its speed increases and decreases over time. The earth completes a cycle of precession every 25,000 to 26,000 years, and the planet is now coming towards the end/beginning of one of these cycles.[1]

Did Pinchbeck and Buckminster Fuller paddle the same river and confer with the stars? Or use the same plant medicine? What is this precessional cycle of the planets? How does the precession of the Earth relate to human life?

Questions bounced around in my head after reading Pinchbeck's book. I read about DMT (dimethyltryptamine), pyramids, aliens, native peoples, past lives, crop circles, Burning Man, and astronomy in Pinchbeck's book, but what was the real thesis of Buckminster Fuller, Pinchbeck, and my river poem?

Pinchbeck writes about the evolution of humans as coinciding with the precessional cycle of the Earth and the end of the Fourth World as described in Hopi prophecies. Pinchbeck inspires hope and empowerment in his audience, along with igniting an appetite for this newly evolved Fifth World. His book, *2012: The Return of the Quetzalcoatl*, brings many mysterious events together with an attempt to ground them all in a real astronomical, evolutionary process.

Whether I agreed with its synthesis of the many mysterious events into a cohesive story or not, I was sold on the book's message. Something in this world had to change. Most modern humans are not living sustainably in sync with our sacred planet, and our Earth may decide soon to shake us free, to find our gravitational mother somewhere else in the galaxy or beyond. The exact year predicted for this change (2012 or beyond) mattered little to me; Earth's timing rarely matches our antiquated Gregorian clocks.[2] What mattered to me was that the shift had begun, and fulfillment of this ache, this longing, this driving hunger in myself (and perhaps other humans) might be found in the newly evolved Earth and her truly *natural* inhabitants.

Knowledge of a possible new world, the Fifth World, along with new way of being in this world, inspired the same hunger that I felt on April 22, 2007, when I went to the Verde River to kayak at night with heady verse spinning around as I rotated and wobbled with the mother planet. However, attempting to understand potential changes in our planetary reality did not really satisfy the painful ache; understanding only increased the hunger. It felt as if there was something I needed to do to assist with the evolution of consciousness of the Earth and all her inhabitants. But pursuing this hunger and its possible resolution in the Fifth World would have to wait.

My exploration into this new age writing about the Fifth World was short-lived, as my life quickly became preoccupied with the daily grind of my medical internship, in what was perhaps the worst year of my adult working life. For one year (which felt like three years), I became a slave of the hospital, upper-level medical residents, and the attending physicians. Mental, physical, psychological, and even spiritual hunger and desperation were the result, because as a medical intern, you do not get enough food, sleep, exercise, or personal time. And you must learn a lot of medicine in this state of mind, staying alert enough that you don't kill or permanently injure someone who comes to the ER, the ICU, the clinic, or the hospital floor. In any other profession, it would be illegal to treat employees in this manner. In some cases, young medical doctors have died while driving home from the hospital, often after spending thirty or more hours taking care of patients and writing orders. My own life was at risk after a long night and morning of being on call (that's twenty-four to thirty hours of work, often with two hours of sleep or less). While driving my blue Prius at forty-five miles per hour, I drifted into brief slumber and veered left of the yellow line just below a small hill. I woke up alive and with my car intact, but that drive could have easily been my last. *It would really suck to die this way*, I thought, handcuffed to my life's steering wheel by insomnia and apathy. Modern medical training was slowly killing my spirit and, at that instant, had almost killed my body as well!

Except for my readings about the Hopi or the Fifth World and my simple life living in my geodesic dome home, I really struggled initially with my life in the world of modern Western medicine—which was 95 percent of my existence. I hated giving screaming kids largely unnecessary circumcisions or toxic shots (full of aluminum, mercury, formaldehyde, and so on). I hated discussing which antibiotic was best for some illness that was probably best left to natural courses. I hated giving pain medications to people who were so overmedicated that they looked like zombies. I hated living in a mostly windowless hospital and sleeping two hours or less at night. I hated working all weekend. I hated the fact that most babies were delivered in hospitals by strange, sleepless medical interns or residents rather than in loving homes surrounded by midwives. While I loved babies, children, and all people, I did not like how the rules of Western medicine treated these patients as if they were all the same, according to something called a "diagnosis." Losing interest in my own life and in medicine, I began to care less and less about what drugs and shots I gave to patients. This type of modern medicine violated my sense of what patients' bodies really needed. I was literally going through the motions to get through this process of medical education. I was checking out and felt I had little to live for. I knew there was a better way to live and a better way to do medicine, but at that time I could only hunger and hope for a different kind of life and medicine in some future day—if I survived my medical internship. In my inner and outer worlds, I was at the point of desperation. (Note: For a medical intern, it is par for the course to drift into depression; mean prevalence for depression averages 36 percent but can reach as high as 80 percent in some training programs.)[3]

In this life of quiet desperation as a young medical doctor, something still burned in my soul as I yearned for a better world, perhaps the Fifth World described by Hopi prophecies. It pulled at me through the challenges of my desperate life. I was driven to understand more about the Hopi people. At the time, I knew a fellow resident physician at the University of Arizona was from the Hopi tribe. I briefly thought about asking my Hopi resident colleague more about his heritage and culture. However, this resident also seemed to be caught up in a grinding desperation; he was slaving away to become a family practice physician to help patients (or earn a better living than that which was possible on the reservation) by prescribing pharmaceutical drugs, immunizations, referrals, lab tests, and all the other diagnostic and treatment tools available to us in Western medicine. From my outside observations, he seemed more focused on his goals in the Western, modern civilization than I, a mostly English Caucasian person with maybe 5 percent Cherokee Native blood, ever was.

A burning question at that time begged for an answer: "Why does any of this medical science matter if our world is soon coming to an end or becoming uninhabitable because of our unsustainable, modern civilized way of living?" Medical doctoring is important but seemed ancillary to the larger questions of consciousness, polar precession, ecological catastrophe, and prophetic destinies.

In retrospect, I may have bought into more of Pinchbeck's writing than I probably should have at the time. Since then, I've found that the date of 2012 and even an apocalyptic end of the Fourth World just isn't the truth, or at least the whole truth. In *The Order of Days*, David Stuart offers a balanced critique of Pinchbeck and other self-appointed gurus who claim to know much about Maya or Hopi religion.

> For Pinchbeck, 2012 is ... a time when people must embrace 'indigenous shamanic knowledge' to ensure human survival and awareness in a time of world crisis ... [His] self-centered writings are a bit hard to take, but they do appeal to many who seek a broader philosophical context for the economic, political, and environmental problems our world now confronts. That may be fine, but it's important to realize that Pinchbeck's claims about Quetzalcoatl's 'return' in 2012 [or anytime near that date] don't really have any basis in authentic Mesoamerican culture or philosophy.[4]

As a medical intern, even if I had read Stuart's critique of Pinchbeck or others like him, such as John Major Jenkins, I would not have given them much thought. Reflecting on that time, I see that I was desperate for something better than my current life of medical training. Pinchbeck's personal-story-infused new age writings gave me some hope and made me want to explore deeper what real truth did exist about the Fifth World.

Perhaps a more direct exploration of the Hopi culture and traditions would provide answers. Even though I had limited reading time and it meant less sleep, I managed to pore through Frank Waters' *Book of the Hopi*. Waters' book, published in the 1960s, is an attempt to unpack much of Hopi traditional views, prophecy, belief, and ceremony for the modern Westerner. In describing Hopi origin, beliefs, and ceremonies and their importance, Waters' book is detailed and excellent. While I did not totally understand all Hopi myths surrounding their ceremonies, I became fascinated with how the Hopi see humans and their relationship to the Earth—as well as the manifestation of the Fifth World.

The Hopi civilization is reportedly one of the oldest living continuously inhabited areas in North America.[5] Historically, the Hopi did not, reportedly, migrate across the Bering Strait land bridge, like many other Native Americans, but emerged from somewhere in the south, possibly having crossed the sea on rafts, moving from island to island.[6] There is also a myth in Hopi tradition, and shared with some other Native cultures, that they ascended from the Third World from an area near the Grand Canyon called the "Place of Emergence" via the *sipapuni*, or "umbilical cord of Mother Earth."[7] The ladder from the sacred kiva structure (the womb space of Mother and child) symbolizes this sipapuni in many Native traditions.[8]

While the mythology of the Hopi origins confuses my rational mind, the fact that Hopi people were one of the most ancient civilizations in North America enticed me to learn more of their stories, philosophy, and culture. I was also drawn by the way they understood their connection to Mother Earth, through the sipapuni.

Waters writes,

> With the pristine wisdom granted them, they [the First People of the Hopi] understood that the earth was a living entity like themselves. She was their mother; they were made from her flesh; they suckled at her breast... Corn was also their mother. Thus, they knew their Mother in two aspects which were often synonymous—as Mother Earth and the Corn Mother. In their wisdom they also knew their father in two aspects. He was the sun, solar god of their universe ... Yet his was but the face through which

looked Taiowa, their Creator. These entities were their real parents, their human parents were but the instruments with which their power was made manifest.[9]

This way of thinking about the human body and its origins from Mother Earth and Father Sun had never entered my medical education. Nor had my parents or anyone in Western Anglo-European culture taught me anything approaching this understanding. Waters continues:

> The living body of man and the living body of the earth were constructed in the same way. Through each ran an axis, man's axis being the backbone, the vertebral column, which controlled the equilibrium of his movements and his functions. Along this axis were several vibratory centers which echoed the primordial sound of life throughout the universe or sounded a warning if anything went wrong.[10]

The Hopi understanding of the human body in the likeness of the Earth was also not something I learned in medical school. Was it an important understanding? If so, why did we modern humans not think of our true parents in this way? Or why did we not extrapolate the characteristics of the Earth in understanding the human body?

I *hungered* to know more. Waters' *Book of the Hopi* enlightened me in my understanding of the human body and the Earth. However, the Hopi prophecies about the next Fifth World, a.k.a. Fifth Cycle, as described in Waters' book, still mystified me. (Of note is that Waters definitely stretches the historical truth about the Hopi, particularly regarding his doomsday perspective of the Fifth World, as well as its connection to Maya and other Mesoamerican cultures. While the Fifth World is a very real Hopi prophesy, the nature of its emergence out of a catastrophic end to the Fourth World—as well as its connection to the end of the Maya calendar—is largely a modern concept that is not grounded in historical anthropology).[11]

While reading Waters' book about the Hopi, I inhabited a geodesic dome located on a mountain above Tucson, Arizona. It was October 2007. Even with limited time between my medical internship work, I would burn a little bit of sage or some other herb on a regular basis outside my mountain oasis. The act of smudging, or burning sage or incense, has been considered an act of prayer or spiritual cleansing for many religious traditions, including Catholicism and Protestantism. Personally, I feel that the smoke or incense prays when I have nothing to say. While sage and cedar are common Southwest smudging materials, I had been inspired by a book about a Yaqui medicine man named Don Juan to also burn copal. Copal is an amber resin from the genus of Bursera, which describes a hundred types of shrubs and trees stretching from the southern United States to northern Argentina.[12] Copal was used traditionally by Mesoamerican tribes, such as the Maya, in sweat lodge ceremonies as well as for medicine.[13]

Curious about this ancient resin, I began looking for a store where I could buy some copal. After searching online, I contacted Native Rainbows in Tucson, which had been owned by a lady named Karin Elliot since 1985. Karin operated the store out of her house, so I made an appointment to go visit her. Serendipitously, Karin told me about her conversations with Hopi elder Dan Evehema, who had died in 1999 at the age of 106. Soaking up every morsel of knowledge about the Hopi available, I listened intently to Karin. From a medical perspective, learning about Dan Evehema and his longevity was enough to inspire interest, even beyond his Hopi heritage.

She told me about Dan's life and how he was always telling her to eat more corn. "Of course, he did," I thought. "The Hopi are all about the sacred maize." Indeed, traditional Hopi regularly sing to the cornstalks and dance for rain in the arid region of Arizona where they live. When I pressed Karin about Hopi Fifth World prophecy and its relevance for humanity and the Earth at large, I received a mysterious response. Karin stated very clearly, "It is their prophecy. We are not Hopi, so it's not our place to share it with the world."

I listened a bit more to Karin, purchased my copal, and some charcoal, and then went back to my geodesic dome home mystified. Learning from the Hopi and other Native peoples might help us understand how to live better without destroying our current planet. Shouldn't we learn all we could about the Hopi prophecies and pass on the message? Frank Waters had certainly sought to elucidate the mysterious lives and beliefs of the Hopi to Westerners.

I walked outside to the porch, burned the copal, and meditated about the Hopi people and my questions for them. Karin had told me about an elder of the Hopi tribe, Martin Gashweseoma, who was the guardian of sacred prophetic stones possessed by the Hopi tribe. Karin told me that she could set up an appointment with some of the Hopi elders if I wanted to see them, but she told me to avoid Martin because he was crazy, or at least a little demented. In the fall of 2007, I made it a point to go find Martin and see these special stones.

While I was making these plans, I was suffering from a severe case of plantar fasciitis. Plantar fasciitis is a debilitating injury, often to one or both feet, which leaves the patient feeling as though he or she cannot walk, stand, or run without burning pain at the base of the heels. As a long-distance mountain runner, I had acquired the condition in medical school during the fall of 2006 after a thirty-three-mile race. I had failed to recover, in part, owing to a sleepless medical student lifestyle. During the fourth year of my medical training and internship, which required long hours of standing and hospital walking, the condition had become extreme. It was so extreme that I almost took a scalpel home and cut my own plantar fascia at the base of my feet. Before pulling out the knife, I considered a few less invasive options. I knew that if I could create overstretch and strain the plantar fascia by running, I could also probably restretch and lengthen the plantar condition by running. However, the plantar fascia would heal after running only if I could keep it stretched out with night splints. I'd also used healing injections directly into the fascia attachments on my calcaneus (heel bone).[14]

Ultimately, more than just a physical condition, my plantar fasciitis, along with some other medical conditions I had (like a left inguinal hernia), was a sign of being ungrounded and malnourished. I was at the end of my rope in my life with modern medicine, and I needed to find some hope beyond just some words in a book. So I skipped a day of my internship and traveled to Northern Arizona for a long weekend of running in Kachina Peaks, and I also hoped to visit Martin Gashweseoma, who held the sacred stones of the Hopi, stones that might shine some light on and hope for a better life in the next world—the Fifth World.

CHAPTER 2

------◆◆◆------

Hopi Peaks, Spirits,
People, and Messages

The Kachina Peaks (a.k.a. San Francisco Peaks) consist of a magical area of volcanic mountains located just north of Flagstaff, Arizona. The peaks are named for the Kachinas, sacred deities of the Hopi, who believe these beings hover in the clouds over the peaks for six months of the year and bring rain to the high, arid desert landscape of their reservation and surrounding areas in Northern Arizona.[1] The Hopi people also believe that the Sipapu (the portal from whence they emerged into the Fourth World) is near the Kachina Peaks, at the beginning of what is known as the Grand Canyon, near the confluence of the Little Colorado and Colorado Rivers. Along with the Hopi, the Navajo, Zuni, and Havasupai tribes consider the Grand Canyon, along with the areas around the Grand Canyon and the Kachina Peaks, as sacred. These mountain peaks are in a national forest area, with a ski slope and extreme hiking trails (with over four thousand feet in elevation change from the base to the summit). The forest around the Kachina Peaks is mysteriously deep and full of large pines that dwindle in size as they near the summit of Humphreys Peak, which stands at 12,633 feet.

In the early years of medical school, I spent a lot of time trail running and backpacking up and around the Kachina Peaks, sometimes experiencing unique energies and seeing some unusual lights while in the area. (To be clear, I do not go looking for UFOs or Native spirits or what people may call "elementals" or any kind of "forest people.") While camping at the base of these mountains, multiple times, I observed lights that were hovering about four feet up from the ground, near the pine trees.

I first saw the lights in 2004, when my wife at the time and I were backpacking up near Mt. Elden, a mountain adjacent to the Kachina Peaks Wilderness area. As the air was getting a little colder and nightfall was coming, my wife noticed these lights on the mountain below us. They appeared to be way off in the distance, primarily because of their indistinct nature. I told her the lights were probably car lights or city lights in the distance. There was nothing to worry about. She and I ate some simple camping food and went to bed in our tent. Whether she felt safe or just trusted my assessment of the situation, she went to sleep soundly. However, I was restless. I had a sense that something or someone was watching us closely. Around 1:00 a.m., I finally got up to urinate a few feet away from the tent. I noticed that these lights were now right in front of me, about twenty-five feet away, hovering next to the tall pine trees! I was now quite certain that the lights were not from a distant city and were not car lights. The lights blurred, and I struggled to focus on them. They seemed conscious—but not with animal, plant, or human energy—and whatever they emitted expressed an intensity of focus on me that felt invasive, even intrusive.

I went back to bed. I figured that if I had not been eaten or attacked yet, this "light being" intended me no harm. Hence, I did not provoke it or investigate it. However, several minutes later, after drifting into a light sleep, I had a dream in which I was beamed in the chest with light. It was like being hit with a soccer ball in the chest when I was a kid. I felt a little breathless for a second, thought about it for a minute, and then brushed it off.

While this encounter with the lights was my closest encounter to date, it was not the only time I'd seen lights like these. In the summer of 2003, my climbing partner and fellow trail runner at the time, Jonathan Cavner, and I would regularly camp each weekend in the summer at the Inner

Basin area on the backside of Humphreys Peak. Cavner and I would run about three thousand feet to the saddle of the mountain and back down the front side of the mountain and then turn around and go back up and down, for a total twenty-mile out-and-back run. We would regularly see lights in the forest, usually around dusk or at night. The lights appeared much farther from us when more people were camping in our vicinity.

In the spring of 2006, after a multiday backpacking trip in the Grand Canyon, I stopped on the way home to camp alone near the old lava caves at the base of Mt. Elden. The lights appeared again, but with an intensity and proximity I hadn't experienced since the prior trip up Mt. Elden. I felt restless and could not sleep, even though I was exhausted after backpacking for several days. Why did this mysterious light being insist on bothering me? Was I invading the land of some ancient spirit or alien? I felt a little bit afraid, but I was not about to get up and leave. I needed rest and didn't know where else to crash. Besides, it was after midnight. Finally I said a few prayers to the Creator and just let go of feeling afraid. Interestingly, not long after my prayers, the clouds moved in, became thicker, and shrouded out the lights; I fell asleep. (When I later shared my experiences with the lights with several friends, they explained that these lights might be from a technologically advanced race of aliens. Their alien technology is, reportedly, so advanced it allows them to travel at rapid speeds, time warp, and even read minds, but that technology does not allow them to enter the next age, a.k.a. the Fifth World. These aliens recognize that an open heart of loving intent is required for entry to the Fifth World; hence they spend a lot of time examining humans who might teach them how to get there. But without intuitive guidance from the heart, these technocratic aliens, as well as some of their human counterparts, remain stuck in the Fourth World.)

In the fall of 2007, I returned to the Inner Basin at the base of Humphreys Peak, understanding the Kachina Peaks now to be in the sacred Hopi territory. I was looking for hope in these ancient Hopi territories in my life of quiet desperation as a medical resident. During this trip, while camping alone, I noticed the lights again. My quest for answers now trumped any initial fear of the lights. When I saw them in the distance, I got out of my tent and followed them. However, the lights moved away from me and then disappeared, later reappearing away in the distance. Unable to get close to the lights, I finally went back to my tent and fell asleep. I woke up the next morning and ran up and down Humphreys Peak for about fifteen miles of trail. I ran down the mountain fast and hard—so fast that I fractured the little sesamoid bones at the base of my big toes—a diagnosis later determined by X-ray. While I enjoyed running among the Kachina Peaks again, I had no great specific revelations from the alien lights, the Kachinas, the mountains, or anything else. Now I was hurt and still desperate for answers—for some truth, maybe about the Fifth World, which might help me find a grounded place in this life.

Yet, in spite of my injuries, I did not feel that my exploration into the traditional land of the Hopi, at that time, was complete. I needed to meet the Hopi people and learn more about them and their way of being, and to visit Martin Gashweseoma. I drove on, in pain, to the current tribal lands of the Hopi in northeastern Arizona. A little more background about the Hopi has relevance here.

> The Hopi are a Native American Nation who primarily live on the 1.5-million-acre Hopi Reservation in northeastern Arizona. The reservation is surrounded by the Navajo reservation. Hopis call themselves *Hopitu* - 'The Peaceful People' … Hopi is a concept deeply rooted in the culture's religion, spirituality, and its view of morality and ethics. To be Hopi is to strive toward this concept, but one never achieves peace in this life."[2]

I wanted to be around some people, such as these Hopi, who had found peace and balance in life and had devoted their way of life to this goal. I had no peace with my current medical residency training and did not fit into Western culture that well. However, as I drove into the pueblo town of Hotevilla, in the Hopi lands, I also felt like a stranger from the outside world. Yet, I wasn't entirely an outsider among Native people; I had Cherokee ancestors and had lived with Dené (Navajo) people for a month during medical school. However, this time, in the Hopi territory, my role among Hopi felt a lot different than that of medical student. I was on a spiritual (and physical) quest for meaning and answers at a critical time in my life and career. I felt lost and out of place, and I almost drove away empty-handed. Still, I was too motivated to give up now. I had to find the keeper of the sacred stones, Martin Gashweseoma, and ask him to explain the meaning of them to me. I felt that these prophetic Hopi tablets, if understood, might provide some direction for my life and maybe the rest of the planet.

I stopped at a gas station and began contemplating my next steps to locate Martin. There I saw a Hopi man who was about my age, smoking a cigarette. Being the ever-vigilant young physician, I asked him about himself and why he smoked cigarettes. He replied with a kind response which I now do not recall, but it ultimately led me to offer him $20 for his pack of cigarettes. He gave me the tobacco, and I then asked him if he could tell me where to find Martin. He hopped in my car, and we drove about a mile to Martin's house. Before parting ways, the young Hopi man offered to sell me a Kachina doll, which I politely declined. (A Kachina doll is a representation of a Hopi deity or its personification in Nature that reminds us of real power and presence; at that time, I thought the dolls were primarily just gifts sold to Arizona tourists).

I cautiously tapped on a screen door, and Martin answered it. When I asked about the sacred Hopi tablets, he pulled them out and showed them to me. He was a kind and friendly elderly gentlemen who, without any prior notice from me, just sat down for about two hours explaining the meaning of Fifth World prophecies and comparing some of the Mayan prophecies. It was interesting, sad, and hopeful all at the same time.

The stone tablets looked like this image:[3]

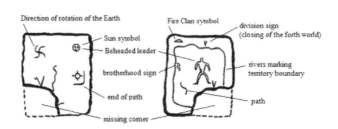

Martin spoke of previous worlds—along with the end of the current Fourth World—as well as the overlap of Hopi and Mayan prophecies, WWI and WWII, an upcoming war with China, Big Brother monitoring us through computers ("a giant spiderweb," a.k.a. the internet and electrical grid), "iron birds" (modern-day airplanes), "snakes of iron" (railroads), "rivers of stone crossing the land" (modern-day highways), and ultimately mass destruction, especially with "gourds of ashes" (atomic bombs).[4] Martin seemed convinced that massive destruction, as part of a great purification, would occur around the same time as humanity's emergence into the Fifth World (a.k.a. the Fifth Cycle).

At the time, I was particularly amazed to believe that I or anyone else was being (or could be) watched through the computer. However, after reading Jonathan Taplin's *Move Fast and Break Things: How Facebook, Google, and Amazon Cornered Culture and Undermined Democracy,* I am now more convinced. The book quotes Kevin Kelly, executive editor of *Wired* magazine: "'Everything will be tracked, monitored, censored, and imaged, and people will go along with it because vanity trumps privacy,' as already proven by Facebook."[5] Of note, when I visited Martin in 2007, Edward Snowden had not yet become known as a whistleblower for reporting the everyday surveillance of US citizens.[6] (If you want more information about how your privacy is constantly eroded by companies such as a Facebook and Google, check out the documentary film *The Creepy Line* directed by M. A. Taylor, as well as *The Social Dilemma*, directed by Jeff Orlowski. With a knowledge of your daily surveillance by tech giants and the governments who are wedded to them, be wise and clever about the content you look at as well as post online. I recommend searching with private web browsers and utilizing Facebook sparingly, if at all. Also, I tend to think of these Big Tech companies in the same way I think about the alien "light beings" encountered near Mt. Elden. While invasive to the mind, they will never be able to access the heart, where the core of a person lives. Just like the aliens, these brainy, heartless Big Tech companies can easily be brushed off and will remain in the Fourth World when the rest of us with hearts transition to the Fifth).

During our visit, Martin also encouraged me to check out Prophecy Rock, a sacred petroglyph located on the Hopi tribal lands, so that I could better understand humanity's journey from the First, Second, Third, Fourth, and upcoming Fifth Worlds. At the end of our encounter, I watched Martin take a large coffee can and walk outside to urinate. In 2007 when I visited him, Martin's house, located on the First Mesa of Hopi lands, had no running water. With limited technology, including indoor plumbing, Martin's way of life emulated that of traditional Hopi people.

The sun was beginning to set as I drove a few more miles to the Second Mesa to find Prophecy Rock. When I found the rock, no one else was around. It felt like a place where modern American teenagers might park to make out on a weekend night. There were no tourism signs, just a big rock face with some unique petroglyphs etched into its side. I took the following photo and stood in front of the rock, thinking about everything Martin had told me, as well as what I'd read about the Hopi.

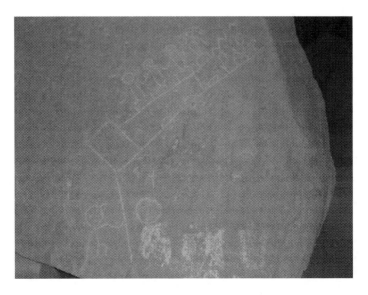

Looking at the petroglyph, I knew that it was important, but I needed to do a bit more research to really understand it. From the book *Meditations with the Hopi*, the following drawing of Prophecy Rock provides understanding the meaning of the petroglyph.[7]

Hopi Prophecy Diagram-Prophecy Rock (Oraibi)

It is believed that Prophecy Rock displays past, present, and future. In this depiction, the Hopi are seen as emerging from underground toward the surface to the First World, Second World, Third World, and current era of the Fourth World. Ascending from the underworld (the far-left vertical line), they must choose between two paths. The lower path is the one that takes them on the Path of the Life, represented by the lower horizontal line, where they live, traditionally, in heartfelt devotion to the Creator, at peace with Nature and close to Earth. The higher path, with the more popular upper horizontal path with five stick figures on it, is the way of the head—particularly left-brained dominant thinking.[8]

This heady, higher path eventually ends, represented by its squiggly trajectory followed by the dots at the end of it to the far right of the petroglyph. However, before that high path disintegrates, any Hopi and other humans in this Fourth World can return to the lower Path of Life, represented by the descending right vertical line. The Fifth World begins when Hopi and people from other tribes and cultures descend (along the far-right vertical line) and join with those already on the continuous Path of Life, which is signified as a sustainable path by the last small circle on the far right, on the lower horizontal line. On this Path of Life in the Fifth World, Hopi, and all peoples with them, enjoy a harmonious intimacy with the Earth—as represented by the lower stick figure planting corn.

This interpretation of Prophecy Rock brings a lot of clarity to the core challenges of the Fourth World (a.k.a. Fourth Cycle or Fourth Age). Many modern humans, for a large percentage of our daily lives, live in our heads, functioning out of the left brain instead of the right, especially as we do focused work on computers. In his book *The Master and His Emissary,* Iain McGilchrist discusses how, in Western societies, the left brain tries to rule over the right brain's understanding of life. McGilchrist believes it should be the opposite. For internal and external harmony to exist in ourselves and our world, the right brain must govern our perception, orientation, and action of our lives.

We already know some of the consequences of a left-brain-governed life that is divorced from the heart. In fact, many humans are overwhelmed by the amount of information they receive through their computers. We know that the time teenagers spend on social media is causally related to their depression levels. The pinnacle of our left-brain computer achievements might best be realized in the virtual world of artificial intelligence (AI), which may someday achieve a merger with our current human natural brains, unarguably a much more complex organizational structure than any computer. Yet many modern people believe the merger of our natural brains with AI will be a big step toward human advancement. But what if this machine–human merger, instead, is more of step toward an artificial (virtual or fake) reality? For example, no *actual* human is on a Facebook page. Our images online are, instead, representations that we objectify with our left brains. The images we see are mere shadows of reality, and when we spend too much time staring at 2D screens or 3D virtual shadows, it means we are spending less time in an actualized, multidimensional reality. Instead of using Facebook, Instagram, or other left-brain diversions from reality, we naturally are designed to use our whole brains to subjectively relate to and spend time with real flesh-and-blood humans, animals, plants, and all the spiritual and material reality in our present-day Earth.

To reiterate, Hopi elder Martin Gashweseoma says there are two paths for humans to follow, according to Prophecy Rock. One path takes them into the ethers of constant mentalization—perhaps of the virtual (artificial) reality—a path that does not lead to a salvific destiny, as it will disintegrate. The other path, a peaceful one offered by the Hopi, leads humans to harmony with the Earth, to the soil, and to an abundance of corn. Ultimately, the path of an integrated whole brain, a loving heart, and higher consciousness leads to a deeper relationship with our fellow humans and all creatures of the Earth, in the Fifth World.

Given that modern industrial society has moved away from farming in the past seventy-five years, what does this Hopi message of the Fifth World really portend? Are we going backwards to a world without computers in which we are all farmers or living in some flower-child fashion off the land?

I do not think the path to the Fifth World is one of a complete rejection of science and technology, but rather one that uses these tools wisely, from an embodied mind, to work in harmony with the planet without overemphasizing their importance. In the Fifth World, a superior form of science—a contemplative science that stems from the spirit, mind, and body—will bring us closer to our Creator (Taiowa); our true Mother, the Earth; our true father, in the sun and sky; and our human brothers and sisters; as well as animals, plants, and other creatures. In contrast, many current Fourth World technologies take human minds and spirits away from their bodies, as well as our bodily connection to the Mother Earth, creating an imbalance of the spiritual and physical along with humans and the rest of the planet. Divided humans (spiritual and physically disconnected with their heads not attached to their bodies) will be unable to access the Fifth World and shall share the destiny of the disintegrating Fourth World. In the Fifth World, the spirit and body are united—a merger which fosters balance in a world that's peaceful, respectful, and loving.

In *Meditations with the Hopi*, Robert Boissiere articulates this Fifth World message from Prophecy Rock:

> If there is a name, a word, that can show the world what Hopi peace is—it is balance. The world must grow, expand, but it must do it in balance…

In the beginning, we are told, Taiowa, the Creator, gave us his life plan, as it is written on the rock of Oraibi, which we call the prophecy....

But next to him, beware of the other way, the way of those who do not pray. *It is easy enough to see that their heads are not fastened on their body, as it happens with people who use their minds instead of their faith in the spirit way...*

When prayer and meditation are used rather than relying on our new inventions to create more imbalance, they will also find the true path. Mother Nature tells us which is the right way.[9]

Even when contemplating all the potential destruction and purification processes foretold by Martin and commentators about Prophecy Rock, hope arose in my mind and psyche. While I agreed with some premises of the Hopi prophecy of the Fifth World, I did not believe that the world would destructively end in 2012. However, I knew that Nature's weather patterns could destroy some of us at any time. Maybe at least some of us humans could truly follow in the Hopi way of peace and balance with Nature and with each other. And this next world, the Fifth World (or Fifth Cycle), might truly exist as a haven of prayer, peace, love, and balance. Instead of embracing the dissociated, investigative, technocratic, scientifically-based Western Fourth World of medicine and culture, I could embrace a higher wisdom and maybe a better medicine—the kind that leads to the Fifth World. While I still might employ some of modern technology, its creation and use would be governed by a higher wisdom, such as contemplation, intuition, heartfelt love, prayer, and meditation. Following my experience with Martin and Prophecy Rock, I began to see light at the end of my dark medical internship tunnel.

After visiting the land of the Hopi, I started the long drive toward home in Tucson and immediately felt an actual physical hunger. I pulled into the only restaurant I saw along the Hopi highway. I ordered a bowl of hominy and ate my food slowly. Being a minority in the land of Indigenous people, I must have looked like a lonely tourist—which I was. A Hopi woman, who was about thirty years old, invited me to attend a ceremonial Hopi dance. It would have been awesome to go to the dance, but I told her maybe another time. With Hopi corn in my belly and a pack of tobacco in my car, I returned to my journey in the Western Fourth World. As I traveled deep into the darkness of night, my body and soul, now satisfied with sacred Hopi corn and dreams about the Fifth World, felt hope.

CHAPTER 3

Osteopathic Coyote Medicine

Before my foray into the mythology and lands of the Hopi, I explored other tribal lands in North America ("Turtle Island," as it is known by some tribes). In the fall of 2005, as a third-year medical student, I briefly came to know an author and physician named Lewis Mehl-Madrona, MD, who was working with Dëne people in northern Saskatchewan.

With his pioneering matrix of mainstream and cross-cultural medicine, Dr. Mehl-Madrona is a unique physician. Originally from Kentucky, he is ancestrally a mix of Cherokee, Sioux, and Caucasian and has had a passion for medicine and science since an early age. At twenty-two years old, he was the youngest student to graduate from Stanford Medical School. Early in his career, Mehl-Madrona even worked on developing some early versions of the MRI machine. Along with his mainstream achievements, Lewis authored the book *Coyote Medicine*, in which he compares his experiences of modern Western medicine, in clinical rotations as a third-year medical student, with his Native American ceremonial medicine, including sweat lodge ceremonies.

In 2005, when I was an early-third-year medical student, I picked up the book *Coyote Medicine* at a local bookstore and began reading the story of Mehl-Madrona. It was a critical time in my early medical school life. The first two years of osteopathic medical school had been a didactic challenge, with hours of study for two or three exams per week; sometimes these tests took three to four hours to complete. I found a way to handle the massive data input and testing by getting away from it on desert trail runs and bike rides on the weekends and, when possible, during the week. However, starting in my third year of medical school, my clinical rotations in hospitals and medical offices lasted all day and even overnight. There was much less time for exploring the desert wilderness, as the indoor life of clinical medicine took almost all my time. Also, because several of my initial rotations included primarily Spanish-speaking patients and Hispanic physicians in the metro area of Phoenix, Arizona, gaining a knowledge of clinical diagnoses and treatments included a lot of extra translation work.

During these challenges, I kept seeing the coyote when I did get outside, even just briefly on my way to school. Where the parking lot of my medical school encroached on the arid landscape of an old orange grove, I would catch glimpses of this schoolyard coyote. Following the path of the coyote into the wilderness with my mind, I hashed out two poems.

Forbidden Wildness

The coyote trots through the orange grove,
Taunting me.
Had I not called his name
Three hours earlier,
Perhaps the draw
Would be less.

The grove, now quickly
Transitioning into a parking lot,
Also feels the teasing—
But both of us cheer
The coyote onwards
And follow his spirit
Into the desert wildness.

Where, oh where
Art thou,
My dearest coyote?
Don't tell us,
For we might love thee less.
And never let us
Make you our pet,
For then we
Might kill you.

Yes, kill and no less,
For coyote and brother wolf
Belong not in cages
But rather among
Lonely hilltops and dry ravines,
High mountains and empty deserts.

But dearest creatures,
Will you ever settle?
Why must you
Wander so far,
So wide, and so deep?
What is that you seek?

Do you not care for
The familiar territories
Where friend and family reside?
Do you not want
The peace of mind that
These structures give?

You will know me by
Following me
Into the wild unknown,
Going beyond the "Forbidden" signpost.
You will never trespass
If you see the wilderness
As your home.

But it is a home—
Eternal flux and change
No belief systems can hold.
Here the winds are too strong,
The running paws too quick,
And the extremes of life too sharp.

Life and death are adjacent realities
That meet
Along a thin razor line.
Those who walk the line
Are those who can love
This forsaken home.

But what of the past, the future?
There's no looking
Back or forward here
Only present, only now
With a fixed
Beautiful gaze.

"Look into our eyes,"
Coyote and wolf offer,
"And you will see."[1]

The Lonely Coyote

The ancient howling
Pierces the desert skies
Across jagged bluffs,
Canyon walls, rocky cliffs;
The echoes carry on.

Riding air currents,
Dancing with vibrations
Of earth and eardrums,
The coyote's cry
Is at one with the wind.

O wind, O cry, O spirit
Ever changing, ever the same,
Beckons forth this longing,
This loneliness, this wildness.

An uncontrollable breath,
The ear-ringing cry,
More than a desert dog;
'Tis the soul of creation.

The howling—
A cry of joy and laughter,
Hope and freedom,
Heaven and Earth,
And the ever
All-oneness (aloneness) of life.

Desire for connection,
For love
Of quiet desperation;
Yes, we all
Want to howl.

Rather than howl,
We run,
Pretending at freedom,
Pretending at connection,
Pretending at life.
Have we forgotten?
Do we heed the coyote?
Can we run or breathe or love
Without the howl?

O look at the horizon,
Meditate on a mountain,
Be with the silence,
Be with thy wind,
Be with All.

O welcoming loneliness,
O how long it's been;
We've tried to hide,
Tried to fly away,
Tried to close the ears, the Earth,
To thy howling, to thy mystery,
To thy eerie stillness.

Seeking satisfying things
Or only the familiar,
But knowing only
You are there.

Might we come home
To nowhere and everywhere—
At home with the howl
With the wind,
A haven of the heavenly airs
With wails of darkness and peace?

Are we but
This eternal force,
This ethereal fire,
Which carries coyote
Dreams, visions, and cries?

Yes, just a dream of a coyote,
Fading quickly
Yet alive forever
In a lonely howl.

Personifying and even spiritualizing the coyote in an almost salvific way, I chased after Coyote in his path of life.[2] Admittedly, I projected my own loneliness, ungroundedness, and despair upon the dry landscape, seeking solidarity in the life of a coyote. During my last two years of medical school, the human world had become much less significant or meaningful. Although Coyote's food and shelter are uncertain, he is free to roam and free to explore the otherwise forbidden landscape. Coyote laughs at those stuck, including me as a third-year medical student, in the status quo worlds of rigid beliefs and doctrines. Coyote beckons me to partake in a more real world of constant change and flux, although in that wilderness, nothing is stable, including food and water, relationships, and survival itself. Yet even with the daily challenge of flirting with life or death, Coyote emanates something so raw and pure as he lives in the present moment.

Meanwhile, I was going through the motions: studying, meditating, running, and commuting to the clinic. My home life did not offer much support or connection. My wife at the time stayed busy with her work, which regularly stretched into the weekends. I would see her for dinner and listen to her daily challenges. We had a few good times together, but our relationship regressed into something more like that of roommates, with each of us having our own agenda. I tried on several occasions to salvage the relationship, but she gave me a calendar and requested I book an appointment with her—which didn't really work. Eventually I gave up on intimate human connections, seeking solace only in a lonely, mythical, and sometimes real coyote who echoed his howl across a desolate landscape. By late autumn of 2005, I had lost most of my passion for life. I was married to someone too busy to hang out, and mainstream medicine left me no time for friends or for trail running. I started to feel I had little to reason to live.

About nine months before I admitted to suffering from depression and inner desperation, one of my friends from medical school, Jake, woke up to his own lack of motivation and drudgery in his pursuit of a career in medicine. Jake dropped out of medical school completely in the early spring of 2005. Even though he was the second highest-ranked student in my class, he'd realized that devoting his life to the role of a physician was not fulfilling; nor was it his passion. Jake had pursued medicine and completed one and a half years of medical school just because he had wanted to please his dad. Jake left this early career path with over $50,000 in school loan debt but in a much happier state of being.

I made an appointment with the same school counselor Jake had been to and explained my dilemma. The counselor kindly listened to me for about an hour. She could see that I had a passion for osteopathic medicine, for healing, and for excellence in my work, but she also understood that I felt trapped, mildly depressed, and out of place within the current clinical rotations offered by the school. It was sobering to see my situation from a third-person perspective. While I did not then know specifically what kind of medicine resonated most with me, I felt that the traditional osteopathic medical approach was more authentic to my identity than the pharmaceutical-based medical practice I observed during my clinical rotations. The counselor asked me, "How much longer is required before you can get out and really do the kind of medicine that is authentic to you?"

I replied, "Two and a half more years." This was the minimum requirement for me to finish my medical school and internship and be eligible for licensure in about 40 percent of the states in the United States. She smiled and encouraged me to press onward. I resolved to stick with medical school and at least complete my medical internship in the next few years. I tucked away my dream of doing more authentic medicine and determined to do as I was told until I finished my training.

Even with this renewed resolve, my feelings of desperation and depression persisted. My lack of motivation, disconnection, ungroundedness, frustration, and dissociation in the world of Western medicine began spilling over into the everyday clinical world. I struggled to participate in rotations in which doctors only prescribed pharmaceuticals and managed patients allopathically. While on a pediatric rotation in downtown Phoenix, some of my raw frustration slipped out of my mouth. Normally I kept my mouth shut and did my best to be cordial to all the patients, allopathic doctors, and staff. However, one day after consulting osteopathically for twenty minutes with a patient suffering from acute sinusitis, I observed my supervising physician enter the room and immediately prescribe an antibiotic. I expressed notable dismay at the doctor's kneejerk use of the medication. My reaction set him off. He verbally scolded me, and then he left the room in an angry, even fearful disposition. A wild canid had awoken in me and snarled a bit. I was sent home from the clinic immediately. The clinic called my osteopathic school and said, "We never want to have another medical student from your school rotate in our clinic again."

A few days later, the medical school faculty overseeing the third-year rotations at my school called me into the office for questioning. I came prepared. I had printed off four journal articles on the proper management of acute sinusitis; I placed them on the table in front of the faculty. The papers explained why antibiotic treatment for sinusitis, even from the allopathic Western perspective, is ineffective and, ultimately, poor management for the condition. Composed of several osteopathic physicians, the school faculty agreed that I was correct in my medical assessment but made it clear that I should not have questioned the pediatric physician. All in all, the school faculty were kind and understanding of the situation and told me that I could finish the rotation in another pediatric clinic. However, as karma would have it, I failed the pediatric test for the rotation. As it later turned out, I enjoyed repeating my pediatric rotation with a traditional osteopathic pediatrician in San Diego, California— while also getting in some quality beach time later during my fourth year of medical school.

Yet, in December 2005, after getting booted from the downtown Phoenix pediatric rotation and gently reprimanded by the school faculty, I questioned the quality of my osteopathic education. With this frustration, I decided it was time to speak to the dean of my medical school, Arizona College of Osteopathic Medicine (AZCOM, the Arizona branch of Midwestern University). The first question I asked Dr. James Cole was "How many osteopathic pediatric physicians do you have training us as osteopathic medical students?"

Dean Cole responded, "We have twelve physicians that work as pediatric preceptors for our third-year students."

I asked, "How many of these physicians are *osteopathic* physicians?"

Dean Cole said that they were all MDs (allopathic physicians). He then went on to explain that, before coming to Midwestern University, he had worked in a clinical practice where he had to work with other physicians, including allopathic physicians. And upon seeing the clinic's patients, he had to conform to the same standards of care held by those allopathic physicians. Dr. Cole also proudly shared that many osteopathic students from AZCOM were getting accepted at top residency programs, including in allopathic programs.

I looked Dean Cole straight in the eye and said calmly, "You sold out, Dr. Cole; you rejected your osteopathic heritage and training. And now I'm paying for it."

Fortunately, I did not get kicked out of medical school. I was confident that they wanted my private school tuition of approximately $39,000 per year, and it would be harder to boot me than keep my money and let me finish the last 1.5 years of school. I also think Dean Cole knew that my conclusions about the state of osteopathic education at Midwestern University and in the United States at large were correct.

I felt so confident in my assessment that I followed up my personal dialogue with him in a letter stating that if I owned a company that had contracted with his osteopathic school to teach me osteopathic medicine, I would have sued his organization for breach of contract.

After that exchange, I knew that my training as an osteopathic physician would now be almost entirely something that I would have to seek out myself. I also felt that genuine osteopathic medicine—with its traditional, integrative approach to the patient—provided some real grounding for my spirit, body, and mind. By embracing osteopathy, with its traditional principles and practice, I believed I could provide authentic healing for patients.

It's worth understanding more of the background behind traditional osteopathic philosophy. Osteopathic medicine was developed in the late 1800s alongside allopathic medicine. Osteopathic philosophy and principles were first articulated by Dr. Andrew Taylor Still, who was trained as an MD but used manual medicine in place of the harsh drug treatments used during that era. Although his practices were accepted by the early medical community, Dr. Still chose to start his own schools because his holistic philosophy was fundamentally different from allopathic practice.

Osteopathic medicine includes four major unique principles:

1. The body is a unit; one cannot treat a part of the body without considering its entirety.
2. Structure and function are reciprocally interrelated. In other words, treatment of the anatomy (structure) directly affects physiology (function), and vice-versa.
3. The body is capable of self-regulation, self-healing, and health maintenance.
4. Rational treatment is based on an understanding of these principles.

In contrast, allopathic physicians, including 90 percent of today's MDs, do not conform to the above osteopathic principles. "Allopathic medicine," which combines the root "allo" with the suffix "pathic" literally means that the physician uses something "other," such as an outside force (e.g., a drug) to address the patient's pathology—his or her condition. While this may seem like standard Western medicine, it ultimately reduces the patient to a disease or condition (from the suffix "pathic") that necessitates outside (from the root "allo") treatment, often delivered in a very commercialized, industrialized way. Indeed, entire specialty careers in allopathic medicine are built upon treating one part of the body—say, the kidneys—to the exclusion of the rest of the body.

Specializing in outside treatment of a disease in the kidney, or any part of the body, to the exclusion of other areas of the body, violates the first principle of osteopathic medicine. Furthermore, most allopathic physicians rarely consider addressing the structure of the entire body when addressing its function, such as the function of the heart, kidney, or lungs. To be clear, an allopathic physician might address the *anatomical structure* of a diseased body part by performing a surgical procedure, but rarely, if ever, does the allopath at the same time address the *health and function* of the entire body, as described by the second osteopathic principle. For the third principle, the allopathic physician does not believe that the "body is capable of self-regulation, and health maintenance," because that concept is antithetical to the entire nature of allopathic medicine—which denotes that an outside (allo-) force is necessary to manage the body's illness or disease (pathology). For the fourth principle, "rational treatment," as defined by osteopathic medicine, cannot be practiced by allopathic physicians, because these physicians do not subscribe to the first three principles of osteopathic medicine. In fact, Dr. Still started osteopathic medical schools and separated them from the allopathic training because he knew that the philosophy taught to new osteopathic physicians was entirely different from the guiding principles of allopathic medicine. Dr. Still chose the root "osteo," which means "bone," as the best way to describe how osteopathic physicians can access and address the body's internal healing mechanisms.

Dr. Still said, "To find health should be object of the doctor. Anyone can find disease."[3] Allopathic doctors seek out diseases to treat with external forces. Osteopathic physicians, in the tradition of Dr. Still, seek out the health of the whole human as a unit. While addressing disease is certainly important, it is not the primary focus of osteopathic physicians, who adjust, by manual therapy, internal structures of the body in a manner that facilitates the body's own self-regulation, self-healing, and maintenance. It's worth noting that Dr. Still, as an MD himself, did not reject the necessity, at times, of using external forces to help patients. Osteopathic medical schools, from their inception, still included training on the use of modern medical techniques and therapies. During WWII, when many US allopathic physicians went overseas, the osteopathic physicians stayed behind and treated patients. By the 1950s, osteopathic physicians treated clinical patients on a regular basis. In their wisdom, the allopathic medical profession opted to include US osteopathic physicians into their mainstream Western medical club. State by state, the allopathic doctors granted osteopathic physician privileges at allopathic hospitals, allowed them to prescribe medications, and eventually allowed them into allopathic residency programs. In the state of California, osteopathic physicians were even encouraged to trade in their DO licenses to get brand-new MD licenses, and most of them complied.

Since the 1950s, many DO's have practiced more like allopathic physicians, as surgeons, internists, or primary care physicians, trading away traditional osteopathic principles in exchange for acceptance in typical allopathic settings. For example, my medical school dean, Dr. James Cole, DO, was "forced to," or at least "expected to," uphold an allopathic standard of care in his 1970s–1990s clinical practice; even he had to reject the core osteopathic philosophy. His argument would be that osteopathy has changed to incorporate allopathic modalities. My argument would be that to reject osteopathic principles for more allopathic practices (particularly using symptom-based treatments of less adherence to the Hippocratic Oath) constitutes a rejection of the essence of osteopathic medicine.

Indeed, largely because of ungrounded nontraditional "osteopathic" practitioners like Dr. Cole, it is rare to find traditional osteopathic doctors who adhere faithfully to osteopathic philosophy and principles. Most of my colleagues from osteopathic medical school now operate pretty much the same as any other allopathic physician, except for about 5 percent of us who are truly authentic osteopathic physicians. Those of us who are traditional osteopathic doctors effectively diagnose and treat patients in a hands-on manner that is often superior to any manual diagnosis and treatment provided by allopathic physicians. For example, in a recent study comparing the standard medical therapy given by traditional osteopathic medical practitioners or internal medicine doctors, osteopathic manual medicine (OMM) helped a significant number of patients use less pain medication and reduce the need for physical therapy.[4]

While traditional osteopathic physicians are guided by osteopathic principles and employ OMM to diagnose and treat patients, there is also a place for the use of "outside" treatments, in conjunction with the body's own healing wisdom, for some medical conditions. To reiterate, by "outside treatments," I am referring primarily to the use of drugs or surgical forces to help balance and heal a patient's condition. The main point is that most of the Western medicine taught in allopathic schools (as well as most osteopathic schools in the United States, except for training in OMM) does not meet the criteria of the four major tenets of osteopathic philosophy, as articulated by Dr. Still. As a result, most osteopathic physicians today work as allopathic physicians and might as well be called MDs.

> MD and DO are basically the same for most purposes. That's the practical answer. MDs and DOs are both capable of seeing patients, prescribing medicine, and doing surgeries. In fact, DOs and MDs are so similar that 4th-year osteopathic medical students and recently graduated DOs are able to apply for allopathic MD residencies, provided that they take the USMLE Step exam. No specialties are off-limits to DOs. Some people have concerns about marching into the most competitive specialties as a DO, but competitive applicants still do. DOs promote their approach as being more "holistic"— but as explained below, this does not always play out in the real world.[5]

While the acceptance of newly trained DO's into the mainstream Western allopathic medical world was deemed a benefit by purveyors of "osteopathic" educational institutions, including Dr. Cole, this attempted merger of osteopathic medicine with allopathic practice constitutes a rejection of the real power and authenticity of osteopathic philosophy and practice. Nevertheless, to pass my postgraduate training and thus gain a license to practice medicine, I had to learn the language of allopathic medicine and fully embrace it, even when the fibers of my being fought against it. While I signed up for training as a true osteopathic physician, I found it necessary to assume the role of an allopathic physician.

Now, in the freedom of my current practice, I view my patients through the lens of osteopathic principles. There are, of course, times when I employ external forces (pharmaceuticals or procedure), but these externals are applied in sync with the innate healing wisdom of the patient, as is consistent with osteopathic philosophy. For osteopathic practitioners who choose to employ outside (allo) forces, osteopathic philosophy, in contrast to allopathy, requires the guidance of the right brain over the left brain, as articulated so well by Iain McGilchrist's book *The Master and His Emissary.* Also, the use of outside (allo) forces by osteopathic doctors must be rationally guided and filtered in a way that honors the patient holistically, treats anatomy and physiology together, and understands how the patient can self-heal.

Another philosophical critique of allopathic medicine is the prioritization of disease states and symbols over patient relationships. In its left-brained, disease-focused approach to the patient, allopathic medicine fails to see the full picture of the patient's condition, as the patient becomes objectified. That is, the patient is reduced to a disease label: "cardiac arrest in room 12." Allopathic doctors spend most of their time looking at "information about the patient" rather than being face-to-face and therapeutically touching and speaking to the person in each room. Allopathic medicine, in philosophy and practice, values the "map," including symbols of that patient's reality (e.g., labs; X-ray, MRI, and CT imaging; other physician reports) over the "territory" (the divine-animal-human spirit, body, and the mind that makes up the life of the patient). In its essence, allopathic medicine, with this symbol-based view of a patient, often fails to elucidate the most accurate and proper diagnosis or treatment of the patient. True osteopathic physicians, while valuing *information about* a patient, prioritize input from their whole brains in order to best relate to, connect with, be present to, look directly into the eye of, and effectively diagnose and treat their patients as equal human beings.

According to Iain McGilchrist, when you look at a Facebook image of a person, you look at it with your left brain but do not connect with the person in the image as a person. You feel no relationship. A person on a screen seems to be a false or exaggerated symbol, not a real person. This dehumanization can result in trolling or Facebook stalking. Overfocus on these online symbols on social media is one of the leading causes of loneliness, depression, and suicide in teenagers.[6] In the same way, burned-out physicians (along with many patients) are depressed by the "care" provided in the current allopathic medical system. These patients and the growing number of mentally and physically unhealthy patients are proof of allopathic medicine's failure as a primary, long-term manner of patient care.

Stepping out of Western mainstream culture, it is possible to envision a medicine, such as osteopathic medicine or Native American healing, where the very real physical, mental, emotional, and spiritual essence of a patient is integrated with the labs, images, symbols, and other virtual representations *about* a patient. One of the first steps toward this "reality-based medicine" involves placing more importance on the time spent with a patient and less on charting "about" the patient symbols and labels. In the current allopathic model, the average medical intern, resident, or hospitalist may spend two to three minutes seeing a patient in his or her morning rounds in a teaching hospital and the rest of the day talking about this patient to other physicians, ordering labs or meds, and then doing discharge summaries. The patient is left alone in the room with a disease to be treated. He or she is then poked and prodded by nurses, who measure urine output and enter blood counts into a computer. The data are scanned for a minute or two later in the day by the medical practitioner. The physician uses this representative data *about* the patient's disease to make potentially life-and-death decisions, utilizing outside (allopathic) forces—maybe a drug or surgery created by an industrialized, commercialized Western society—to manipulate the body back into a "normal value" on the computerized charts. Then the patient is sent home and told to continue taking that magical cocktail of drugs until the protocol is considered unnecessary by an outside clinic physician.

An example of the ludicrous nature of this form of hospital-based allopathic medicine occurred during my residency. I had a four-hundred-plus-pound Hispanic male patient with hypercalcemia. Hypercalcemia simply means elevated blood calcium. For about a week, our medical team of resident physicians just kept this obese, but otherwise healthy, individual in the hospital day after day, watching his corrected calcium score go up and then plateau at a higher-than-normal level. Eventually I sat down with the patient and asked about his normal daily diet. After a little dialogue, he reported drinking a gallon of milk each day. His mom would even bring it to the hospital for him. After a week of looking at his labs, we finally chatted long enough with the patient to know the source of his high calcium level! (Go figure). His allopathic physicians wasted thousands of dollars of this man's livelihood because no one really explored some of the most basic aspects of his everyday life before putting him back in a hospital room. How many other lonely patients are locked in windowless rooms, getting unnecessary tests looking for expensive zebra-shaped symbols in hospitals every day? (In Western medicine, a "zebra" is an "unusual, often rare diagnosis." Looking for zebras, instead of a more likely diagnosis ("horses"), can be time consuming, expensive, and ultimately detrimental to the patient and hospital resources).

In 1903, Thomas Edison stated, "The doctor of the future will give no medicine, but will interest his patient in the care of the human frame, in diet, and in the cause and prevention of disease."[7] There is some value in a type of medicine that incorporates symbols, such as labs and fancy imaging, as well as outside forces such as drugs, surgery, and other procedures, but what if we practiced, using our whole brains and our hearts, looking at the diet, routine, and real life of the patient *first* before creating symbols like labs, diagnoses, or external pharmaceutical or surgical procedures? What if we believed what Edison articulated in the early twentieth century? We believed in Edison's brilliance when he invented the lightbulb; why not believe in his brilliant and wise perspective of medicine? Edison sure sounds as if he is advocating for osteopathic medicine. What if the allopathic physicians started looking to the traditional osteopaths, or at osteopathic philosophy, to properly understand how to best care for their patients?

Ultimately, a central thesis of this book is that there is a better way to understand and practice medicine than allopathy. As that new medicine manifests and the "doctors of the future" show up in conjunction with the evolutionary cycles of our Mother Earth, we will begin to thrive in what the Hopi people call the Fifth World.

Finally, osteopathic medicine, in its manual practice as well as its philosophy, as articulated by Dr. Still, MD, DO (1828–1917) in the late nineteenth century, was derived from traditional Native American bodywork. What Dr. Still named "osteopathy" was originally known as the bone-setting methods of the Shawnee.

> Indeed, Dr. Still lived his life, like the Native Indians, by a Nature-centered belief. And when he started his medical practice, he advertised himself as a "magnetic healer" and "lightning bonesetter" before naming his methods Osteopathic Medicine. Today, much of the traditional healing of the American Indians has been lost because the Christian missionaries called it devil worship. However, what has survived in pockets around the country (along with Zuni and Navajo healing and bone-setting) is Cherokee bodywork, which was surely similar to Shawnee practices....

47

Cherokee bodywork today is practiced and taught by Dr. Lewis Mehl-Madrona, M.D., Ph.D., of Cherokee and Lakota heritage, professor at several colleges and universities, medical researcher, and author of many books, including *Coyote Medicine*. His thesis, along with some of his colleagues, is that Dr. Still learned much of what would become osteopathy during his years helping his father in his medical duties among the Shawnee. Dr. Mehl-Madrona, who is seeking to honor and preserve Cherokee bodywork, came to this conclusion after experiencing and seeing the many similarities between Cherokee bodywork and osteopathy.[8]

Understanding that osteopathy had its roots in Cherokee and Shawnee bodywork, it is no surprise that my pursuit of authentic osteopathic practice led me to also pursue a greater understanding of Native American medicine, from Dr. Lewis Mehl-Madrona. After reading his book *Coyote Medicine* in my third year of osteopathic school, I *hungered* to spend time with him and learn more about how to be true healer of the mind, body, and spirit.

CHAPTER 4

Wolf Medicine

I t wasn't until the American Indian Religious Freedom Act was signed into law by Jimmy Carter, on August 11, 1978, that Native Americans were allowed to freely express their spiritual practices.[1] Native American religious practices had been specifically outlawed since 1895.[2] In comparison, the First Amendment guarding freedom of religion, meaning the religion of the Anglo-European settlers, became constitutional law on December 15, 1791.[3]

In the early 1970s, during the third year of his medical training, Mehl-Madrona attended a sweat lodge and spent time with Native healers in Wyoming. Even when it was illegal to practice Native American spirituality, Mehl-Madrona found it essential to understand his Native American heritage and healing practices. In *Coyote Medicine*, Mehl-Madrona shares his experience of the sweat lodge—an ancient ceremony of thanksgiving, healing, and purification practiced widely by Native peoples around the world. Constructed of willow tree branches covered by canvas or hides, the lodge looks like a dome but is technically the top part of a sphere stretching under the ground. Stones are brought into the lodge under the direction of a Native healer (known as a shaman by some cultures) and water is poured over the stones. The stones release their energy into the sweat lodge participants.[4]

Mehl-Madrona contrasts hospital-based Western medicine with the medicine of the sweat lodge. "The brightly lit, sterile rooms of Western Medicine, couldn't have been further removed from the darkly mysterious sweat lodges." Early in his career as a third-year medical student, Mehl-Madrona recognized a philosophical (and spiritual) basis for healing, in lieu of his allopathic training. He also recognized the allopathic problem of prioritizing *objective* information *about* the patient over a *subjective* relationship *with* the patient. In *Coyote Medicine*, Mehl-Madrona writes, "We were well on our way to being paragons of 'scientific objectivity,' holding onto sacred hard numbers instead of a subjective worldview."[5] He later writes,

> Riding through Powder River, Wyoming, population 10 or so, I began to realize what kind of doctor I wanted to be. I wanted to walk both roads, the Anglo and the Indian, though I realized that I ran the risk of being rejected by both cultures. I could stay out of trouble by acting as if both views have their place—one in the hospitals and the other on reservations—but at the moment I was too much in love with the world to do that. Through the sweat lodge, the tipi ceremony, and my morning run along the hilltop, the whole world had spoken to me. The earth had swept through me and left me changed. I would no longer accept the view that people are only the incidental occupants of a set of organs.[6]

This is a pivotal point in the life of Mehl-Madrona, and his words resonated strongly with my own disposition about practicing medicine during my third year of osteopathic school. After his experience in the sweat lodge, Mehl-Madrona had to incorporate an understanding that his patients were spiritual *and* physical beings into his daily practice as a physician. However, he also knew the inherent challenge of synthesizing sterile Western Medicine with the Native medicine that was core to his identity and heritage.

I attended osteopathic medical school over thirty years after Mehl-Madrona did. Being of Generation X, I did not care about allopathic medicine. I did not want to walk the "Anglo-road" of allopathic medicine. I had been sold on the philosophy and practice of true osteopathic medicine, but my school, in many respects, had trained me like an allopathic doctor. Understanding these drawbacks of Western allopathic medicine, I had hoped that Native American healers might be able to give me some insight into what true, whole-person, sustainable healing might entail. In my state of desperation, Mehl-Madrona's book *Coyote Medicine* inspired hope, as well as a powerful desire to learn directly from Native American healers.

During my third year of medical school, when I discovered that Mehl-Madrona offered weekend-long intensive workshops, I considered attending one of these workshops. Mehl-Madrona had previously worked with Andrew Weil's Integrative Medicine Program at the University of Arizona, so I figured he might still live in Arizona. However, when I reached out to him, in late autumn 2005, Mehl-Madrona told me he was working with Native people in northern Saskatchewan. Serendipitously, Mehl-Madrona mentioned he had to give a lecture in Tempe, Arizona, the following month and suggested that we chat in person at the conference hotel.

I arrived at the hotel in Tempe somewhat nervous. I was finally going to meet one of my heroes, a physician and author whom I deeply admired. If lucky, maybe I would even get to learn from this enlightened healer–physician for a long weekend. I waited patiently in a hotel lobby chair. Finally I noticed a man with long hair walk hurriedly into the hotel and stop in the middle of the lobby with his head over a Blackberry phone. I then swallowed the stark reality that Mehl-Madrona was very much a part of this modern world, not some hippie doctor running around with coyotes in the desert. After a few minutes, he walked over and sat down across from me.

I explained, in brief, my challenges with Western medicine and my desire to learn from Native healers. I also shared that I felt a little lost and directionless in my career and wondered whether I could participate in one of the healing intensive retreats that he offered over long weekends.

Dr. Mehl-Madrona listened with empathy and sincerity. I felt like he really heard and understood some of my challenges. After about twenty minutes of dialogue, he asked, "Do you want to come do a rotation with me?"

I replied, "In Saskatchewan? Are there healers up there?"

He said, "Yeah." There was a silence after his reply that made me wonder what kind of healers were up there. I sensed an underlying nonverbal message from Mehl-Madrona that beckoned me to let go of control a bit and just "wait and see."

I thought about his invitation to journey to the north country of Saskatchewan, where I could work with Native people and maybe meet some authentic healers. It was a great offer but was riddled with unknowns and some very cold temperatures. (The average low temperatures in February in northern Saskatchewan can be -20° to -25° F). But maybe this rotation would reignite my passion for healing and medicine, as well as teach me how to treat patients holistically in a very ancient way with sweat lodges and other ceremonies. Maybe this rotation could give me a purpose and direction that would help bring me back to life from a restless state of despair.

At that time, I shared the same sentiment Mehl-Madrona writes about in *Coyote Medicine*: "I had signed on to be a doctor in a culture that separates physician and priest. I dreamed of combining their roles as a healer."[7] Perhaps a faraway rotation in the remote lake country of northern Saskatchewan with an esteemed mentor could help me realize this goal. Yet, since living in Phoenix for the past three years, where the average low in February is 45° to 50° F, I did not even own a heavy jacket. This was going to be a journey from an extremely hot, dry landscape to an extremely cold one.

In late February 2006, I stepped off a puddle jumper plane from Saskatoon, Saskatchewan, onto a bitterly cold, windswept runway. I was ready for it. I had purchased a lightweight but sturdy windbreaker fleece jacket and borrowed a large down jacket and pants from a mountaineering friend. The goal of being away from the civilized distractions and immersed in the frozen village of Stony Rapids was exactly what I wanted. I was ready to be stripped away to the core to find my real identity and my true career path in a faraway land where no one knew me.

After five days or so, I wrote the following email to a friend, sharing my initial impressions:

> I'm finally here in Stony Rapids, Saskatchewan (northern Canada). There are mostly Native peoples here—in a string of tiny towns along some big lakes. Today, I helped the doctors here sew up a young guy with a knife wound.
>
> I've yet to explore the wild places around here and the locals have warned me about the packs of wolves—which allegedly ate a geology student last fall. The desire to explore, wolves or no wolves, persists in me—hell, that is why I'm here. They won't let Americans carry guns, but I may be able to hire out some Native people to take me out in the wilds. Also, I may get to go on a Caribou hunt—not for shooting, but to take photos of a 10,000 big herd. (I am giving up the vegetarian life here out of necessity).
>
> Temperatures today are mild—about -13 C or 0 F with lots of snow. Not quite equatorial but livable.

I stayed in a small house with two foreign medical physicians who were great individuals. They would work for two weeks straight on call and see a variety of patients at the local hospital, and then go back to live with their families in a warmer southern part of Canada or the United States for two weeks. Therefore, for a few days at a time between the physician rotations, I would be the most qualified person in the whole area, as a third-year medical student. My mentor, Dr. Mehl-Madrona, spent most of his time in Saskatoon teaching at the University of Saskatchewan. I never even saw him that rotation month; we just communicated by email. I would visit patients at clinics locally and at the hospital in Stony Rapids, and I sometimes took a puddle jumper to neighboring villages.

While I saw mostly psychiatric patients, I practiced Western medicine of all types, including taking care of patients with various types of medical conditions: pregnancy, stomachaches, cancer, back pain, and headaches. I even tended to patients in need of surgery. The critical ones were put on a plane to the nearest big city of Prince Albert. I practiced osteopathic manual therapy on many of their structural conditions and listened to many of them with empathy, looking for spiritual and physical causes of their conditions. I had to employ Western medicine, including pharmaceuticals, at times, to alleviate these patients' physical ailments. Saskatchewan had no health food stores where I or patients could buy natural herbs or supplements, and only a few Native patients told me they knew of herbs that could help them. I had journeyed to the northern Canada to find healers and found myself being a Western doctor. I had been tricked by the Coyote of medicine, Lewis Mehl-Madrona, MD!

Yet with an openness to the magic of a medical approach that stretched beyond the tools of Western medicine, I found myself making house calls, with Mehl-Madrona's mentorship, and engaging more deeply into the psychospiritual challenges of the Metis and "Treaty Peoples" living in the Northern Hamlet of Stony Rapids and on the Black Lake Dëne Sųłıné Nation (pronounced Dene-su'-lee-neh) as well as surrounding Indigenous communities.

It was a tough life these tribal peoples endured, especially since the Dëne Sųłıné people of Black Lake had been forced to settle into a nonnomadic life by the Canadian government only about fifty years previously. Before that time, these northern Dëne peoples were nomadic hunters of caribou throughout a wider range of northern Canada into what is known now as the Northwest Territories and Nunavut. The traditional lands of the Dëne Sųłıne̋ also likely extended south into what is now Arizona, where their Dëne relations continue to live. In the sacred stories of the southern Dené (Navajo) and Indé (Apache), as well as the northern Dëne peoples, it is clear that Indigenous peoples once moved throughout their ancestral lands unrestricted by artificial colonial borders. The Anglo-European colonizers literally invaded and stole these ancestral lands to establish "North America" and then resettled the peoples whose lands they stole on "Indian reserves" in Canada and "reservations" in the United States.

As part of their settlement agreement with Canada in 1899, the Dëne Sųłıne̋ peoples were promised that they could maintain their ceremonies, healing practices, and traditional way of life, which included hunting, fishing, and gathering in their traditional lands. The Dëne Sųłıne̋ were promised by the Canadian government an Indian reserve and a school for their children if they decided to settle in one location. Their settlement on an Indian reserve occurred in 1949 after the Fond du Lac Band, as they were called at treaty signing, separated into the Fond du Lac and Black Lake Bands (now referred to as "Denesuline Nations"). Today, a majority of the Dëne Sųłıne̋ people continue to live upon their Canadian government–established reserves.

Despite government promises that their traditional way of life would not be interfered with, the early fur trade brought alcohol and disease, especially phthisis (now known as tuberculosis), along with beads, guns, and other manufactured goods. In their interactions with the Western colonizers, profound change was inevitable for these Dëne peoples and all Indigenous tribes in North America. Once established in their traditional lands, Catholic missions accelerated these way-of-life changes for the northern Dëne by introducing foreign religious and cultural traditions. In fact, by the time of their treaty signing in 1949, many band members had converted to Catholicism in spite of the tribe's recognition of the need to preserve traditional spiritual beliefs and practices. Dëne parents sent their children to Catholic mission schools, where they received basic education in English and so-called Christian lessons, along with regular insults and molestations by priests and nuns. It is reported that for every Dëne child molested physically or sexually, each adult victim could potentially pass the cycle of abuse on to approximately fifty-six others.[8] When I arrived in Stony Rapids, I encountered many peoples haunted by traumatic memories of rape, incest, and other crimes. Also, the cycle of prejudice by the Canadian police against these northern Dëne people was and still is strong, perhaps as strong as the racism against African American people in the Southern United States in the 1960s.

Even with this prejudice and abuse, the influence of the Catholic Church remains central in many northern Dëne people's lives; one of their former priests is immortalized in the government-funded school in Black Lake. In contrast, few northern Dëne people have yet to experience their own traditional healing ceremonies and dances, which once lasted days and nights during which people "danced their sicknesses into the fire."[9] But memories and remnants of the old ways still existed among the elders of the community even when I lived among them near the Black Lake settlement. The older Dëne people still remember wearing caribou-hide clothing and hunting with small teams of three to six dogs while travelling fifty to sixty miles in a day just to feed themselves and their families. The healing energy of the drum is still powerful and present in many of their tribal gatherings. It is still whispered among the people that their ancestors once "danced their enemies into the fire," too.[10]

Why did I care about the challenges of these Indigenous peoples of Canada? What was resonating in me that felt connected to the life, spirituality, and medicine, as well as the tragic histories of these northern Dëne people and other Indigenous peoples like them?

Along with my search for authentic healing practices, my interest in Native culture has roots in my personal history and my ancestry, particularly as it relates to religion, health, and spirituality. My mother, the youngest of nine children, is part Cherokee on her mother's side. Born in 1939, she was raised in Turtletown, Tennessee, near the largely unheard of Ducktown. (My father's ancestors were primarily English). No one knows exactly how much Cherokee blood runs through my mother's veins, but her mom and brother possessed enough kinship to collect benefits from the nearby Cherokee Nation. Most of my mom's kin escaped the infamous nineteenth-century forced march for over sixty thousand Native Americans, known as the "Trail of Tears," a march that led to death or enslaved life on a reservation in or nearby modern-day Oklahoma. When the Anglo-European settlers routed these Indigenous peoples from their land (for a small purchase price), most of my Cherokee ancestors retreated deep into the Snowbird Mountains of North Carolina, along with approximately four hundred other families of the Wolf Clan of the Cherokee Nation. The Snowbird Mountains, near Great Smoky Mountain National Park, are located about fifty miles from where my mom was raised.[11]

Perhaps my strong *connection* with the stories of Indigenous peoples, including my own Cherokee ancestors and the northern Dëne peoples, was the reason I felt so *disconnected*, at times, from the Anglo-European people and even present-day Western culture. Perhaps my connection to these Indigenous peoples was the same reason I did not resonate with the philosophy of Western medicine but hungered for something more. This ancestry, at one time deeply hidden in my blood, arose more distinctly to the surface of my life when surrounded by other Native peoples, culture, medicine, and spiritual practices in the far north territory of Canada.

Looking deeper into my Cherokee heritage, I noted that some of my ancestors were very powerful people. According to the ancestral chart of the family of my mother, whose maiden name is Martha Jean Reid, one of my ancestors, Amatoya Moytoy, was supreme chief of the Cherokee Nation during the mid-1600s. Chief Moytoy was married to Quatsy W-O-T-W-C (Woman of the Wolf Clan), and they had a son named Kana Ga-Toga, in

1690, who was also a Cherokee chief. Perhaps these powerful grandfathers and grandmothers were speaking to me through my feelings and hungers, beckoning me to not buy into the Anglo-European medicine or even that dominant culture's way of life. (Of note, three months after leaving the north country of Saskatchewan, I was told by a psychic acupuncturist, a holistic osteopathic doctor, and a medium that a Native grandfather was present with me as a guide).

While I discovered that medicine and life did not have to be exclusively either Native American or Anglo-European, I found it very challenging to unite these distinct forms of medicine, spirituality, and worldviews. Most of my colleagues, teachers, and even patients identified me as just another prospective Anglo-European physician who needed to learn medical science and to obey the rules guiding Western standards of care. However, given my hunger and Native ancestry, those standards of care set by Anglo-European doctors just weren't good enough. To fully embrace Western-minded doctoring would be to forsake my blood, my identity, and my core nature as a spiritual and physical being.

Even the coyote and the wolf had their roles in steering me down this path toward a higher standard of medicine—what I might later call Fifth World medicine. One may note that until the early twentieth century, wolves ranged widespread across North America, including the Southeastern United States—the historical lands of my Cherokee ancestors.[12] During that time, the predominant canid species in the Southeast was the red wolf, genetically a cousin of the gray wolf, which is still present in Canada, Alaska, Russia, and the Northwest United States, although in size and color, the red wolf resembles a coyote. (In spite of a reintroduction program in North Carolina during the early 2000s, very few, if any, of these red wolves are still alive, primarily because of the actions of poachers).[13] Hence, the coyotes in Arizona who distracted me from my Western medical studies, reminded me, in a primal way, of the kin of my Cherokee ancestors, the red wolf.

Speaking of wolves as kinship creatures—or, later, as they became domesticated canids, as "man's best friend"—is nothing entirely new to Anglo-Europeans. In my own childhood, I had a "super dog" named Smokey, an Australian blue heeler mixed with dingo, who played rough with me, and together we explored as much of the fields and forests around my home as possible. (My parents owned sixteen acres of land and a ten-acre lake adjacent to our home in Georgia). Smokey was part wild dog and could round up cattle with ease, as well as hunt game in the woods.[14] He would fiercely protect us against anyone that came to the house; some UPS delivery men would not even step outside their trucks. Not only was Smokey a great protector, but he was also my best playmate. He and I would roll around in the yard wrestling or chase each other. One day when I was nine, he ran off with my kite, and I chased him with a small stick. When I caught up to him, I tapped him on the back with my stick, and he reflexively turned and nipped at me. His bite caught me in my right cheek. I put my hand to my face, and it was covered with blood. I started crying and went into the house, where my mom immediately called my dad at work, and we rushed to the hospital. Twenty stitches in my face later, I asked my parents what would happen to my super dog. They told me that he would be taken away. They did not tell me he would be taken away and euthanized. But I knew that Smokey was gone. I never saw him again, but Smokey left his mark on me, physically and spiritually. To this day, his wildness, loyalty, and love live on in my body and soul.

As much as I loved my super dog Smokey, I would dare say that this deep friendship and kinship barely scratched the surface of the kind of relationship my ancestors had with the wolf. That is, to ascribe a name of one's tribe or core identity to the wolf, as my ancestors from the Wolf Clan of the Cherokee Nation did, implies an even deeper kind of relationship than just a respectful friendship with domestic or wild canids. In *Wolf Nation*, Brenda Petersen writes,

Many Indigenous peoples—from the Hopi and Navajos of the South to the Southern Cherokee and Seminole, the Northeastern Penobscot and Algonquian to the Midwestern Chippewa tribes—believed the wolf was a spiritual guide and ally.[15]

The tribes' designation of wolves as spiritual guides and allies resonated much more with how I was thinking of the wolf and coyote than perhaps most of my Western medical peers or culture. In general, most Western Americans simply do not think of wolves as brothers and sisters (totems) in their physical and spiritual nature. Even fewer people think about how wolves might teach us or even how we might take care of these wolves. But in my confusion about how to practice an authentic and higher standard of medicine, I *hungered* to learn from the wolf, while in northern Saskatchewan, with her spiritual and physical presence so close to me.

It is quite common for Native peoples, traditionally, to learn from their totems, including the wolf. An elder named Fred Woodruff, from the Quileute Reservation near La Push, Washington, states, "We learned from the wolf how to survive and how to be mere human: how to honor our elders, to protect and provide for our families—and we learned from the wolves the loyalty you need to really belong to a tribe."[16] How most early Anglo-European settlers related to the wolf was, and in many respects still is, quite different from how Indigenous peoples, including my Cherokee ancestors relate to the wolf. Early Anglo-European settlers did not hold the same respect for the wisdom, relationship, or life of these wild canids, but many prided themselves, and still do, on their abilities to hunt wolves under the badge of protecting families, livestock, or land.

It is noted that livestock protection forms a large part of the rationale for allowing wolf hunts (a.k.a. wolf "management") in Minnesota, Michigan, Idaho, Montana, Wyoming, and Western Canada, despite these sacred animals having been on the endangered species list for most of the past fifty years. In truth, wolves kill very few livestock in comparison to the numbers that exist. In the documentary film *Medicine of the Wolf,* it is cited that in a recent year, one hundred sixty-five thousand cattle existed in Minnesota. Of these cattle, verified wolf kills amounted to eighty-two cows.[17] Even if the numbers of verified kills are only half of the actual toll, wolf kills amount to one tenth of 1 percent of the total number of cattle in Minnesota. If we can afford to feed our domestic canids, our dogs, cannot we at least offer a few livestock from our abundance to care for our brother and teacher, the wolf?

Unfortunately, in the eyes of many Westerners, the Anglo-European settlers and many today, wolves are savage, bloodthirsty beasts closer in likeness to evil demons or dragons than respected teachers and spiritual guides. These Westerners fear the darkness and death wolves bring and cheer on the knightly heroes (hunters) who valiantly root out these beasts along with any of their kin, such as the Indigenous peoples who were also hunted and removed from their territories like savages.

Thankfully, in the history of American civilization, a few Anglo-European peoples woke up and began to see the world more clearly through the eyes of a wolf. One of these former wolf killers, Ernest Thompson Seton, later a founder of the Boy Scouts of America, authored a book, *Wild Animals I Have Known,* in 1898, in which he writes about the wolf, "… a moral as old as Scripture—we and the beast are kin."[18] Another early Anglo-European settler, Aldo Leopold, regarded now as the father of wildlife conservation, was a former wolf hunter who killed a mother wolf and caught a "fierce green fire dying in her eyes." He claimed that upon looking into her eyes, he was changed forever. Leopold gets credit for later saying, "To look into the eyes of a wolf is to see your own soul—hope you like what you see."[19]

In the north country of Canada, I, metaphorically, looked straight into the eyes of the wolf and with the eyes of a wolf as I interacted with the Native peoples of that land. Revealing the core of my soul and body, the experience was haunting and powerful, and I found it challenging to face my kinship with the wolves and peoples living in these frozen lakeside territories, as well as with my own ancestors in the Wolf Clan of the Cherokee Nation. Perhaps these Indigenous peoples of Canada and my brother wolf had wisdom and knowledge to teach me, and maybe I also had a role, as a mixed breed, in their lives. If Native wisdom about medicine, spirituality, and life could be integrated into my otherwise Western medical education and culture, perhaps I would be then able to, with the powerful guidance of the wolf, honor, respect, and protect the lives of all my relations with true, authentic medicine—a type of medicine that stretched beyond the Fourth World.

In an email to Dr. Mehl-Madrona, I described my experiences working with these Native "Treaty Peoples":

Hi Lewis,

Again, it has been an honor to be up here in Stony Rapids. Visiting the mental health patients and others has been quite an engaging and creative challenge. Having an hour or more sometimes to really sit with the patients and explore all their relationships and the parameters of their lives has been excellent. It can be quite fulfilling to see what happens to individuals when simply given a lot of love, attention, and motivation towards their next steps of healing.

Regarding the Native healing, the land and its inhabitants have great teachers. From the northern lights to windswept frozen lakes and stalwart pine trees and other beings, all have been nourishing friends up here. The wolf has certainly been present here, and the medicine of the wolf feels strong. Working with at least a few patients, I have felt the wolf's presence. One patient got a little angry at me and accused me of being an undercover police officer. I looked back at him with the wolf's deep eyes and told him that I wasn't afraid of his anger and sent him as much positive love as possible. He walked away upset, but I think the anger was an important release. Better with me than someone else. There was a rage deep in him that I didn't fight, but I also, perhaps like the wolf, held my ground.

There's a lot of rage here. And many individuals hold the pain inside or try to numb it with alcohol or drugs, or even prescription meds at times. The psych doctors in Prince Albert tend to pass out the drugs all too readily— at least that's what I hear from some of the mental health workers here. Listening intensely and working with the mind does take time and energy, though there is sometimes a place for psychiatric meds. The rage is, however, quite a multigenerational challenge that affects whole communities. I feel like there are perhaps ten or more patients struggling for every one that is seen by the mental health workers. This type of systemic rage will take time to overcome, especially when that rage stems from sexual, verbal, and physical abuse. Seeking answers to why this rage is so big in these communities has led me back to the residential schools where lonely, needy nuns or priests had their pedophilic ways with several kids who later did the same to later generations of individuals. Celina, in charge of the Aboriginal Healing Foundation, talked to me at length about not only the sexual but physical abuse in these schools, as well as the separation of families, etc., that occurred at that time. You know the stories. Arlene, a researcher and grant writer for the Healing Lodge in Black Lake, tells me that the residential schools have had a major impact on the present-day situation of that community. It's amazing in some ways that these Native people have done as well as they have. They certainly are handy for surviving in this cold.

Arlene is of Austrian descent, but she is the wife of a Cree man from Prince Albert. She is visiting Black Lake now until her grant work is complete. She has shared with me a lot about Native spirituality, which she practices regularly. Her adopted brother is a native healer whom she has invited me to come back and meet with sometime in PA. Also, Arlene and I plan to meet tomorrow with Eileen Bruno, a Dëne woman who knows a lot about traditional ways and seeks to preserve them. Eileen has also set up a time on Tuesday night where the elders will speak as a group about the traditional ways of healing and life. If the group wants it, we will video the talk and get it to you.

Best regards,
John

Along with getting more deeply involved in the lives of the northern Dëne, I also began going further and further into Nature on my trail running excursions around Stony Rapids. The trail running seemed to purify my soul from the challenges of everyday patient struggles. Here there was no mountainous desert landscape to explore as in Arizona. I ran on frozen lands and in the nearby forests. There I was alone with my thick wool socks, lightweight fleece pants, ear coverings, and down mittens, panting along the lightly snow-covered ice in the -10° to -20° F weather. The farther away from the small civilization I ran, the more I felt the wilderness and the living beings, such as wolves, present there. On my first few runs, I took bear mace with me. The thought of being ripped apart by wolves on the ice did not appeal to me. However, I finally got tired of being afraid of the wolf and embraced whatever destiny might come. If I were to own the wolf in myself and my heritage, I had to be willing to let the wolf, if necessary, consume me. I had to love the wolf in a spiritual–physical kind of way.

I did not see a wolf on this journey but did see their tracks and feel their presence when I entered their territory. I hashed out the following little poem about the juxtaposition of my internal fire and that of the wolf's landscape of frozenness and cold.

The Core

Crystal lake,
Brilliant light,
Sparkling glitters,
No heat outside,
Only cold.

Frozen...
All about is
Subzero,
Except the core.

The core
Has this fire
Which burns
Hotter when stoked.

Crystals of snowflakes
Inspire the
Core's fire
To balance
Out the cold.

Internal and external
Purification,
The core's purpose
Is clear.

Burn away dross,
Burn away fear,
Bring forgiveness to the soul,
Bring light to the darkness of cold.

May crystals
Settle and fly
All about
On lakes and hills,
On paws and noses
Of wild and furry kin
Who are ever present
With us…
At the core.

At that time, I did a little more investigation of what the presence of wolves represents metaphysically and allegorically for us two-legged creatures. The following resonated with my psyche at the time:

Wolf is the pathfinder, the forerunner of new ideas who returns to the clan to teach and share medicine … If you were to keep company with Wolves, you would find an enormous sense of family within the pack, as well as a strong individualistic urge. These qualities make Wolf very much like the human race. As humans, we also have the ability to be part of society and yet still embody our individual dreams and ideas …

If you have drawn the Wolf's card, you may be able to share your personal medicine with others. Your intuitive side may also have an answer or teaching for your personal use at this time. As you feel Wolf coming alive within you, you may wish to share your knowledge by writing or lecturing on information that will help others better understand their uniqueness or path in life. It is in the sharing of great truths that the consciousness of humanity will attain new heights. Wolf could also be telling you to seek out lonely places that will allow you to see your teacher within. In the aloneness of a power place, devoid of other humans, you may find the true you. Look for teachings no matter where you are.[20]

With the power of the wolf igniting in me, I gained more confidence in my work as a future osteopathic physician and healer. I felt this energy when speaking and listening to patients. I wanted to understand more from these Native tribal peoples about their ancient ways of survival and how to help them recover from the trauma of civilized life, as well as find the healers among them. With the help of some locals, I interviewed the elders of Black Lake while living there in Saskatchewan in February 2006. We even got the local health authorities to pay $50 to each elder for his or her time. Below is an excerpt from the meeting. See the appendix at the end of this book for the entire interview. A few notable comments follow.

Elders' Meeting with Doctor in Training John Hughes[21]
J. B. Bigeye (Elder from Black Lake)

Today we have lost our own way and are trying to fit in
with the white man's way. Today we are not well mentally,
physically, spiritually, and emotionally. People are not
listening to one another, and the young people are doing
things that are not right, because no one is lecturing them.
It's getting worse. How are we going to solve problems
nowadays?

… Long ago, there were people that were healers, and
they foresaw the future. There were spiritual people, and
they knew what was going to happen … Today it's like
I'm listening to them and following them. We lost our
cultural way of life, in the 1950s and 1960s, and ever since
then our way of life is the white way of life. But we don't
understand the white way of life, and that is why we are
very sad people … The elders used to say that the white
way of life would destroy our people.

Elder Pierre Nilghe

Long ago when people were very sick, there was a true
healer, and they cured the people from the land. And if
that person was meant to recover, then they would recover.
Nowadays, I see lots of people from the hospital and they
pass away …

What you said—culture is lost—this is very true. Long
ago, the people followed the caribou. That was a happy
time. They didn't sit around. Now people sit all day.

The Dene people used to meet at Christmastime and New Year. That was when they would bring food and eat together. We were poor, but that was a happy time. We would have a drum dance, and people would exchange things.

Elder Elsie Skull

Long ago, there was traditional food, but now there is food in the store that makes people sick. I survived cancer, but I lost my daughter to cancer. There were so many spiritual healers, but she still died, because that is God's way. Traditional food is healthy food. I have so many prescriptions from the doctors and the nurses, and if I take those pills, it makes me nauseated and makes me want to throw up. We don't understand that medicine.

Elder Mary Jane Yooya

I worked with the children for ten years, and I helped Chief Freddie Throassie with the canoeing trips. I teach the children in traditional and cultural ways. I know that if you teach them in this way, that the children listen. I know that when they go to sleep at night, they ask for help from the Creator. By teaching the young people in the cultural and traditional way, they will listen. And I like to help the young people because I know that they can listen. I am a Dene teacher and elder at the school for about ten years. And I have seen how the students are very sad. But I have seen how happy they were on the canoe trip.

Elder Pierre Brussie

> Long ago, people were happy, even though there was not money. But I saw how happy people were. People used to wait for winter in the fall time. People made their own skates, but it was not from the store. People made their own games from caribou bones. There are five caribou toes, and you make that into a game …
>
> But long ago was a happy time. But today it is too much for me, what I see and what I hear. Long ago people travelled up north with dog teams. I saw dog teams floated on the water because you couldn't put them on the canoe. It was a hardship, but those days were a happy time. Today we have everything, but we're not happy.

The comments these tribal peoples provided were distinct to their ancestral heritage, of course, but I wonder how much their daily struggles adapting to the North American modern life, including allopathic medicine, reflect those same challenges of Western society overall. For example, J. B. Bigeye's comment "Today we are not well mentally, physically, spiritually, and emotionally" tends to be true for many people in Western society. When looking at each of these mental, physical, spiritual, and emotional elements even in young people, Native or Anglo-European, living a Western lifestyle and using allopathic medicine, the results are not always so good.

Regarding mental and emotional health, the degree of illness is severe, especially among children. According to a survey conducted by Citizens Commission on Human Rights, "More than 20 million school children worldwide are said to have a mental disorder that requires them to be chemically restrained by powerful mind-altering psychiatric drugs."[22] A new government survey in 2015 found that approximately one of every thirteen children takes at least one medication for emotional or behavioral problems. Today's statistics have that number closer to even one in eight children using powerful mind-altering drugs, and the number is continuing to increase. "Over the past two decades, the use of medication to treat mental health problems has increased substantially among all school-aged children and in most subgroups of children," researchers wrote in a Centers for Disease Control and Prevention report.[23]

John Horgan, a writer from the Center for Science Writings at the Stevens Institute of Technology, articulates the following commentary about *Anatomy of an Epidemic: Magic Bullets, Psychiatric Drugs, and the Astonishing Rise of Mental Illness in America*, by the journalist Robert Whitaker:

> As recently as the 1950s, Whitaker contends, the four major mental disorders—depression, anxiety disorder, bipolar disorder, and schizophrenia—often manifested as episodic and "self-limiting;" that is, most people simply got better over time. Severe, chronic mental illness was viewed as relatively rare. But over the past few decades the proportion of Americans diagnosed with mental illness has skyrocketed ... This epidemic has coincided, paradoxically, with a surge in prescriptions for psychiatric drugs. Between 1985 and 2008, U.S. sales of antidepressants and antipsychotics multiplied almost fifty-fold, to $24.2 billion. Prescriptions for bipolar disorder and anxiety have also swelled.[24]

Clearly, the use of drugs for mental health disorders has drastically increased in the past two decades as these psychiatric drugs have become more widely available and accepted in Western culture. The question to answer is, Are the drugs really working? Whitaker has an answer, particularly regarding SSRI drugs, which are widely used for depression.

"When patients stop taking SSRIs, they often experience depression more severe than what drove them to seek treatment."[25] According to a study by the World Health Organization, chronic, regular antidepressant usage leads to high risk of long-term depression. SSRIs also cause many side effects, "including insomnia, sexual dysfunction, apathy, suicidal impulses and mania"—effects that cause many patients to also seek treatment for bipolar disorder.[26]

Indeed, the literature confirms what the elders from Black Lake stated: Western allopathic psychiatric medications do not work long-term for Native people; nor do they work very well for Westernized people. However, the real question is: Why are so many patients now seeking the use of these medications? In other words, why is the mental health of Native and Western people failing? Think about it, and I'll revisit that question later in the book.

Along with the failing mental health of both Western and Native people, the physical health of these populations is also rapidly deteriorating. In *The Last Child in the Woods*, Robert Louv says it directly: "As far as physical fitness goes, today's kids are the sorriest generation in the history of the United States."[27] Angela Hanscom, in *Balanced and Barefoot*, echoes Louv: "The cold hard truth is that when you compare today's kids with past generations, they just can't keep up. Children are getting weaker, less resilient, and less imaginative."[28] It turns out that these children are just emulating their adult parents. The number of overweight adult Americans is at an all-time high. A 2013 study by the Institute for Health Metrics and Evaluation published its sobering results in the *Lancet*:

> An estimated 160 million Americans are either obese or overweight. Nearly three-quarters of American men and more than 60% of women are obese or overweight. These are also major challenges for America's children—nearly 30% of boys and girls under age 20 are either obese or overweight.[29]

While obesity is a problem for Native and Western humans, other chronic health problems also continue to increase in prevalence. In 2018, the National Institutes of Health reported the following:

> Trends show an overall increase in chronic diseases. Currently, the top ten health problems in America (not all of them chronic) are heart disease, cancer, stroke, respiratory disease, injuries, diabetes, Alzheimer's disease, influenza and pneumonia, kidney disease, and septicemia. The nation's aging population, coupled with existing risk factors (tobacco use, poor nutrition, lack of physical activity) and medical advances that extend longevity (if not also improve overall health), have led to the conclusion that these problems are only going to magnify if not effectively addressed now.[30]

The trends in the declining health of Americans as well as most Westerners are clear and easy to identify. The big question is rooted in etiology. What is behind the chronic illnesses arising across all demographics of Western societies? This question shall also be explored in a later chapter.

Regarding spirituality and health, for centuries, a large percentage of Westerners cared for and expressed their spiritual essences through organized religious practice. However, in recent decades, many humans have experienced a loss of connection to traditional organized Western religions, such as mainstream Protestant and Catholic churches, as well as Jewish synagogues. In 2015, a Pew Research Study revealed that numbers of mainstream Christian religious believers are declining, while numbers of those with no affiliation to a belief system or a religious community are rising.

> In 2007, 78.4% of U.S. adults identified with Christian groups, such as Protestants, Catholics, Mormons, and

others; seven years later [in 2014], that percentage fell to 70.6% … The biggest declines have been in the mainline Protestant tradition and among Catholics. People who self-identify as atheists or agnostics (about 7% of all U.S. adults), as well as those who say their religion is 'nothing in particular,' now account for a combined 22.8% of U.S. adults—up from 16.1% in 2007.[31]

Many Westerners are rapidly moving away from organized religious beliefs and groups. Considering the devastating impact of child abuse perpetrated by spiritual leaders of the Catholic Church, as well as some Protestant churches, who can blame Native or Westernized peoples from steering clear of these traditional religious structures and their doctrines? While religious organizations can and do offer some amazing services to aid the poor, as well as uniting like-minded communities, their beliefs and doctrines are losing relevance with most demographics across the United States, especially the younger generations. The question now is: What is replacing the former religious beliefs and organized mainstream structures? Where is the energy that use to be behind organized religious beliefs and structures going? Are Native and Westernized people becoming more spiritual in other ways, or are they losing faith in the Creator, a higher power, or anything greater than themselves?

Another Pew Research study from 2017 states the following:

About a quarter of U.S. adults (27%) now say they think of themselves as spiritual but not religious, up 8 percentage points in five years…. This growth has been broad-based: It has occurred among men and women; whites, blacks and Hispanics; people of many different ages and education levels; and among Republicans and Democrats."[32]

If all demographics of Western peoples are more "spiritual than religious," where is that spirituality now focused? And what has become of the spiritual health of most Westerners? Has it improved or worsened as Westerners have migrated away from the mainline religions of Christianity? I think the answers are literally up in the air. My theory is that Westernized peoples know what they don't want from mainstream Judeo-Christian religions, but they are still exploring what it means to be spiritually grounded outside of these institutional structures.

Some of those who are "spiritual but not religious" are looking to mystics from the Scholastic era, such as Meister Eckhart. Beth Daley writes about this newfound quest by former religious persons to follow the teachings of Eckhart in her online article "Why a 14th-century mystic appeals to today's 'spiritual but not religious' Americans." She states, "The percentage of Americans who do not identify with any religious tradition continues to rise annually." Many of these Americans seek to indiscriminately mix diverse religious traditions "to form a personalized spirituality, often referred to as 'cafeteria spirituality.' This involves picking and choosing the religious ideas one likes best."[33]

What appeals to the average person, as well as what other modern-day explorers of noninstitutionalized spirituality may be seeking from mystics like Meister Eckhart, is the lack of codification, necessary dues, or even hierarchical structure that is characteristic of mainstream Western religions. Many of the spiritual pursuits of nonreligious Western people have been very individualized, piece-it-together, ungrounded, cafeteria-style, and divorced from a community and ritual. At least since the 1960s in the United States, there has been a rejection of what were thought to be religious truths in favor of a variety of other spiritual or not-so-spiritual teachings—some of them articulated by liberal postmodern philosophers, and some of them as uncovered mystical paths from centuries ago. The downside is that many former religious people have gone down paths leading further away from truth. The upside is that some of those stepping away from mainstream religions might find something better, and more spiritually healing, in their mystical spiritual pursuits than what is offered by mainstream Westernized religions.

When I went to the north country of Saskatchewan, I also wasn't spiritually satisfied or necessarily healthier, even with my extensive studies of and childhood devotion to mainstream Judeo-Christian religions. I had pursued Judeo-Christian religious studies deeply, earning a master's degree in theological studies from Duke University's Divinity School just before starting medical school. Yet I needed to know whether stepping outside mainstream religion and into the world of Native American spirituality and healing practices could lead to greater spiritual *and* physical health. Could it be that Native American spiritual and medical practices not only address health in a spiritual way but also address the physical and mental aspects of sustaining and healing life? I had seen enough fat pastors preach the "word of God" from their Judeo-Christian Bibles and then immediately denigrate the temple of the "God," their physical bodies, with lack of exercise and the junk foods served on Sunday mornings. In fact, Western pastors and other clergy represent some of the unhealthiest people in Western culture.[34] In contrast to such pastors and many Westerners, who believe that spiritual practices pertain only to the fate of the soul, my consensus is that unless your faith affects everything in your life (including your diet, actions, relationships, and mental state), what good is it? Hence, authentic, healthy spiritual practice must correlate with mental and physical health. (Note that sometimes because of genetics or karma, an individual's outward physical well-being, even with those who are spiritually healthy, does not always demonstrate perfect health. Still, a trajectory of wellness—in a spiritual, mental, and physical way—effuses from those who are on a path of health and long-term well-being).

Given today's vast array of choices in spiritual paths, is there hope for humans seeking consistency with their faith in a spiritual, mental, and physical way? Is there a spirituality that leads to greater wellness in all aspects of human life and perhaps that of the entire Earth and heavens? Does Native American medicine and its associated spiritual practices have wisdom we can learn from as Western peoples?

At the end of my interview with the Elders of Black Lake, in the North Country of Saskatchewan, Elder Betty May Toutsaint commented: "We have to take action and meet with the leadership. We're going to bring up housing and teaching and take steps to get back to the land … There is a sense of God's presence here. We can close with a Dene prayer, or whatever you want."

There was something very spiritually moving and inspirational about meeting with these elders from Black Lake. It had felt like a heartfelt group prayer session in a sacred place. If you could have heard and seen the interview, you would have seen the elders light up as they talked about teaching the children how to dry meat, make traps, or cook without a frying pan. These cultural skills evoke an archetypal spiritual power that enhances life and happiness.

After the elders' interview, I drove with my friend Arlene back toward Stony Rapids, which was about twelve miles away from Black Lake. We stopped along the road. It was at least twenty-five degrees below zero, and the northern lights streamed across the entire sky, as big and bright and deep green as I'd ever seen them. They were majestic in their color and expanse across the cold winter night sky. Many Native peoples believe that these lights are emanations from their grandfathers' and grandmothers' spirits. With such beauty, these lights felt alive and reflective of the happiness of the ancestors, as well as of the Earth spirits. As they lit up the night sky, ancestral spirits had also been present in the meeting of the elders. Ultimately, we all recognized the presence of the Creator, and something shifted in us.

Following the experience with the tribal elders and the northern lights, I felt the spirit world calling to me even more. I was ready to visit with a Native healer, a local shaman, and participate in a sweat lodge. I wanted to go down this path into the unknown, into the darkness of the womb of Mother Earth. There was a desire, even a desperation, to truly find a purpose and direction for my life.

Arlene told me about her "adopted" brother, Gerald, a shaman who performs sweat lodge ceremonies when someone requests help from the spirit world. Gerald's heritage is Dakota Sioux on his father's side and Plains Cree on his mother's. In addition to performing sweat ceremonies, Gerald has an extensive knowledge of traditional healing medicines, which he picks and prepares according to the spiritual traditions of his ancestors and specific instructions from the spirit world. While having only a fourth-grade formal education, Gerald is well respected as a healer for local tribespeople on the Dakota Sioux Reserve outside of Prince Albert, a small city located an hour-and-a-half flight from Stony Rapids.

Even though many people receive healing help from his medicines, ceremonies, and spiritual advice, Gerald humbly explains that the Creator, the grandfathers, and the grandmothers are the ones who do the healing, not him. Arlene asked Gerald whether he would be willing to "do a sweat" with me. After confirmation from Gerald and the go-ahead from Mehl-Madrona, I boarded a small plane to spend a few days with Gerald on the Dakota Sioux Reserve near Prince Albert, Saskatchewan.

CHAPTER 5

Exodus

How did I get here? How did I end up in a sweat lodge in northern Saskatchewan on the Dakota Sioux Reserve with Gerald the shaman? In other words, how did I physically, mentally, and spiritually get to the place in my life where I hungered for greater teaching and wisdom from a creosote tree, the coyote, the wolf, my ancestors, a shaman, and Dene and Hopi elders over the more formal education provided by my early life of religious and scientific studies, medical school, and Western culture? To answer this question, it is worth exploring my personal exodus from mainstream Western religion, culture, and medicine.

Both my parents were raised poor. My grandfather on my dad's side was raised in the era of the Great Depression and worked as a low wage earner at a railroad station for most of his life. Like most people from his generation, my grandfather counted every nickel he ever earned and spent. My mom's family was even less fortunate. Her father died when she was four years old, so she was raised by her older siblings and her mother in a small drafty house with only a wood stove for heating water and cooking food. They had no toilet, only an outhouse. She and her family slept on beds made of cotton sheets wrapped around corn husks. They grew nearly all the corn they ate and used for bedding. Her mom and sisters also made quilts, which they piled high upon those beds. My mom's family ate cornbread with almost every meal as a staple, paired with eggs or an occasional chicken. Sometimes her brothers would kill a squirrel for additional protein. Unfortunately, my mom lost hearing in her right ear at an early age as a result of pneumonia. Antibiotics were not readily available in that era for poor families like hers.[1]

My father was raised in the conservative sect of Protestant Baptist tradition. My dad and mom were married in a Baptist church in downtown Atlanta in 1967. My parents, sisters, and I attended a Baptist church until we moved in 1980. Then we began attending a slightly less conservative United Methodist Church in my hometown of Conyers, Georgia, near metropolitan Atlanta. My mom taught Sunday school at the church, and we all actively participated, attending church on Sunday mornings, evenings, and even other days for choir practice or other events. We also had family devotions every night before bedtime, along with an occasional story. I was usually an obedient child who pleased my Sunday school teachers and my parents by memorizing books of the Bible and applying scriptural knowledge to my life. I became a person of faith at an early age and was baptized and confirmed in the Methodist church.

In addition to my religious education, my parents raised me and my older sisters about twenty-five miles from the city of Atlanta on a ten-acre lake with sixteen acres of land that included creeks, woods, and pastureland, along with cows and a vegetable garden. My parents' house, built on the cusp of the energy crisis, in 1980, had passive solar heat and light. My mom made clothes and fresh-milled bread for our family. Daily wholesome nutrition and supplements were staples in our household. My father, although religiously conservative, stepped outside the mainstream world after reading books by Dr. Weston Price, DDS, a dentist who traveled around the world in the 1950s to discover and document how primitive peoples, eating diets close to their sources, boasted much better facial anatomy and fewer dental cavities than white modern peoples, who ate white bread and sugar-filled diets based on "foods of commerce."[2] As a dentist himself, my father followed Weston Price's recommendation to get back to natural ways of living and to consume natural foods. He was also one of the first dentists in his area to recommend the removal of amalgam fillings, also known as silver–mercury fillings, which contain over 50 percent mercury, along with nickel and other heavy metals, making them toxic to patients as well as dental office staff. Mercury fillings are now banned in over twenty-eight countries around the world.[3] Unfortunately, some dentists still use amalgam fillings in patient's mouths daily in the United States.

My father's not-so-mainstream health interests led him to explore the writings of many other cutting-edge philosophers and physicians, including Dr. Deepak Chopra; Dr. Norman Cousens; Dr. Wayne Dyer; Dr. Bernie Siegel; Dr. William Donald Kelley, DDS; and Anthony Robbins. On family vacations, I was regularly exposed to these holistic thinkers, as well as Nature-loving musicians, such as John Denver, as we drove many long miles across the United States in our conversion van. While my father read books from these outside-the-box thinkers, he practiced mostly modern dental care, without the silver fillings, and participated in a conservative church. My mother focused on natural food preparation, homemaking, Christian education, and Bible study. Growing up as part of the Traditionalist Generation, they were, in many ways, products of their era.

When I was five or six years old, my parents brought the entire family to self-hypnosis classes, where we learned how to master our sense of pain, reactions, or moods just by counting some numbers and deeply relaxing. As part of the training, I found I could make myself feel heavier and even perform better in my soccer games, especially if I could "drop into" this kind of relaxed, altered state of consciousness. I used self-hypnosis regularly to handle pain and outside stressors with more ease. Self-hypnosis skills even came in handy when my father would drill on my teeth during a dental exam or filling. While he offered me local anesthesia, my father almost always encouraged me to instead use self-hypnosis to mitigate the pain. It worked almost all the time! I would feel the sensation of the drill or other dental procedure, but the feeling was framed mentally as "no big deal."

As a well-behaved, studious child for most of my early childhood, I made good grades and followed the rules. I excelled at school, church, soccer, and Boy Scouts. I also played in the woods, swam and fished in the lake near my house, climbed and jumped out of a lot of trees, and rode my bicycle with no fear on my family's land. I watched TV shows like *The Fall Guy, The Greatest American Hero*, and *MacGyver,* with dreams of working as a scientist or stuntman someday.

About the same time in my childhood development, I became keenly interested in reading some of the free books and literature available at the health food store. On trips there with my mom, I remember reading about the amazing benefits of garlic, desiccated liver, ginseng, and other herbs or nutrients popular at that time. My father already had the whole family taking vitamin C, digestive enzymes, trace minerals, and a multiple vitamin—a plan he'd set in place when I was five. Our kitchen cabinets had lots of other supplements, too. Given my early use of these supplements, I naturally felt comfortable in the health food store and soon knew the store owners by name. As I became older, I convinced my mom to buy, or let me buy, natural treats and supplements to see what kind of health benefits I could gain from them. A healthy lifestyle started to attract and define me in my adolescent years. At the age of ten, I made a commitment to stop eating refined sugar. I became obsessed with the labels on any processed foods that came into the house. At Halloween, I collected candy, but I then sold it to my sisters. By the time I was fourteen and started high school, I was probably more of a natural health nut than my mom or my dad.

At that time, my friendships from my early years began to change. While most of my friends became more interested in girls, parties, and other social appearances, I matured slowly. I spent much of my time running, bicycling, or just being alone in the woods. My sister, Joni, who was seventeen and a senior in high school, took me to a few of her high school friends' parties. Watching one of her friends vomit in a garbage bag while riding in the backseat of our car on the way home from a late-night party, I decided that being around alcohol, cigarettes, drugs, and drunk people did not constitute fun. At fourteen, I had my first kiss with a girl who dumped me a month later, which helped me conclude that dating high school girls was too much work and emotional drama.

Whether I knew it or not, I was starting to embrace an ascetic, nearly monastic life that separated me from many of the otherwise attractive elements of a young adult living in Western culture. By age fifteen, I had stepped away from Western culture's foods of commerce (especially sweets and junk foods), typical high school social gatherings and teenage romance (which often involved alcohol, drugs, and sex), and allopathic medicine (with its mostly toxic pharmaceuticals). Later, I also stepped away from mainstream religious traditions (Protestant and Catholic beliefs and ceremonies).

Biologically, I was far behind almost all my male classmates in height and weight throughout most of high school. Even in my final years of high school, my voice had not yet deepened, and I still sounded like a boy. My best friends from elementary and middle school were now popular high school kids, but because of my small physical size (weighing 100–120 pounds and standing 5'2" to 5'10" through most of high school), as well as my atypical interests, I did not fit in with any group. I participated in cross-country, soccer, and wrestling, as well as church activities, but I could tell that something was different about my relationships. I started to spend more time bicycling and running by myself, sometimes for hours. By the time I was seventeen, I had developed a condition called Osgood-Schlatter's disease, in which the bones of my developing knees began to get inflamed with activity because they were slow to develop. I had to stop playing soccer completely, as well as stop running or playing any impact sports, until my knees finished developing. I began bicycling during most of my free time, riding around town and in the semirural areas in the neighboring counties and cities. I often got in trouble with my parents for bicycling after dark. I began backpacking regularly with my friends, fellow Boy Scouts, and with my dad in my later high school years. Many of these weeklong and weekend backpacking trips were in the ancestral territory of the Cherokee (the southern half of the Appalachians). I have always felt at home in those mountains.

As I grew older, my interest in health activities began to grow. I became a vegetarian to avoid the antibiotics and hormones that store-bought animal meats contained. I gained an interest in medicine, particularly in the more holistic ways of approaching health. It quickly became apparent to me that most pharmaceutical medications just treated the symptoms of disease and rarely, if ever, provided curative care. At that time, I held the perspective that Western pharmaceutical companies focused on making profit from sick people by artificially creating a demand for their commercialized products rather than looking for the actual cause of their disease.[4]

Even today, in my current medical practice, I will ask a patient, "Why do you think you got cancer?" Most patients eventually think of some potential etiology, but seldom before they have undergone chemotherapy, radiation, or surgery on the advice of mainstream physicians. With cancer, most allopathic physicians are not trained to ask a simple, logical question about the origin of a patient's chronic illness, perhaps for "good" economic reasons. While the even the American Cancer Society admitted, at one time, that diet and environmental factors (such as toxic food, pesticides, heavy metals, noxious oil and gas emissions, industrial pollutants, and cell phone EMFs) are responsible for over 50 percent of all cancers, doctors are not taught to investigate industrial or environmental sources of carcinogens or even critique the industries that produce these compounds.

My interest in changing the current medical system was already entrenched in me by the age of fifteen, when my dad and I had regular discussions about employing nontoxic ways to help patients heal. My father encouraged my passion for a more integrated approach to medicine, but he would often remind me that I had to "live in this world" and resist becoming too opinionated, especially before I was licensed to have a medical opinion. While he was incredibly open-minded, he was also part of the conformist Traditionalist Generation. Being part of Generation X, I was determined to "buck the system of old" and foster the medicine of a future world where I, along with other physicians, would care for patients in a Hippocratic manner with integrity, truth, love, and respect rather than just treating symptoms of their "disease."

At sixteen years old, my father introduced me to some role models of healers who practiced more natural Hippocratic medical care. After attending a lecture by Dr. Nicholas Gonzalez, a Cornell-educated cancer doctor from New York, I realized the power of a natural, holistic way of practicing medicine. Dr. Gonzalez, who derived many of his protocols from a dentist named William Donald Kelly, reported a 70 percent five-year-plus survival rate when using nutrients and specialized diets to treat advanced metastatic cancer patients. His protocols reconnected his patients to traditional diets to improve autonomic nervous system balance and restore the body to homeostasis and good health. If the person had Inuit heritage, for example, a traditional diet of 80 percent saturated fat was helpful for restoring their balance (between the parasympathetic and sympathetic systems) and eliminating cancer. The fact that Dr. Gonzalez looked at each person's heritage, diet, lifestyle, and environmental toxins stood in stark contrast to the mainstream "kill the cancer" pharmaceutical approach common to Western oncologists. Gonzalez had literally stepped "out of the box" of his Western medical paradigm into a whole different world of medicine. Although I was only sixteen, I was more than impressed not just with Gonzalez (and others like him) but also with the healing wisdom and power revealed by his alternative view of medicine, especially in 1991.

That next year, I became a staunch vegetarian and attempted to eat lots of organic foods from the garden. I even stumbled upon a summer job working with a homeopathic laboratory. I learned a good deal about homeopathy, and I also encountered a generally negative and polarizing attitude toward the allopathic medical system, among alternative health providers. Even as a young high school student, I respected the necessary use of mainstream Western medicine, in a limited fashion, although I favored the rapidly growing tributary of holistic and natural medicine—a tributary which had its source largely from Native medical traditions and belief systems.

Around the same time in my adolescence, my spiritual and religious focus also began shifting. Instead of attending the church of my parents, I opted to attend a church that was less traditional in its worship setting and more focused on foreign missions. The church met in a rented warehouse, and no one really dressed up in anything more than casual attire. While every other word in the church seemed to be about Jesus or "getting saved by Jesus," I loved the freedom to dress as I pleased and the uniqueness of these hippie-like "Jesus freaks." I loved wearing a bandana around my head to church and reveled in the serendipitous miracles and faith healings reported by parishioners who had returned from foreign mission trips to Nepal, Africa, or other impoverished areas of the world. I later came to learn that these missionary healers were part of a movement that came to be known as the Third Wave of Pentecostalism.

With my church preference differing from my former United Methodist affiliation, I also began to explore Nature with a more transcendental perspective. Although they lived almost two centuries before my era, authors Henry David Thoreau and Ralph Waldo Emerson became some of my best friends in helping me step outside, literally, of the milieu of modern commercial life. After reading *The Tracker* by Tom Brown Jr., I felt as though my home was truly in the wilderness, a landscape where I could live a more primitive, simpler, sustainable life. In the early 1990s, I felt there was so much materialism in secular American culture that I wanted to escape. Even my parents had stopped gardening regularly, raising cows, and making bread or homemade foods, and had bought more into the materialistic culture. While in middle school, I went from wearing name-brand shirts and designer khaki pants to wearing sandals or moccasins with cut-off sweats. While my parents had provided me with a 1979 Datsun car, worth about $2,000, I was happier hiking or riding my bicycle everywhere. I saw the value of Western culture, especially in the realm of science, but felt I felt that this culture was polluting and destroying so much of Nature—including the health of human bodies. Apart from my inner dialogue with literary authors like Emerson and Thoreau, I felt alone in this "impure" world that did not seem to be living in harmony with Nature or the Creator.

At eighteen, as my interest in being alone with Nature and backpacking continued to grow, I became set on the idea of hiking the entire Appalachian Trail (AT). The AT offered solitary respite from the overly materialistic and hedonistic world created by modern society. I found a role-model hiker and dialogue partner living near my hometown, Dan "Wingfoot" Bruce. At the time, he had hiked the entire AT seven times and authored a yearly book called *The Thru-hiker's Handbook*, which provided much-needed information about the towns and necessary resupply areas along the trail. Dan became a great conversation partner, as well as an inspiration that fueled my passion and rationale for hiking the AT. Dan even published my name in the credits of his 1994 edition of *The Thru-hiker's Handbook*, as John "Lightfoot" Hughes.

The summer after graduating from high school, I hiked nine hundred miles of the Appalachian Trail. Emerson's quote summed up my own philosophy: "The civilized man has built himself a coach but has lost the use of his feet."[5] With Thoreau and Emerson as mentors, I ventured into the woods to find health in a solitary and spiritual way. Ten weeks of living in the semi-wilderness of Appalachia had a dramatic effect upon my outlook. While I escaped one society's paradigm of thought, to a degree, I quickly entered another. Ironically, in the solitude of the wilderness where I could think freely, my excitement about social connections with fellow hikers or Appalachian folk grew. In other words, I realized that there was something good about entering a small town after hiking for ten days in the woods. As I enjoyed chatting in the evening with fellow hikers at a common shelter, I postulated that society, even American society, still had some merit because it fostered significant social connections. Even so, I maintained that many of society's paradigms, particularly in its Western mainstream medical system, had a lot of problems, largely owing to a disconnection from Nature.

Entering college at the liberal arts school Furman University two weeks after completing my nirvana-esque AT journey, I was ill-equipped to handle the social barrage of dorm life and the scholastic demands of university classes. In high school, I had developed into the prototypical science type with few social distractions or skills. Now in college, my romantic idealist outlook (fed all summer by the AT experience) opened me up to experiential, subjective life, and this experience began to chip away at my scientific naturalism. In short, relationships with people, Nature, and God became increasingly more important than the science work I had so valued in the past. I double-majored in biology and chemistry, as I believed science was the most valuable knowledge at that time, but I graduated from college burned out by school and burdened with an identity crisis of sorts. Meaning eluded me. The paradigm created by scientific study did not motivate me or offer fulfillment.

While at Furman, my religious friends and church community were largely fundamental and even rigid in their beliefs. Even though I really enjoyed getting to know these intellectual religious friends, they believed strictly in the authority of the Bible and the theological interpretations of their Calvinistic ministers. In a way similar to how science seeks objective truth, the general goal of my religious friends was to find a kernel of objective truth from a Bible study or a church service in order to reveal their own sins and the sinful ways of the world. The end goal was to aid people, including themselves, to repent from those sins and find salvation and healing through Jesus and the love of God. These religious friends rejected the world, with its sinful ways, and encouraged believers to focus on a spiritual place called heaven, along with praising and worshipping God. However, everyone else, unless they asked for Jesus to save them and repented from their sins, could go to hell. In many ways, this religious rejection of the world, along with daily introspection to search out impurities, corresponded with my natural health pursuits (seeking pure medicine) and my desire to escape to an outdoor world (my heaven) quite well.

This fire-and-brimstone teaching had a strong hold on me until I started to find chinks in the armor of the church's doctrine. Always one to question everything, I repeatedly asked the pastors why something they said did not match up with the multitude of Bible verses I could quote at that time during my college years. As I started to question the black-and-white nature of God's authentic message to humans, my world expanded to more open-minded people outside my sect of Protestant Christianity. While I did not buy into the idea of moral relativism, the belief that humans can decide for themselves ultimate moral truth, I understood that little details from the Bible, such as women wearing head coverings in churches, are largely irrelevant to the core truths of the great master, Jesus Christ. From the book of John, in what Christians call the New Testament, Jesus states that those who love and follow him are those who do what he commands.[6] In the book of Matthew, Jesus boils down his entire message into two primary commands:

> "Love the Lord your God with all your heart and with all your soul and with all your mind." This is the first and greatest commandment. And the second is like it:

> "Love your neighbor as yourself." All the Law and the Prophets hang on these two commandments.[7]

These simple commands are the same as, or at least remarkably similar to, the teachings of all the great avatars, sages, and teachers. Hence, it is likely very true that many people are following a path to the divine, as articulated by Jesus, Krishna, Buddha, or other sages. Yet, for all their simplicity, if one explores these words spoken by Jesus or another avatar a little deeper, questions arise. What does it mean to really "love?" What does it mean to love God with all your mental (mind), physical (heart), and spiritual (soul) self? Also, who is "God?" And who is your "neighbor?" Does your neighbor include just humans or all other creatures in Nature? Do mainstream Western culture and its predominant Westernized religions instill greater love for God and one's neighbor in an embodied way? Similarly, are practitioners of Western medicine really loving God and their patients?

These questions have no easy, articulable answers and thus beg for more philosophical exploration—an exploration which shall occur in later chapters of this book. When I was a young college graduate, now free to explore the world in an experiential way, these questions kept me from fully embracing a Western lifestyle, including its culture, religion, and medicine.

Hence, at twenty-two years old, when attempting to find a career path in a Western world where I didn't feel as though I fit in, I struggled. I had graduated from Furman University in 1997, having earned dual degrees in both biology and chemistry, but I felt pretty confused about the direction of my life. While I wanted to go to medical school eventually, the idea of again bonding myself to an institution where I would be told what to do, how to think, and what to study gave me pause.

Right after finishing college, I told my parents that I wanted to work in a bicycle shop. Even after spending tens of thousands of dollars on my undergraduate education, they were okay with me working at a bike shop; they knew I was still figuring things out. I loved cycling and the natural world. My passion had led me to create both a cycling club and an environmental action club at Furman University. Now I wondered what I could do outside the academic world, but I had no clear direction yet.

Instead of working at the bike shop, I started a business to help people cut energy costs—mostly by selling them energy-efficient lighting projects. With my little bit of savings, I rented a live-in warehouse and moved out of my parents' house. Unfortunately, I was burning through my cash. By the end of my first year out of school, I'd spent about $30,000 without making much profit. It was discouraging. I spoke to friends, family, and business owners about reducing energy costs by changing out all their lightbulbs to more efficient ones, and there was some interest, but not enough. I was in the Southeastern United States in the late 1990s, and many Southern people weren't aware of the benefits of reducing energy use or the coal pollution due to the massive consumption of energy used for lighting, air conditioning, hot water, and more. (A commercial building could spend 50 percent of its energy bill in lighting costs during that time). I did find a few like-minded colleagues at an organization called Southface Institute, a nonprofit based in Atlanta that focused on helping homeowners design houses with sealed ducts, low-E windows, and efficient lighting and appliances. But eventually, without cash flow, my business trajectory followed that of 80 percent of all small businesses whose owners' passionate ideas are ahead of the culture. I had to give up my warehouse and business operations and then find a job where I would be told what to do—for a small hourly wage.

Just before shutting down my business, Integrity Energy Conservation, I did manage to land a partnership with another business called Landmark Energy Associates. This organization was a Virginia-based company that installed lighting retrofits for large corporations. They had just landed a big deal with a large phone company. I went to Virginia and spent time with the CEO and was impressed by the company's passion to stop ecological pollution by reducing energy consumption. They felt I might be well-suited to sell energy-efficiency projects to engineers who worked in the large high-rise buildings in downtown Atlanta. These projects included big lighting projects and water-efficiency projects, including toilet retrofits. I was on board; all I had to do was show these engineers how much money they could save by retrofitting fluorescent or incandescent lights with more efficient LEDs (which had just come on the market) or upgrading their toilet parts. I thought I could make back the money I'd spent on my business and help reduce airborne coal pollution from power plants. It was an exciting possibility. But I still had to work and make some cash.

I first went to work for a chiropractor in my hometown. After a month, the chiropractor said that it wasn't working out and he wanted me to leave. He said he felt as though I wanted his job instead of the one I had as a chiropractic assistant. I was bored to death anyhow. After that job ended, I went backpacking for a week or so. Then I jumped from odd job to odd job, doing electrical contracting work, delivering Sheetrock, selling coupon books, selling newspaper subscriptions, and serving as a courier. I took whatever job was available in my little town. I would work until I got bored (usually after a few months) and then go off to learn some other trade.

In the meantime, on my days off or in between odd jobs, I called building engineers and decision-makers about big building retrofits. These guys rarely gave me, a twenty-three-year-old kid, the time of day, but I did sometimes make progress. I even got a call from the national energy manager for AT&T once. Finally I struck oil (or gold). A church friend of mine worked at BellSouth and introduced me to the building engineers there. They called me, and I met with them to discuss a $1.5 million lighting retrofit project, as well as a $102,000 toilet and faucet retrofit project. After 1.5 years of budgeting talks with the engineers, I landed the water project for my partnered firm, Landmark Energy Associates.

We did the project over eight days, during the holidays, and Landmark received a check for the work performed. I was supposed to make about $50,000 on the project. But after two months, no check had arrived. When I asked the Landmark firm to send me my distribution, they told me that the check was in the mail, but it was only $28,000. At twenty-four years old, there was a big difference between earning $50,000 and $28,000. I explained that to one of the owners of the company. He said to write a letter to the CEO, which I did. The company's attorney wrote back threatening to sue me. Along with the financial challenge, this was emotionally challenging. I had trusted these people. When I told my father about my situation, he hired an attorney. I eventually won a judgment against the firm, in my hometown, for $80,000 (my partnership distribution plus legal fees). The Landmark Energy Associates partners never paid. My attorney garnished $8,000 from their bank account, but they hid the rest of their funds in another corporation. This experience was an eye-opener, revealing the devious nature of big-money so-called friends or partners, and the Western business world in general. My early foray into a cutthroat, real-life business world had ended, in more ways than one, poorly.

CHAPTER 6

God, Philosophy, and Medicine

While taking on odd jobs and selling big toilet projects with questionable business partners, I also read a lot of theological and philosophical books in my spare time. When my girlfriend enrolled at Duke University's Divinity School in 1998, I became motivated to understand more about what she was learning about God and how my philosophical interests could also be explored. When I realized that I could get a degree for writing and reading theological and philosophical books, I enrolled at Duke in the year 2000. Since my business ambition had been quenched with a sour deal, I realized that being told what to do and think in an institution was perhaps better than getting my money stolen in the business world. Thwarted by the "real" Western world of business and money, I wholeheartedly embraced the challenge of theological graduate school. Little did I know at that time that I would become a professional student for the next eight years of my life.

Duke is a United Methodist theological school located on Duke's main campus in Durham, North Carolina. The professors are first class, well published, and recognized worldwide. In fact, one of my professors, Reverend Dr. Stanley Hauerwas, PhD, was even applauded by *Time* magazine as America's Best Theologian.[1] I loved Stanley's classes and his contrarian attitude, intensity, and manner of speech. I think he must have passionately dropped the "F-bomb" three or more times in every class. It was great. Hauerwas had many disciples, mostly PhD aspirants, who wanted to be just like him and regularly espoused his theological approach of a story-formed community and ethic. In his era at Duke, Hauerwas and his teachings had a powerful influence over much of the Divinity

School, and not many critics of his views ever stood a chance with him in a theological debate.

Speaking of divinity school debates, I enjoyed watching my fellow classmates get fired up about their religious beliefs as they defended their views in front of the professors or classmates. Having a calculating, scientific reserve, I could sit back and argue for just about any side with emotion, and then switch to the other side in a minute. I loved all the philosophy we studied—from ancient church mystics, to Plato, to modern-day thinkers. I gained an incredible perspective on the foundations behind North American Judeo-Christian society as I learned about Hebrew People, the Greeks, the Catholic Church, and the Protestants.

In my theological studies at Duke, I entered a philosophical world with a much broader expression than anything I'd ever experienced in a church setting. For example, many preachers and churches are devout in believing one specific atonement theory to explain why Jesus Christ existed or died on a cross. At Duke, I learned that more than seven atonement theories exist.[2] One theory, called the moral exemplar theory, states that Christ's moral example is salvific, in itself, for the atonement of his followers. The implications of this atonement theory suggest that Jesus Christ did not have to die on the cross for human salvation. Instead, the cross might be viewed as just another form of capital punishment, or murder, that many of today's Christians are still so passionately (no pun intended) promoting. What if the true disciples of Jesus are not those *who believe Jesus made a sacrifice for them* but rather those *who are actually following the teachings of Jesus* in their daily lives? Hell, these true disciples might not even know Jesus ever existed but may be better followers than regular churchgoers who look for Jesus to forgive them from sins, particularly the sins of Western culture.

At Duke, I also learned that the Catholic Bible has seven more books than the Protestant Bible.[3] Okay, now, which Bible is the authentic word of God? And who gets to decide any of this?

In the spring of my first year at Duke, I entered a course called Theology and Medicine. The class was taught by two professors: Joel Shuman, PhD; and Keith Meador, MD, ThM, MPH. Dr. Shuman, formerly a physical therapist, had left his PT career to pursue a PhD at Duke under the contrarian theologian Dr. Stanley Hauerwas. Dr. Meador was a psychiatrist at Duke with a master's degree in theology and public health. The class was also filled with some sophisticated attendees, many of whom were already practitioners in the health-care field. One was a physician fellow at Duke, and another, Warren Kinghorn, had finished his third year at Harvard Medical School. There I was, an idealistic entrepreneur and odd job worker with biology and chemistry degrees who had recently left his parents' house and read a few philosophical books about God.

Most of my other divinity school classes at Duke included other students focused on careers as United Methodist ministers in mainstream churches around the nation. I had no desire to become a minister. While I still was interested in medicine, I still had no clear direction for my life. However, this course by Shuman and Meador that mixed theology, philosophy, and medicine piqued some of my core interests. After a year of making excellent grades in my other theology courses at Duke, I knew I could read high-level material and hold my own in debates with some of the most articulate intellectuals I'd ever met.

While confident in my ability to make effective arguments in class, I generally refrained from espousing my own religious beliefs. Instead I wrote creative papers that received high marks. I was there to learn all I could and embodied Aikido's humble mental posture of *Onegai shimasu*, which may be translated as "Please let me train with you," or "Please teach me."[4] However, in the Theology and Medicine course, I engaged more in class discussions because I felt as if they had more application to my previous studies of science, medicine, and the physical world we inhabit. The class discussions played a key role in helping me understand and detach from hidden Western culture belief systems, such as naturalism. Naturalism is the belief system that only through the five senses, as articulated by the scientific method, can humans understand the physical world. In the face of my questions about naturalistic Western belief systems, the Theology and Medicine course at Duke helped me discover ancient epistemological understandings of the spiritual and physical world, particularly in relation to science and medicine.

When the class was asked for commentary and summary of one of the main course books, *Body of Compassion*, written by my professor Dr. Shuman, I confidently volunteered for the endeavor. I worked on the paper for a solid week, and on April 5, 2001, the entire class discussed my professor's book and my commentary about it. The following quote is from my paper on Joel Shuman's *Body of Compassion*.

> Humankind, since the 17th century, has explained the ontology of the material world solely in terms of "science."[5] Newton, who claimed his research into the laws of Nature "proved" his faith in God,[6] instead helped introduce a contorted epistemology[7] that, over time and with contributions from Bacon and Descartes, effectively removed religious tradition from the dialogue of material ontology.[8] In place of the clergy, positivists[9] and deists[10] propagated this Enlightenment epistemology to gain hegemony over material matters, in particular, the human body. Today this hegemony finds vivid expression in the modern practice of health care, with one addition: practitioners now attempt to use the language of "science" (falsifiable knowledge gained by making observations through the five senses)[11] in order to describe autonomously both material (physical) and immaterial (spiritual) reality.[12]

The above philosophical words, if fully comprehended, take the reader on a deep journey that unravels how Western humans see, live in, and understand the material world. Shuman's message about humanity's disconnection from our bodies, along with the Earth and the entirety of material reality and the spirit, including the soul, has relevance to all peoples. And hence, Western humanity's disconnection from the body, known since the seventeenth century as Cartesian dualism, has profound implications on the practice of medicine. Indeed, it is this dualistic division of material and spiritual that may be the reason for medicine's continued failure to help patients nurture their physical, mental, and spiritual well-being and live fulfilling, fit, and healthy lives.

An adaption to Ghost Wolf's quote (as stated at the beginning of this book) by Silvia Browne is "There is a time coming, beyond the weather. The veil between the physical and the spiritual world is thinning; it is coming back to life ..."[13] Ghost Wolf and Browne articulate the same kind of reality that Shuman describes as the unity of the spiritual and material (physical) world, a unity which is deeply already expressed in our bodies and the Earth. Medicine of the Fifth World includes, beyond philosophical discussion, the actualization of a united spiritual and material reality at the individual, community, and planetary levels. Simply put, healing this planet and all its inhabitants requires a renewed juxtaposition of what we consider as spiritual and physical. The Fifth World is a place of health, wellness, and sustainability for humans and the Earth because it is where we have learned to live with an integrated mind, body, and spirit.

Yet in the Fourth World (the Western world as we know it), the merger of what is spiritual with the physical constitutes a real challenge and even threat to the way of life for many humans because it requires an abandonment of core epistemologies that divide our spiritual and material realities, including Cartesian dualism as well as Newtonian and Baconian science. To clarify, for at least the past four centuries of the Fourth World, Western humans have erroneously believed in the epistemologies of dualism (and its distinct division of spiritual and material reality) and objective science to authoritatively describe that material reality of Nature. This hegemony of these post-Enlightenment epistemologies is particularly apparent in Western medicine and science and the "experts" in these fields.

Modern medical schools train their practitioners to treat the body only within the framework of dualism. Dualism, as descended from Descartes, views the mind as immaterial and the body as wholly material and governed by physical law. The philosopher Alasdair MacIntyre writes, "When the body is understood as material and passive, it can readily be seen as an object for or an exemplification of the results of scientific research."[14] As an object for study, "knowing" the body comes only through a detached observer.[15] These observers, over time, acquire the title of "expert." These experts, knowing "the *real* order of things" possess an esoteric knowledge hidden to others, and they receive an authority through knowledge not rooted in spiritual or religious tradition, but rather observation and cognition.[16]

Can we really trust so-called experts in science and medicine, who have no connection to the spirit world, to tell us how to care for our sacred physical bodies? And why do many Westerners prioritize the messages by these so-called scientific or medical experts over teachings by a guru, shaman, priest, or any human who is connected to both the spirit world and physical reality? Clearly, many Western dualistic humans have been deceived into thinking that truth about the physical world derives from experts who claim authority over the body and the rest of the natural world—an expertise based on "objective" science.

Ultimately, what dualism does by dividing body and spirit is promulgate the idea that humans, along with the Earth and the rest of Nature, are primarily material entities about which the only accurate knowledge comes from empirical research—that is, using the five senses through the scientific method. The practitioners of this erroneous dualistic philosophy, including medical practitioners and most scientists in Western society, become experts or specialists in the material objects that they investigate with the five senses, often in order to manipulate these objects—through symbolic data from those investigations—for utilitarian human purposes. However, if humans and all of Nature are integrated as spiritual and material beings, this scientific, evidenced-based knowledge and the manipulations derived from it are only half true and insufficient to heal humans and Nature. Shuman confirms that the objectification of the body leads to inaccurate diagnoses and treatments. He also contends that since the scientific viewpoint of modern health care cannot discern "what the body *is* teleologically," modern practitioners cannot say "what [the body] is *for* in order to care for it faithfully when it is sick."[17]

Teleology is the study of ends. "Ends" may denote the actual end of a life, or the purpose and final goal in the trajectory of life. Shuman quotes the Catholic saint Thomas Aquinas, who states, "… the end is the measure of things ordered to the end."[18] That is, the teleological purpose of all of Nature (including human life) is uniquely intertwined with a daily existence oriented toward that end. Aquinas describes this "ultimate end" as "human flourishing in a certain kind of friendship with God."[19] In short, it is impossible to separate Nature's (including humanity's) *existence* from its *purpose*. Hence, addressing all of humanity and all of Nature's continued existence must include an understanding of the purpose of our existence, an existence that stretches beyond what is perceived physically by the five senses, through the scientific method. Western science, as practiced in the Fourth World, does not and cannot deal with ultimate ends or purposes of humans as unified spiritual and material beings. And because it deals only with objective "facts" *about* physical reality, this Fourth World science and its experts cannot speak truthfully about Nature or human lives or what to do with it all. Consequently, in the Fourth World, we have a lot of confusion about what is "good medicine," and a lot of people are suffering. Mother Earth, also, is in crisis.

The suffering of Fourth World humans and the Earth are synonymous occurrences. Under Shuman's tutelage, I realized we are, when integrated physical and spiritual human beings, deeply attached, *pro eo primaria*, to the body and spirit of the Earth, as well as to the Earth's destiny.[20] Wendell Berry articulates my thoughts in his essay *The Body and the Earth*:

> While we live our bodies are moving particles of the earth, joined inextricably both to the soil and to the bodies of other living creatures. It is hardly surprising that there should be some profound resemblances between our treatment of our bodies and our treatment of the earth.[21]

One may also argue that even when we are dead, we remain as recycled particles of the Earth and our spirits share a destiny common with that of the Earth and the rest of Nature. If this truth is understood, it is a wake-up call for many in Western society who believe that our souls just float away to some heavenly salvation, divorced from the spiritual and material well-being of the body of the Earth and the rest of Nature. Influenced by Cartesian dualism and Platonic philosophy, Christian religions have largely been responsible for the Western belief that human spirits just fly away to heaven at the end of life, leaving the Earth to a blissful, sacred destiny. In his book, *Art of the Commonplace,* Berry makes this message clear:

> Religion, in this part of the world, has promoted and fed upon destructive schism between body and soul, Heaven and Earth. It has encouraged people to believe that the world is of no importance, and their only obligation in it is to submit to churchly formulas in order to get into Heaven. And, so the people who might have been expected to care most selflessly for the world have had their minds turned elsewhere to the pursuit of a "salvation" that is really only another form of gluttony and self-love, the desire to perpetuate their lives beyond the life of the world. [22]

Berry does not mince words here as he explains how Western humans have embraced dualism, such as the erroneous division of material and spiritual, body and soul, heaven and Earth, humans and Nature. Many religious persons, even those from the predominant Western traditions, focus their attention on spiritual knowledge, including the beliefs, rules, and doctrines that allegedly help them enter heaven for eternal life. Turning their backs on their Mother Nature, many Westerners have bequeathed all authority over truth about Nature, including human bodies, to experts in empiricism, such as dualistic scientists and medical practitioners, who believe that what is true about the physical world derives only through what is perceived by the five senses. Embracing dualism, Western religious people, scientists, and medical practitioners have abused and manipulated the world horrifically. Berry continues, "The Heaven-Bent have abused the earth thoughtlessly, by inattention, and their negligence has permitted and encouraged others to abuse it deliberately."[23]

And it is hard to blame dualistic religious people or scientists. Western scientists, governed by disembodied scientific "reason," regularly and daily assert authority about human bodies, the Earth, and all of Nature and what to do with it. These scientists and religious followers simply do not possess the necessary embodiment to allow them to know, love, and respect their bodies and the Earth as temples of the divine.

Nonreligious persons see the lack of physical grounding in mainstream religions. Indeed, the demise of mainstream religion in the United States and other Western civilizations may happen in the next few decades. When religious groups fail to synthesize the harmonious unity of the spiritual and physical, the nonreligious see no benefit to these formerly dominant institutions and seek spirituality, along with authentic material connection, elsewhere. Unfortunately, many of these nonmainstream spiritual pursuits are also not grounded in physical reality because many Western spiritual seekers, often unknowingly, believe in dualism. These seekers frequently possess an inner desperation for authentic truth about the spiritual and physical world. But because of dualism, Western religious pursuits as well as alternative spiritual quests are not grounded in the physical manifestation of the sacred in daily life.

The results of what Cartesian dualism has done to medicine are literally sickening. As discussed in chapter 4, many humans, as well as the many parts of the Earth, are sick and getting sicker. This sickness is a direct result of humanity's embrace of a dualistic philosophy purporting that physical bodies (including the Earth and all Nature) are separate from their spirits (souls). And out of this dualism, humans have allowed science, and its medical practitioners, to objectify their bodies and manipulate these bodies (and the Earth) away from disease. Modern scientific manipulation of the body and Earth as objects leads to imbalance of the Earth and its inhabitants. To sum up the cause of this imbalance, I reiterate: (1) Dualistic medical practitioners do not have full knowledge of human beings and the Earth as body and spirit—only *about* the body or Nature as physical data. (2) The gathering and use of these physical data occur purely through the five senses; for these dualistic practitioners, there is no higher way of accessing what is physically true or knowledge about what to do with it. (3) Dualistic medical practitioners try to use objective science to gain control over and master Nature instead of working with Nature. They fail to understand that Nature's healing forces are the same healing powers for all humanity. 4) Finally, dualistic medical practitioners, bound to evidence-based scientific knowledge, have no words for the spiritual nature of humans or the Earth. Without an understanding of the spiritual world (which is inaccessible to the five senses core to the scientific method), dualistic medical practitioners have no idea how to treat humans as spiritual–physical beings.

Western humans continue to default to science and manipulation of the human body and the Earth in their failed attempts to solve diseases, such as infectious diseases, cancer, obesity, heart disease, stress, depression, acid rain, pollution, or whatever. While new scientific discoveries, inventions, and manipulations of the physical human and Nature can be helpful, these endeavors will only lead to imbalance if not performed with a true spiritual intention and authentic connection to the Earth. The following commentary by Robert Boissiere on the Hopi Prophecy Rock beckons for humans to look for answers beyond Western science in treating diseases or approaching life in general: "When prayer and meditation are used rather than relying on our new inventions to create more imbalance, they will also find the true path."[24]

Traditional Hopi understand that health and the sustenance of all life require the realization of the unity of the spiritual and physical nature of human lives as well that of the Earth. Traditional Hopi people understand that the health of humans and the Earth ultimately can be found in radical, subjective, relational connection—humans as physical–spiritual beings, humans with Mother Earth (and all of Nature), body–soul, humans as communities, and humans as one with the divine. In contrast, scientific dualism creates a division of the body and the soul that inaugurates "an expanding series of [destructive] divisions."[25] Wendell Berry writes,

> The modern urban society is based on a radical series of disconnections between body and soul, husband and wife, marriage and community, community and the earth. At each of these points of disconnection, the collaboration of corporation, government, and expert sets up a profit-making enterprise that results in the further dismemberment and impoverishment of the Creation ... Only by restoring the broken connections can we be healed. Connection is health.[26]

Like the Hopi and other like-minded Native peoples, Berry argues that health depends on rekindling core connections of lives—a task which cannot be accomplished through dualistic scientific inquiry and manipulation. Dualistic, disembodied scientific inquiry cannot restore health and balance, because it requires a third-person standpoint—a standpoint in which the observer and the observed are separate. This separation, implicit to Western science, leads to a disconnection of humans from their ecosystem, other humans, the spirit world, and the rest of Nature. Dualistic science disconnects because it *objectifies* core connections—connections which are essential for life. Finding true health requires stepping beyond dualism-based scientific knowledge and restoring these broken core connections through *subjective* relationships.

But what is the pathway for healing and balance? How do we develop a harmonious relationship with our spirits, minds, bodies, animals, plants, and the rest of Nature in a way that fosters health as a result? That is, if Western science is old school (a.k.a. Fourth World), what do healing and balance look like in the Fifth World?

CHAPTER 7

Spirituality and Medicine: Silence Is Power

The endless cycle of idea and action,
Endless invention, endless experiment,
Brings knowledge of motion, but not of stillness;
Knowledge of speech, but not of silence...
Where is the wisdom we have lost in knowledge?
Where is the knowledge we have lost in information?
T. S. Eliot, *The Rock*

In 2002, I graduated from Duke with a master's degree in theological studies. Toward the end of my time at Duke, I realized that the lengthy philosophical papers written and read were just words on a page. The more philosophical these words became, and the deeper I went into exploring them, the fewer people could understand or care about these lofty words. In short, while my theological and philosophical understandings were truly self-enriching, these pursuits resided in the ivory tower of academic intellectualism—or, crudely, mental masturbation. It just didn't feel to me as if philosophical writing, while intellectually valuable, created much material change in my life or the lives of those around me. While I loved the study of philosophy and religions, I craved an application, in physical reality, of those teachings in my everyday life and the lives of those around me.

After leaving Duke, I moved with my fiancée to Phoenix, Arizona, to pursue a degree in osteopathic medicine. The philosophy of osteopathic medicine resonated well with my theological, Duke-inspired understandings of the body, mind, and spirit. After a few prerequisite courses, I started osteopathic school in 2003 at the Arizona College of Osteopathic Medicine. For the next two years, I again embraced the world of didactic scientific study, including hundreds of hours studying biochemistry, physiology, immunology, anatomy, pathology, pharmacology, psychology, neuroscience, and osteopathic manual therapy. Shifting from philosophical training to the rigorous medical sciences was not the easiest step. Instead of writing fifteen- to forty-page papers that expanded the mind largely by looking broadly at multiple possibilities and arguments, I took an average of three multiple-choice tests (usually with six or more answers for each question) where the goal was to use the left brain to converge upon one single, best answer. If you recall my background, before going to Duke, I had lived and breathed the world of science. I took more science courses than anyone in my high school and was even awarded a local Rotary club award for these achievements. I also completed more science courses than anyone at my college, graduating with dual Master of Science in biology and chemistry from a small private liberal arts school known as Furman University.

At one time in my early scholastic life, I perceived that the only valuable knowledge in life was derived from scientific research and inquiry. However, my theological training at Duke, particularly from Dr. Joel Shuman, unraveled my former reliance upon science for true knowledge. But the study of biology, chemistry, and now medicine, with its scientific dependency, was my briar patch—my turf. And even with a head full of challenging philosophy, I was pretty good at the mental operations required by the world of science and medicine.

After leaving Duke, another aspect of my core being—a spiritual aspect, which arose in my everyday life, in between the rigors of medical science study. Stepping outside the language of theology or philosophy to understand this kind of spiritual experience, I found myself trail running in the desert landscape around Phoenix on a regular basis, seeking wisdom in lonely, desolate, quiet places. At a local bookstore, I found the *Soul of Nowhere* by Craig Childs, a skilled writer and adventurer who explores lonely places of the world. *Soul of Nowhere* describes Childs's experiences and contemplations in the desert—especially as they contrast what Western humans hold as scientific and definitive. For example, Childs writes about how we understand the nature of time:

> If you sat in the desert for a year with a clock and a Gregorian calendar, you would find that that your time does not match what you see in the world around you. The snake, the stars, the sun, and the moon belong to an interlocking design.[1] We fool ourselves with our inventions. The gears of true time are not round like those of the clock. The earth travels at different speeds during different times of the year, slinging faster and slower, making European winters eight days shorter than those in Australia. Lunar and solar cycles set up a complex rhythm obeying doublets and triplets, not the singular boxes of weekdays and months. We are made to look like simpletons with our artless time of minutes, hours, and days, leap years thrown in to jury-rig our twelve months so that they don't fall into disrepair. We add and subtract sixty minutes of daylight-saving time to our seasons to make our work days more efficient, our heads buried in business while around us these flawless patterns pass like the hand of God.[2]

Childs's understanding of time is particularly brilliant, as it helps us recognize that much of Western world is not totally accurate about "facts," including chronological time, which most humans would never question or even think to question. The reality about God, Earth, and the rest of

Nature is much more sophisticated than Western science alone can really uncover, and Childs beckons us to invest into this mysterious reality.[3] The Earth, while impacted by our inventions, ultimately beats to a much higher order than we humans can fully understand. Certainly, "we fool ourselves with our inventions," as well as other constructions about the nature of reality.

At the beginning of medical school and a medical career chock full of dualistic scientific explanations and evidence-based medicine, I began investing more time in the spirit world as well as the mysterious desert surrounding my home—along with its sometimes exhausting 110° F or higher heat. I craved more and more time in the desert. During the early years of medical study, I lived close to an area called South Mountain Park, a seventeen-thousand-acre park in Phoenix, Arizona, which qualifies as the largest city park in the world. Two to three times a week, I would run or go mountain biking in this park. Being alone most of the time on my adventures, I embraced the vitality of what, at first glance, seemed like a lifeless desert. Yet I found life and even abundance in this desert haven. I even developed a relationship of sorts with a particular creosote bush that resided on top of a little mountain I regularly ascended while trail running. Here's a little poem I wrote about my creosote bush friend.

Like the Creosote

I like the creosote,
Scraggly and rugged,
Wild and free,
Yes, the creosote like me.

Survive in the desert;
There we grow,
Full of mystery
But hardly a show.

Oh, deafening silence!
Oh, luscious wasteland!
Oh, sucker of life!
Oh, giver of peace!

To blend, to meld
With this gentle harshness,
Is the path of survival
Of joy, love, and ... life.

A school of learning,
The desert looms;
To journey onward
Demands a profound integrity.

The creosote has it!
With rock-colored limbs
And many leaves dry,
It commonly rejoices
In the big desert sky.

The creosote
Smiles on
Through fire, wind, sun,
Snow, rain, heat, and cold,
Beckoning wonder from
All who dare behold.

Thy determination, strength,
The hardy mission of this flora
Enlightens a passerby,

Yet the question remains:
Whereupon dwells
Thy vigilant core?

Few call her beauty;
Most overlook her,
Yet some know her secret:
Yes, the creosote's secret
Unites her with all,
For it holds high
Her nature as "I."

Revealed often by rain,
The creosote's secret,
"Her essence,"
Carries enchanting harmony
As she merges with me.

Might all who breathe
In this creosote free
Be open enough to grow
Into unified diversity.

The subjective relationship between the physical and spiritual aspects of the creosote, the desert, the sun, the rain, the heat, the air, and my life existed as dynamic, mysterious, and beyond anything objective science might describe. These features of Nature guided, tested, taught, and nurtured me in ways that no objects of science could ever do. Akin to the ancient desert monks or traditional Native people, I found peace and love as well as a home in wild places with prickly cacti and thorny, dry bushes.

Along with these spiritual and physical journeys into the desert, I began some other contemplative spiritual practices introduced to me by some local ministers. Contemplative spiritual practices, used by mystics and shamans from all religious traditions, have effects like meditation on the mind and body. These practices sometimes involve quietly repeating a mantra, a phrase or teaching with deep meaning. Contemplative practices bring one closer to the divine in a way that expands awareness and allows one to decrease the volume on the constant mental chatter of the mind. Along with the silence of the desert, these contemplative meditations began to nurture my spiritual essence and provide clarity about my core identity.

After years of making philosophical arguments and even more years of going to churches and listening to pastors and parishioners (including myself) preach, talk to God, talk about God, and sing songs about God, it was time for my mind to just shut up a bit and listen. I embraced silence in the mind through the desert experiences and contemplative training. Through silence, I sought the divine in parallel with a few other ancient philosophers and modern teachers. Saint Thomas Aquinas, the scholastic philosopher who wrote numerous texts, reportedly never spoke or composed any more writings after his experience of divine presence at the Mass of Naples in 1293.[4] Wayne Dyer, a motivational teacher who composed over forty books, shares a message about silence that is resoundingly clear. Silence is indivisible, and it is one of the few things that cannot be broken into parts.[5] If we seek a reunion of the spiritual and physical, mind and body, humans and Nature, Earth and the heavens, we must look to silence.

The oneness of silence is characteristic of the divine and pure Nature. When the Creator speaks, it is primarily through silence—a silence that often includes the quiet sounds found in Nature.[6] What is silence? In his recent book *Seeing Silence: The Beauty of the World's Most Quiet Places*, Pete McBride writes, "We tend to think of silence as the absence of sound, but it is actually the void where we can hear the sublime notes of Nature."[7] I would add that in silence we also glimpse the sublime presence of the Creator.

If theology is the study of God, then maybe the purpose of spoken or written philosophical words about God is to help us better understand silence—the silence of the Creator and how to be silent ourselves as well. After writing and talking a lot for my master's degree in theology from 2000 to 2002 while at Duke, I discovered the power of silence in my pursuit of a deeper connection with the divine and Nature. In this silence, I found truth, love, and peace as my mind became still and less addicted to thinking and talking. It was an incredibly potent experience—one of freedom from outside challenges but also a sense of oneness with all—an experience shared by many wise saints and gurus over the centuries. The following quote—one of my favorites, from Emil in Baird Spalding's *Life and Teachings of the Masters of the Far East*—describes it: "Silence is power, for when we reach the place of silence in the mind, we have reached the place of power—the place where all is one, the one power—God. 'Be still and know that I am God.'"[8]

A silent mind is an open, humble, and clear mind without preconceived judgments or conceptions about present reality. The silent mind is one's natural, original mind—a beginner's mind directly connected to its divine and Earthly source. Yet how many humans know the joy and power of silence in the mind? How many of us know the Creator or Nature through a silent mind? How many, including medical practitioners, instead try to use mental ramblings to overcome problems or diseases in our world?

What is getting in the way of silence? Zen-style spiritual teachers argue that it is attachments that get in the way of our access to the divine through silence. For many of us, it is our attachments that create noisy, extraneous commentary about a thought, feeling, or desire that may naturally arise in the mind. All of us, as living humans, have regular, natural mental processes that derive from true hungers of the body or interactions with others. Attachment shows itself when we *feel the need* to make extra comments about those natural processes, signals, or any other desire. Attachment makes us believe extra mental commentary can gain what we truly desire. However, when self-centered extra chatter enters regularly into our minds, we forget about silence and our core connection to the divine. Instead of trusting in silence, the language of Nature and the Creator, our attachments create a noisy cacophony of mental ramblings that we erroneously believe will bring to us the object of our desires and hungers.

True and authentic connection with the Creator, Nature, or each other results when a silent mind is integrated with the body. Silence does not mean that thoughts or desires do not arise in the mind. When we hold thoughts or desires in mind in a contemplative manner instead of needing to make extra comments about these thoughts, we honor the silence and our true connections. With a silent, detached mind, thoughts or desires manifest but we don't have to try so hard individually to attain them. We remember that there's something higher at work behind all our desires, feelings, and thoughts—some power beyond what we truly can comprehend. Understanding this truth, our minds begin to trust in our innate divine wisdom and learn patience for anything we desire in life, including medicine and healing.

Embracing the power of silence over mentation is a challenging endeavor for any intellectual person of science, philosophy, and medicine, especially an aspiring physician, as I once was, who might have once prided himself on the ability to think and make an argument. In 2003, I realized my attachment-derived mental chatter had to take a backseat to silence so that a more authentic divine self could show forth. In silence, I gained trust in the divine to provide me true wisdom about medicine or anything else in life. In silence, I realized the necessity to let go of some my own baggage—particularly that about "being right"—along with other emotions and fear. When I let go of a *need* to "be right," I also released some lingering bitterness regarding my previous business partnership. I called my old partner in the energy business, whom I had sued for failure to pay per our contractual agreement and told him that all funds owed were forgiven. I just craved silence and peace and did not want any extra thoughts or attachments getting in the way. I experienced the divine present and within me through silence. And in this silence of my core being, I surrendered deep-seated fears, even fears about death, success, or anything else in life. Ultimately, all fear is just fear of death. I was so at peace with my eyes closed and in a silent state. If this quiet, motionless state was death, it did not seem like such a bad fate.

My spiritual quest for a silent mind and a life free of attachments is nothing new among spiritual mystics and monks over the ages. Many of these teachings about silence and nonattachment originate from the Four Noble Truths of Buddhism:

1. All existence is suffering (or *dukkha*). ("Dukkha" can be translated as "suffering," "struggle," "pain," or even "desperation.")

2. Suffering comes from craving or attachment. Humans may blame our difficulties on things outside ourselves; however, their actual root is found in the mind itself. When our minds become attached to things and crave them (or, alternatively, push them away), this leads to more suffering.

3. Cessation of suffering results from the cessation of craving. In short, suffering ends when we let go of attachments—our minds' cravings.[9]

4. To end suffering and let go of lifelong attachments and cravings, one must follow the Eightfold Path. This Eightfold Path includes having a right view, right intention, right speech, right action, right livelihood, right effort, right mindfulness, and right concentration. This path leads to liberation from suffering and, ultimately, to nirvana, or enlightenment. Enlightenment, for Westerners, might be described as "flourishing in a certain kind of friendship with God."[10]

As I let go of more of my mental cravings, I found myself simply "being." I had *let go* of my desires, fears, and attachments and found that there was nothing to really do. I did not need to "do" anything to "become" someone. I felt complete and at peace with my life internally. I even was ready to die if that was my imminent fate. My mind was clear as I emptied it daily of anything that seemed important. I let go of everything that came up to the mind.

Interestingly, the external world of medical studies at that time in my life contrasted with my private world of spiritual evolution through silence. In medical school, I filled my head full of the scientific knowledge of medicine to overcome suffering in future patients. In my spiritual life, I meditated and emptied my head to gain relief from suffering and ultimately to find peace, healing, and even enlightenment. I found myself checking out of my outside world more and more. The outside world just didn't mean as much to me as the internal world behind closed eyes. As a spiritual being, I really did not need or crave anything externally. If I could find this much peace and healing in my own life by letting go of desire and attachments, then perhaps everyone could find the same peace. Perhaps authentic medicine might involve guiding patients, or anyone, down this Buddhist path of detachment toward the relief of suffering and realization of enlightenment.

Regarding the practice of medicine and Zen path of enlightenment to overcome suffering, the relevant question is: How can one facilitate authentic healing in spirit and the physical world with a silent mind? Is there not a place in medicine for scientific thinking and reasoning? I would argue that there is a place for it but that this scientific reasoning cannot be practiced in a disembodied or objectifiable manner. In place of this Western science, an ancient science exists—first articulated by the philosopher Aristotle as "ultimate science"—that derives from silence and contemplation. Aristotle's ultimate science necessitates an integrated spirit, mind, and body which can attune to the rational cosmic order to accurately know the Creator and Nature and thus practice effective, authentic medicine. For those who seek to practice ultimate science and the medicine derived from it, know that "attuning to the cosmic natural order of life through reason" is not the same as "rational thinking" or "rational control" from a disembodied individual Western mind. To "reason," for the ancients like Aristotle, means to align with the "cosmic order," an organization of the universe that exists beyond one's individual noisy mental chatter. In this sense, to "reason," for those who practice ultimate science and medicine, is a lot more like contemplation than anything else. And to really gain mastery over contemplation, it is necessary to begin with a silent, unattached, and open mind—a beginner's mind integrated with the body.

There's much more to discuss about ultimate science and contemplative medicine. In fact, because this ancient science is so important, I devoted a second book to the subject: *Fifth World Medicine: The Science of Healing People and Their Planet*. For this chapter, however, let's continue to unpack why Westerners have traded authentic knowledge and the medicine that derives from silence and contemplation for the authority of disembodied rationality and objective science.

As previously discussed in chapter 6, Cartesian dualistic reasoning and linear scientific thinking ultimately are ineffective by themselves for gaining the whole truth about medicine or any of our physical and spiritual reality. The understanding of Western reason's limitations is a fact missed by the most brilliant people in all of society. Disembodied reason and linear scientific thinking define a large part of the Western scholastic and intellectual culture—including my undergraduate studies of biology and chemistry, graduate school in theology, and medical education—in an imposing manner. That is, many higher-education-trained experts, through the power of this disembodied reason, along with scientific empiricism, claim sole authority to make truthful assertions about the nature of reality. If a student, for example, proposes ideas or thoughts that deviate from Cartesian reason and its linear processing of symbolic content-based information, that student's insights, revelations, or intuitions are rapidly excluded from any intelligent discourse. Those who espouse nonlinear, subjective truths have no place in the Western culture of reason-based higher education, medicine, or, for that matter, much of the Western world.

As I have been confined by the boundaries of an academic culture governed by modern Western science and dualistic reason's authority, it is easy to understand why I have sought exodus from this Western culture and its medicine. Dualistic rational thinking and linear science, along with the Western Fourth World governed by it, failed to satisfy me as a young student eager to learn whole truth about my life, medicine, or love. I *hungered* to find a way of life and even a new world (a Fifth World, perhaps) beyond the noisy rational and scientific chatter that is so predominant in the Western mind and culture.

Yet in Western societies, relatively few people have made exodus from the mainstream culture and its so-called expert authorities. The masses still look to those academic intellectuals or institutions to bequeath their "expert" knowledge of truth about physical, and sometimes even spiritual, reality. Since the seventeenth century, these institutions have proclaimed authority over truth, with their left-brained data analysis and case-controlled scientific studies, replacing former authorities from prior ages—including religious leaders, Eastern sages, and Native shamans. As Western culture and its peoples attached priority to the mental chatter of experts in dualistic rational and scientific thinking as their primary authorities, much of the wisdom, truth, and way of life from traditional Native, Eastern, and Judeo-Christian traditions had to be rejected. And of necessity, silence, the language of Nature and the Creator, was also rejected.

It is not without justification for at least the past three centuries that Westerners rejected and continue to reject traditional authorities and the practices of Native, Eastern, or religious leaders in favor of those claiming to be experts in rational thinking, including that of science and medicine.

Disembodied reason and objective science have given many the perception of mastery over their physical bodies and physical world. Many Western peoples believe that this technical mastery over life is a good justification to bow daily to the power of dualistic mental rationalizations. However, when one ascribes authority to disembodied reason and objective science in life or the practice of medicine, it is impossible to also "be still and know" the Creator or Nature in a truthful manner.

At the end of my college days, I had a head full of scientific and rational mental noise. My core being sought answers to the question: What really is my purpose here and what is the meaning of it all? With my rational, analytical mind, these questions took me on an exploration of theology, philosophy, metaphysics, and ontology. In my study of these subjects, I even identified myself with the rational thinking mind in the role of a professional student for many years. These philosophical interests ultimately led me to Duke's Divinity School to seek some mental clarity about what is truth and the meaning of it all.

As a graduate student at Duke, I continued to believe that rational mental chatter offers a path to the highest level of meaning and truth. But dualistic reason, along with all the intellectual disciplines that come out of it—including science, medicine, theology, and philosophy—does not lead to the whole truth about complex matters, including truths about God and health. With a priority of focus on symbols (and concepts) as abstractions from everyday life, dualistic reason operates predominantly from what is commonly termed the "left brain." Unless it is properly integrated to the right brain, the content-filled left brain remains disconnected from the larger context of reality. The role of the right brain is to maintain a relationship with outside world as it comprehends the big picture of one's spiritual and material reality. Apart from the right brain, many left-brained dominant academics waste a lot of energy and time "mentally masturbating" with excessive content to discern what is scientifically or philosophically true. Without a whole-brained approach, these academics often miss the forest as they are so focused on the details of every tree. They miss the context of an argument and often the larger spiritual and physical big-picture truth.[11] To learn more about the distinctive functions of the left and right brain, check out *The Master and His Emissary: The Divided Brain and the Making of the Western World* by Iain McGilchrist.

Interestingly, my theological studies at Duke facilitated intellectual conclusions about the division of the objective and subjective, body and soul, matter and spiritual—particularly how medical science and its institutions care for humans. However, what theological study did not do was to critique its own tool of Western reason and abstraction. Theological school did not teach me about how to let go of the noisy chatter of a disembodied mind by embracing silence. It was only later, through spiritual study and practice, that I learned how to let go of attachments, particularly ones that led to false conclusions. When I let go of these attachments and trusted in the wisdom of a mind ruled by silence, I lost interest in ivory-tower intellectualism of daily wrestling with various philosophical concepts. I realized that my master's degree in theology did not necessarily promote spiritual or physical development but instead pointed me down a path of increased reading and writing and more philosophizing. When I finally detached from the necessity of making arguments and philosophizing, I began to discover my core identity as an integrated spiritual and physical being.

In letting go of dualistic reason's control over my thoughts and life, I also learned that truth, contrary to the belief of purely rational Westerners, cannot be confined to what is only "objective" knowledge based on left-brained processing of symbols or language or even numbers. Truth is found in the subjective, holistic connection and inherent relationship a human has to the Creator, another human, or any being in Nature. To learn truth, I had to detach from rational or scientific thinking about medicine as well. I had to abandon the need to "know" or to "be right."

Letting go did not come easily. My ego resisted; it took hours and days and months of meditation and contemplation. I had to abandon any thought, belief, or knowledge that came to mind that seemed important. If a thought was important and critical to my life, it would return as a core truth. But I did not have to know or believe in any core truth. The core truth, of my life or God or medicine, existed whether I thought anything or not. When I finally let go of the need to believe or know anything, I found silence.

How many doctors, scientists, theologians, and philosophers have no rational answer when they are questioned? How many of these practitioners encourage silence as their greatest medicine, healing, or path to enlightenment? How many practitioners know the power of silence over rational, scientific thinking?

Unfortunately, so much of our intellectual Western Fourth World remains trapped in the confines of reason, to the detriment of the physical and spiritual health of humans, animals, and the rest of the planet. A significant purpose of this book is to encourage Western humans, including practitioners and patients, to detach from dualistic rational thinking and embrace superior wisdom, health practices, and ways of life that derive from contemplation, love, and silence. Note that a silent mind and open heart do not preclude thinking, planning, or mental judgments. Instead, silence allows us to function out of a whole mind which is integrated with a vibrant body and spirit. With this spiritual–physical juxtaposition, the authority once held by Western reason and science falls by the wayside. As Westerners let go of their devotion to dualistic reason and objective science and the so-called experts in those disciplines, we suffer less, grow spirituality, and begin our journey from the Fourth World to the Fifth World—a sustainable world in harmony with Nature and the Creator.

Why have Westerners, especially in the past three hundred years, been unable to transition to this Fifth World way of understanding, loving, living, and being healthy? The answer is that we accept so much of what we think we know as a matter of fact. That is, many Westerners are unchallenged about their core concept of reality. Even still, however, many people still *hunger* for more meaning to their lives. Thoreau echoes again, "The mass of men live lives of quiet desperation."[12] No matter the states of our lives (rich, poor, famous, or unknown), if we look deep within, we eventually admit to being unsatisfied and incomplete in a Fourth World governed by modern reason and science.

We are unsatisfied, quite simply, because life is so much more than data points. We must *hunger* for something more—more than a rational, technical, and scientific perspective of the world or each other. When we look deeper, we comprehend that our very spiritual, mental, and physical health, along with the destiny our of lives, as well as the life of the planet, rest on an authority that exists beyond rational or scientific babbling.

Yet even my lofty written words are not enough motivation for anyone to detach from rational thinking; there must be an innate willingness to let go of symbols, mentalization, and objectivity to embrace something more subjective, mysterious, unknown, and silent. How do we let go of the core concepts—concepts deeply imbedded in Western culture and ourselves—about reality?

I cannot make a *rational* argument to encourage one to abandon one's attachments to Fourth World reason and science and embrace silence. The best I can do is to share my own spiritual path and understanding of the Four Noble Truths of Buddhism. On this path, I have surrendered so many of my fears, anger, desires, and attachments and resolved to just "be." Even when "going through the motions" of scientific study during my first year of medical school, I realized that there was nothing to do and nowhere to go in the silent state of beingness. There was also nothing to say or believe. All was just automatic, as I had truly let go of control. There was nothing but stillness and peace; akin to death, I was literally resting in peace. I thought this was the ultimate end, and I was truly ready to die or continue in life; it did not matter.

During this time in my early medical school life, this spiritual path of detachment and silence was the best medicine for me and possibly good medicine for potential patients. In this state of self-emptiness, I literally had no more baggage. I later realized that a state of complete detachment is what Buddhists call the "void," or "*Śūnyatā*" in Sanskrit.[13] Śūnyatā literally means "emptiness."[14] In my experience of the deep emptiness of the void, the following poem bubbled up in my awareness.

The Void

Alone. dark. nothingness.
Motivationless.
Where? Who? How? When?
All echo into silence.

The response simply Is,
Which takes one nowhere,
Yet everywhere exists
Just all at once.

Spirit prevails.
Yet it is handleless
And wild
Like ethereal wind.

Transcendence?
Or simply existence
Why such loss,
But such attraction?

All is lost,
Yet all is found
Deep in the dark—
The dark, meaningless void.

"Go to the goal;
Pursue something,"
Calls out the outside cry
Because the void doesn't satisfy.

The ego lessens its hold
And looks for home,
And the wrestling
Settles down.
All simply stops.

Absolute zero.
No answers come
But the magnetic pull is high.
Simple physics, yeah?
So where's the motion,
The excitement,
The emotion?

Where's the Logos, the Shabd,
That which connects us all,
That through eternity
Communicates end to beginning?

Rest, rest, rest,
Peace be still.

Oh, might this depth continue.
Oh, please let it.
Although unmanageable,
All else is frill.

Yet so all exists here.

There's no search needed.

No need to go, do, think, move, believe.

Just be

I

You

…

Yet life exists

In and through the void.

Let us not settle

For less.

It shall occur …

Nothing.

Let go.

Is this it? Is the void the ultimate state of freedom and thus enlightenment?

The void is indeed an amazing state of being, but in my own experience, something felt missing. Following a path of detachment from everything, I had found silence and found peace. But, in a state of complete emptiness, I had a sense also of ungroundedness. It was as though I could float away with the wind into a divine nothingness of the void. My spirit had its nirvana, but my human form wasn't quite there yet. While I'd reached a state of detached enlightenment, my spirit was still not yet integrated with my physical body or the rest of the physicality of the Earth.

Despite what many gnostic and New Age spiritual teachers may say, authentic "beingness" qua "being human" requires physical embodiment as well as a connection to the divine, infinite love that is the source of all of life. In short, to be a human being, at least on this side of death, means to show up physically to chop wood, carry water, and even use medicine to take care of that body and other bodies. In this sense, the healing path of enlightenment is nondualistic, as it fosters an integrated spiritual and physical world; it is not an escape from the world. The endpoint of authentic spiritual pursuits brings sages, shamans, and enlightened medical practitioners face-to-face in deep connection with the raw physicality of life. Even though the enlightened are no longer attached, at an ego level, to the attractions of this life, they still are fully embodied in this world through the power of divine love.

To remain in the physical human body and world of form, I had to go deeper into the silence. To go deeper, I had to even *let go* of "letting go" of the noisy mind. With no intention at all of thinking, doing, or letting go of anything, the mind lost its place of importance. Out of the stillness of the mind, the body took on more priority. I had greater awareness and guidance from the body, as well as what is considered the seat of the soul, the heart. I realized the sacredness of the body as well as all its connections in the Earth. Deep in the silence, the body grounded me in the physicality of life. However, now with a truly silent mind, the body's health, motions, senses, and destiny became much greater priorities in my life.

Indeed, the path of true enlightenment, for Earth's inhabitants, does not lead to an escape the body or Earth but embraces it and all its relationships. And to live in a spiritual and physically enlightened state, one must live out of love from the heart—a physical, beating heart of a living creature. In place of a disembodied mental, rational, or scientific chatter, heartfelt love for the Creator, Nature, and others is what guides our thoughts, actions, and healing on the path to enlightenment and the Fifth World.

CHAPTER 8

Love: The Medicine of Enlightenment

In contrast to objective science and disembodied reason, love from the heart does not dissect or analyze the world in a disengaged manner. Instead, love, with its physical and spiritual nature, necessarily involves subjective interaction with the oneness (a.k.a. all-oneness) of all life. While Fourth World reason, in particular scientific reason, seeks to gain objective truth from external senses and descriptions, love guides its practitioners to more accurate, whole truth. The truth discovered through love is more complete because it involves *knowing* rather than a *knowing about* something or someone. The subjective quality of love allows one to intuitively know the whole truth about humans or anything in Nature. *Knowing and having relationship with another* is superior to *knowing about something or someone.*

When practitioners in all disciplines of life, including medicine, embody love over dualistic reason, it dramatically changes how they act as healers. Manifested as the primary way to care for patients, all humans, and the Earth, love dissolves the division of current medical dualism (of matter and spirit), in which patients are examined and treated as only physical, bodily, scientific objects. Love encourages the practitioner to engage with patients subjectively and intuitively in a more authentic way than through Western reason and science.

Approaching patients with compassion rather than purely reason, a.k.a. "scientific rational control," sounds incredible. Loving physicians and other practitioners can now clearly see their patients without a need to resort to massive amounts of informational content (in the form of symbols) about the patient or other patients. Understanding patients through love, Fifth World practitioners do not necessarily require content-heavy "evidence-based" studies to support their care for patients, other animals, or all the Earth. Yet there is still a place in medicine and other disciplines for asking questions, making observations, and formulating theories to understand humans and all of Nature. What is critical to realize is that these scientific experiments do not necessarily lead to the entire truth about a matter and that, when divorced from the spirit, love, intuition, and other more subjective ways of knowing, such experiments can lead to erroneous, irrelevant, and detrimental conclusions.

Unconditional love, as it derives from the heart, trumps disembodied reason or science as a means of understanding and engaging with patients. Yet, owing to the way Western medicine is set up currently, even practitioners who may claim to be loving, are bound in a Fourth World system of intellectual reasoning and science in place of the practice of heartfelt love. Medical dualism that divides the body and spirit prevents the true subjective connection of love as a basis for diagnosis and treatment.

The delivery of scientifically based diagnoses and treatments by medical practitioners is largely due to their demand by patients. Instead of loving methodologies and its practitioners, most Western patients desire a rational, scientific, and even technological approach to medical care, seeking proven content-filled studies for all their chosen treatments. Western rationality and the scientific, evidence-based studies that derive from it are the currency of modern medicine even among most osteopathic and alternative medical practitioners. As a result, most medical practitioners, pharmaceutical companies, and associated industries are rationally trying to prove something—some health effect from a drug, supplement, diet, or device. Where is the love in this modern content-overloaded, intellectually governed practice of medicine? Where is a focus on the patient's story (the context), an enlightened spirit, a sacred body, and a personalized, hands-on approach of doctoring that cannot be replicated in some data-driven scientific paper?

At least since the seventeenth century, the institutional expression of love and other higher-order consciousness states has largely been relegated to the domain of religion and spirituality. While originally practiced by monks and nuns, medicine has stepped away from love as its original motivation and methodology. In place of loving monks and nuns, scientific experts have taken over much of the ethos of the Western world and medicine. The post-Enlightenment Western world even developed the term "facts" for physical, empirically derived information. Before the seventeenth century, a scientific "fact" did not exist, because no such word as "fact" had been coined. Alasdair Macintyre writes, "Facts, like telescopes and wigs for gentlemen, were a seventeenth century invention."[1] And a result of dualism, facts, particularly scientific facts, took the place of previous truths that derived from what is spiritual and imperceptible to the five senses (a.k.a. unprovable, such as love). For the Western mind, imperceptible, spiritual, loving, or intuitive wisdom about medicine or anything in life has relevance for those in religion or for those on spiritual paths. For Western people stuck in the Fourth World, unconditional love belongs in the realm of mystics, saints, and devotees to Christianity or other religions. Today, nothing but scientific fact-based reason is systemically allowed in medical clinic or hospital settings.

Yet to practice Fifth World medicine requires that one prioritize love as a way of being and acting over Western science and reason. What is keeping medical practitioners from operating out of love? This is almost the same question I asked before: What is keeping any of us from silence?

It is our attachments that produce mental chatter that keep us from silence. For medical practitioners who have filled their minds with knowledge on how to overcome suffering, to embrace a state of emptiness or unknowingness, especially when treating patients, is a very difficult move to make. One of my teachers, Viola Frymann, DO, did master this kind of emptiness in her approach to patients. She taught that osteopathic medical practitioners should approach patients without the perspective of knowing anything at all about them.

What if most doctors did adopt an emptiness of the mind, expressed as "I don't care to be right, to win or to be admired, and I don't know?" Would anyone in the world listen to these types of physicians? Why haven't more physicians embraced this path of enlightenment to the end of both spiritual and physical suffering?

To embrace the path to emptiness—the path to the void—takes a lot of humility and trust in silence. But while the void is awesome, it takes more than complete detachment to learn truth and practice authentic medicine. That is, although the enlightenment path of nonattachment and self-emptying through silence leads to inner peace and personal spiritual healing, one must embrace the loving connection in all things in order to care for and love patients. In other words, at the end of the void, one's path shifts from a path of *detachment from everything* to a path of intimate and subjective *connection and oneness with all*, including one's body, others, and the rest of the Earth and cosmos.

An experience of this connection to the oneness of all things, understood through ultimate love, has long been a characteristic primarily of spiritual people, such as monks, sages, shamans, and ones who are intimately connected to Nature. Regarding how oneness may occur through a silent mind, Bill McKibben writes,

> Our minds can actually fall quiet, and when they do, I have noticed something odd: animals seem to notice. Or, in way, to not notice—we begin to blend in with the world around us. Suddenly, birds are alighting nearer, and deer barely glancing up as one wanders past, as if turning down the volume on our inner monologue somehow lets us fit it more easily with everything else.[2]

Unfortunately, because so many Westerners live in a world of continuous mental chatter as well as external noises, they have failed to comprehend the loving interconnectedness of life through Nature and the divine. Our path to love, the medicine of enlightenment, has been thwarted by an addiction to noisy stimuli in our minds and a developed Western world far removed from pure Nature.

Finding sounds, or music, that connects and heals us through silent love can be a daunting task. Mystics of varied traditions, often through deep meditation, have discovered a divine music derived from silence that facilitates love as the interconnectivity of all beings. In Native American lore, this sacred music is termed "the sound of the Creator." In Sanskrit, it is *Nada Brahma* (the sound of God); Sikhs refer to it as the "Cosmic Tone." Heraclitis, the Greek philosopher, referred to it as the "Logos," and the Bible refers to it as the "Word." In the Hindu tradition, the term is *"Anahad Shabd,"* or just *"Shabd,"* which translates to "unlimited tone" or "sound current."[3]

In my experience, the path of enlightenment involved complete detachment from whatever *I thought I knew* and even what *I thought was myself at the core.* I had become dissatisfied with the noises of a Western mind and Western world. Following silence, I traveled deep into the void, but I did not hear any sacred music or experience the sound current there. Recall the lines from my poem in Chapter 7:

> Where's the Logos, the Shabd,
> That which connects us all,
> That through eternity
> Communicates end to beginning?

The path of detachment did not carry me forward into a life of love in tune with the music of the heavens and Earth. It was only when I surrendered the void and its peacefulness that I could feel and hear the Shabd and embrace the love as the core nature of my being and all reality.

To really be loving, I had to show up in a physical body and in a physical world of chaos. The loving step from a spiritual, inner void of detached darkness and peace into a wild spiritual and physical world where I experienced oneness with all beings was not easy. It took several years of my life before I could really honor the sacredness of my physical body and the interconnectivity of life. My previous monk-like psyche put up a lot of resistance, and I experienced a lot of emotion: sadness, joy, burning, vulnerability, fear, wildness, and even confusion. At the same time, I also felt a sense of empowerment. The following poem, written a year after my experience with the void, best describes this push–pull challenge, as a spiritual and physical human being, of allowing authentic, unconditional, divine love to rule my life and intimately connect me to all in this wild world.

O Love

She exists here,
Here and everywhere,
The Golden Glow,
Beautiful Mist.

Ever the draw
Majestic Power,
Holy Wonder,
Living forever.

The Presence fills
Air, sky, hills, fields,
Even humans
Sometimes.

All the time
And in no time,
She finds us.

The consciousness
Of closeness,
How it wrestles
Off the veil.

The hermit's cloak
Loosens up
And disappears.

Light, flames, fire
Flash all about
Until finding their focus.

Blazing fire,
Mystical unity,
Burning energy.

O divine Self,
Now revealed
How wild,
How free
You are.

O Self, O Love,
What now ...
What now
Without the cloak,
Without the solid ground?

Light just comes out,
The Hermit,
One with the Light,

Is home
And lost
All at once.

O heaven and Earth,
The connection
Is true indeed.

Why so uncontrolled?
How did you
Get in, O Love?

How did you
Break open the walls
Of this cave?

Oh, the beauty
Of the darkness,
Its safety
And peace.

Who let in the light?
It's okay
Without the light.

Why so vulnerable
Do I feel—
So nostalgic,
So winsome,

So aching for
A Void
That's gone
"Poof."

And indeed,
It's the nature
Of voids
To nonexist.

Truly is this Light
As good as Darkness,
The darkness of the cave?
Is She worth the risk?

Especially when She goes
Unnoticed
Or gets confused?

Why, why, why
Why are their tears
In my eyes?
Being, yes.
Too much,
Too overwhelming
For this lost hermit.

Oh, but the
Adventure,
The liveliness,
The roller-coaster ride.

She can take you—
She pulls you.
You want her more,
Though you've always
Been with Her,
Even in the cave.

But now She's ready
To blossom
And fly,
And be.

Oh, do follow her;
Follow her
Into the pain,
Into the mystery,
Into life.

The All-oneness,
Yes, She's there.
You are Her.

Remember this:
You became real.
You walked into
The Light
Outside the cave.

You took off
The cloak;
You stepped
Off the cliff
And began
To fly.

And flying
Is wild.
You were overwhelmed;
You tried to go back,

Tried to find the cloak,
But to no avail.
Where to fly now?

You know,
But there's so
Much challenge there.

O Self,
Be with the Silence,
Be with the Love,
Be with Her/Me.
It's scary, but
True amazing glory
Is the reward.

Many philosophers, theologians, shamans, great masters, physicists, poets, and teachers over the ages have described a loving, intimate connection with Nature and the divine as a state of healing and flourishing with all life. Some religious persons believe this state of pure love and oneness with the divine can be realized only after the end of their lives in some heavenly realm. The truth is, however, anyone on the path to the Fifth World, including medical practitioners, can experience this oneness in everyday life. For those physicians willing to take a step into *unknown silence* as well as authentic *love* for all that exists, they will find a world of great healing and connection at the innermost levels.

If expressed immanently, an individual's present oneness with all of Nature and the Creator is the natural destiny of his or her life to the very end. In the words of Aquinas, "The end is a measure of things oriented toward the end."[4] For Aquinas, this end, now and forever, is a healthy flourishing through oneness with the Creator. Aquinas is not alone in this perspective about the interconnectivity of all life. Several poets, including many of those from the Romantic period, share about a divine oneness that permeates time, space, and all the natural particles (including humans) in this universe. I really like some of the following poetic quotes.

William Blake writes, "To see a world in a grain of sand and heaven in a wildflower. Hold infinity in the palm of your hand and eternity in an hour."[5]

Henry Thoreau states, "You must live in the present, launch yourself on every wave, find your eternity in each moment."[6]

The Mistress of Vision by Francis Thompson reads as follows:

> All things by immortal power
> Near or far
> Hiddenly
> To each other are linked
> That thou canst not stir a flower
> Without troubling a star.[7]

These poets, along with Aquinas, are, arguably, describing the same "holographic universe" articulated by the twentieth-century theoretical physicist David Bohm. To better understand these poets, Aquinas, and Bohm, it is key to know a little bit about holograms.

A hologram is a physical recording of an interference pattern that uses diffraction to reproduce a three-dimensional light field, resulting in an image which retains the depth, parallax, and other properties of the original scene.

> Bohm believed that although the universe appears to be solid, it is, in essence, a magnificent hologram. He believed in the "whole in every part" idea, and just like a hologram, each part of physical reality contained information about the whole ... In stark contrast to Western ways of thinking about the nature of reality as external and

mechanistic, Bohm considers our separateness an illusion and argues that at a deeper level of reality, we, as well as all the particles that make up all matter, are one and indivisible. For Bohm, the "empty space" is full of energy and information. It's a hidden world of the implicate order, also known as the "Zero Point Field" or the "*Akasha*".[8]

Derived from a Sanskrit word meaning "space" or "sky," the term "Akasha" refers to the "spiritual Primordial Substance that pervades the whole space, and from which the cosmos is developed."[9] George Lucas, with his character Yoda from the film *The Empire Strikes Back*, depicts Akasha as "the Force" that connects us all:

> Size matters not. Look at me. Judge me by my size, do you? Hmm? Hmm. And well you should not. For my ally is the Force, and a powerful ally it is. Life creates it, makes it grow. Its energy surrounds us and binds us. Luminous beings are we, not this crude matter. You must feel the Force around you; here, between you, me, the tree, the rock, everywhere, yes.[10]

Accessing Akasha (a.k.a., the Force) in an appropriate way constitutes the primary theme of the Star Wars films. And as we know from the characters in the films, using this cosmic energy field requires a powerful state of consciousness—a state often realized only by the Jedi (in Star Wars) and mystics (in the nonfiction world). In contrast to the mechanistic way Western practitioners dissect and dissociate from their patients with scientific methodologies, mystics or avatars who join with the Akasha realize an innate, loving connection to all beings in a holographic universe. Those who trust in the power of this cosmic field regularly receive an indivisible instant knowingness about humans and all life. The message of many poets, saints, or spiritual gurus over the ages is that we, including everyday physicians, can also through love ally, like Yoda, with the Akasha, as the cosmic field that binds us all together.

Can you imagine your physician, acting out love, being able to hear the Shabd, the sacred music of the Creator, and tune into the Akasha, the power that connects us all, in approaching your spiritual and physical health? Would you choose your science-based rational doctor or Yoda-like mystics and shamans to help you truly heal? Who has more power?

Fifth World medicine can be described as the evolution in consciousness and form in humans, the Earth, and Nature. As humans and the planet transition to superior ways of being and acting in harmony together, we all pursue a path to greater love manifested in the holographic interconnectivity of all beings.

Love leads us to subjective oneness, knowingness, and holographic connection through the Akasha, but what happens next? Is this relief of spiritual and physical suffering possible? Maybe the oneness of all reality has relevance only for sages and mystics who meditate all the time, or perhaps it's just spiritual, psychological, or metaphysical healing? We still have a physical plane—with real physical injuries to the body that need good medicine. How does understanding an infinite oneness with all things play out in the physical world?

Ultimately, at the highest level of enlightenment, the juxtaposition of the spiritual and physical occurs as divine love manifests in the material bodies of humans, the Earth, and the cosmos. Indeed, the transition from the Fourth to the Fifth World shall occur as a direct result not only of the transcendence of one's spirit but also the reemergence of that spirit into a physical Earthly form.[11]

Hence, Fifth World medicine calls for healers, shamans, and other medical practitioners to embrace infinite love as their core identity and as something expressed in the interconnectivity of all beings in Nature. With the advent of the Fifth World as reality, hermits, sages, and mystics shall no longer retreat from the world but can return to live in society.

These teachers, along with enlightened shamans, healers, and medical practitioners will teach us what is essential from the technological world and how to abandon what is unnecessary and limiting—including how we communicate with each other, understand science, treat the Earth, help to heal one another, and love each other.

As I personally began to embrace the power of divine, unconditional love manifested in the oneness of all things, I finally realized that *being*, as a human on the path to enlightenment and the Fifth World, did not just mean sitting in darkness with infinite stillness and divine love but instead required that I extend this medicine of silent love into the world around me in a spiritual and physical way.

Returning to osteopathic medical school, I conducted an email survey of any classmates who had interest in a "spirituality and medicine club" at the school. With affirmation from many classmates, I started a club to support aspiring physicians to help themselves and patients, as physical and spiritual beings, to follow a path of enlightenment to overcome suffering—a type of training much overlooked by my osteopathic medical school and, for that matter, any Western medical school. My spiritual path, once just an internal, quiet journey, had evolved, now manifesting in my physical world with a small tribe of other medical students in its wake.

CHAPTER 9

Healing Ceremonies: Spiritual–Physical Medicine

To kick off the Spirituality and Medicine Club at my osteopathic medical school (AZCOM), I invited Howard Silverman, MD, coauthor of the book *Healing Ceremonies* to speak at my school in the spring of 2005. I met Dr. Silverman at an integrative medicine conference led by Andrew Weil, MD, held at a local hotel in the outskirts of Phoenix. At the time, Dr. Weil and Dr. Silverman were both associated with the University of Arizona's Integrative Medicine Program. Dr. Silverman spoke eloquently about his experience with Native people and their healing ceremonies.

It was great to finally see someone from a mainstream university openly share about spiritual and medical practices under the label of integrative medicine. Integrative medicine, as the art of combining Western medicine with ancient, Native, Eastern, and often less invasive healing modalities (e.g., acupuncture, herbal medicine, homeopathy, nutritional therapy, Ayurveda, and yoga), enamored my young medical school mind. Perhaps integrative medicine could serve as a bridge to Fifth World medicine—a medicine based in the unity of the spirit and matter. However, because Western thought and its evidence-based medicine overemphasizes a materialistic, scientific understanding of reality, I was not so sure that even integrative medicine could overcome this hurdle to allow for more of a Fifth World style of medicine, particularly in the realm of spiritual practices. There is very little spirituality in the system of Western medicine, even though most of its practitioners would acknowledge that humans, and all of life, are composed of both spiritual and physical elements. In fact, unlike Native or Eastern medical practices, Western medicine fails to see anything that cannot be measured with the five senses as valid scientific evidence. Unfortunately, spirituality does not fit within these "evidence-based parameters."

Indeed, Western Fourth World allopathic medicine is strictly governed by a disembodied rational mind with an incessant desire to control a wild, unruly physicality. Silverman explains that, in a typical physician–patient relationship, the physician uses his or her scientific reason to address an ailment in the patient's body. It is this disembodied part of the physician, the rational mind, as separate from the rest of its human physical nature, that attempts to create a positive health or symptomatic change, usually by a manipulation or exploitation of a natural process in the patient's body. A good example of this kind of allopathic medicine is when a Western physician notices a patient's blood pressure is elevated and then prescribes an artificial substance, in the form of a blood pressure medication, to manipulate the patient's kidneys in order to cause the body to urinate more fluid so that the blood pressure is lowered. It is pure manipulation of a natural process in the patient's body, which works in a variety of patients across the globe. There is not that much skill or engagement required by the physician with a particular patient to make this happen.

Unfortunately, there are a lot of other disconnections in this Fourth World allopathic medicine approach.

1. The physician has little physical connection to the outcome of this treatment.
2. The physician does not necessarily have a personal experience with the condition or this treatment.
3. The physician does not have to have any connection to Nature, the Earth, the patient, or the patient's community.
4. The physician, hence, does not need to work with Nature or understand Nature to diagnose this condition or treat it.

5. There is no, or limited, investigation as to why the blood pressure of the patient is higher than average (including etiologies such a toxin, virus, pain, etc.) or how to treat the condition naturally (e.g., lifestyle changes, etc.)

6. The patient, as an actual physical being, really does not even matter. The patient is a diagnostic symbol, an object, that the physician treats as a representation of reality out of his or her left brain.

7. The physician rarely talks *to* the patient or engages personally with him or her; rather the physician mostly talks *at* the patient, now known as a "symbol."

8. The physician and patient now become part of a larger commercial enterprise, including pharmaceutical companies, drug stores, or insurance companies, entities which have no higher purpose than profit.

9. Finally, there is rarely any acknowledgment of the spiritual aspect of the patient by the physician because their diagnosis and treatment is based on an understanding of the patient as an empirical symbol.

In contrast, as Dr. Silverman explained in the lecture provided at the Spirituality and Medicine Club at my osteopathic medical school in the spring of 2004, the shaman directly engages his or her body, mind, emotions, and spirit with the patient's body, mind, emotions, and spirit. The shaman's goal is alignment with the patient, in a way of solidarity, to allow a higher power from the heavens, ancestors, four directions, animal spirits, or Earth elements to channel through him or her to manifest healing as the patient also opens to these powerful forces.

In *Coyote Medicine,* Mehl-Madrona explains a little more about how shamans understand how healing works. "True medicine men and women know that only the Creator and the spirits, or the patient can really take credit for the healing. The patient must do seventy percent of the work of getting well," he (the shaman) states. "The Creator does twenty percent, and I do ten, which is barely worth mentioning."[1] The healing process and paths undertaken by shamans, their patients, and all those related (Creator, spirits, animal totems, plants, fire, rocks, water, and other earth elements) rarely involves repeatable, case-controlled evidence. In *Coyote Medicine,* Mehl-Madrona quotes another shaman: "Look at birth—there is disorder, mess; but from this chaos comes new life, new beginning. Before you can become a healer, you must make friends with chaos."[2]

How to make "friends with chaos" is a lesson never taught to me by any of my Western-minded medical school professors or anyone else in the realm of scientific, rationally practiced medicine. Western medical students learn to use scientific reason to minimize risk and attempt to maximize control over Nature and natural forces, including those in the human body. This position of controlling Nature with disembodied reason, instead of embracing her freedom, wildness, and "chaos," is endemic not only to Western medicine but also to all modern societies governed by science. Our Western minds want to know what is out there in Nature and control it, whether it is a virus, bacterium, heart irregularity, wild animal, wild plant, or any other natural process. We want to use science to harness and tame the world so we can live life without fear. Chaos is dangerous and high risk and has no place in a world that one must know objectively and control to feel safe. Silverman writes,

> We have invested science with providing all the answers. We have come to believe that the secrets of life can be known only through proven quantitative means. As a result, we have created a culture in which we subordinate the subjective experience of our lives to objective reality, even though that "objectivity" flows from *fact* fragments based on someone else's perception of what is probable.[3]

Science seeks to quantify, objectify, and separate persons from an experience or experiment. Yet life is lived in the subjective, and ultimately, these ideas of "scientific objectivity" and "scientific facts" tell only, at best, half the story about medicine and life, and these so-called facts are derived from a worldview that began only in recent centuries. Recall the quote "Facts, like telescopes and wigs for gentlemen, were a seventeenth century invention."[4]

By believing in a modern world based primarily on an ever-moving target of "scientific facts," Western humans lose an understanding of the necessity of radically subjective spiritual–physical experiences—such as those that occur in ceremonies—that foster optimal mental, physical, emotional, and spiritual health. Healing ceremonies are the kind that help us "make friends" with the chaos of all of life and death—including love, health, disease, and disorder—as they merge what is physical and spiritual in a single experience. Some ceremonies are actual events that occur only on special occasions. Other ceremonies include simple daily rituals as offers of gratitude or acknowledgment of the power of the divine. These kinds of rituals serve to make us whole as human beings—as divine wild animals. Instead of trying to control Nature, ceremonies allow us, as wild beings, to ride waves of uncertainty, chaos, and risk and make peace with the unpredictable challenges of life.

In *Healing Ceremonies*, Silverman and his coauthor Carl Hammerschlag argue for a loosening of the grip of Western science and medicine over the control of human bodies and beckon us toward the wisdom found in authentic ceremonies as a path to health. They encourage an understanding of Native American and Jewish ceremonial traditions as a helpful guide for Western peoples, and they explain the benefits of these rituals. Silverman and Hammerschlag explain that every religion and premodern culture has ceremonies to make sense of life and find meaning. Indeed, ceremonies provide a space for guidance, community, looking within, touching each other, dreaming, and visioning along with helping to build courage and inspiration.[5] The long-term effect of ceremonies facilitates participants to "reconnect with dreams of their lives, cleanse old expectations, and make new commitments."[6] Quoting Rabbi Lawrence Kushner, they write, "We realize that we are part of something much larger than our daily decisions. With or without our consent, we too are players in a kind of divine scheme for just a moment or two, it is as if we rise to encounter our destiny: It is not you [our ego] who sent me here, but God!"[7]

Unpacking Kushner's message, what happens in an authentic ceremony, even momentarily, is uniquely akin to the long-term development of consciousness for those on the Zen path of enlightenment. We see our world with a divergent, big-picture gaze (instead of scientific focus) and have whole-brained subjective relationship with it (instead of objective distance from it). The spiritual connection felt in ceremonies expresses itself with very real physical healing outcomes (while scientific rationalism leads only to more disembodiment). Ceremonies lift us from doubt into a world of magic and faith; give us hope, dreams, and vision; and bring us, if they are practiced regularly, to higher consciousness states.

For traditional Native Americans, a ritual of reverence and prayer is practiced for the physicality and spirituality of animals and plants encountered in daily life. This is undeniably a contrast to the many Western humans who unconsciously slaughter and eat poorly treated cows, caged chickens, or monocropped food plants. Westerners regularly consume assembly-line-produced, overly processed fast foods made by commercial corporations. Perhaps it is not so much *what* toxins are in these foods (including dioxins, antibiotics, growth hormones, and GMOs) as it is *how* these foods are so unceremoniously consumed. If we do not consider animals and plants as our kin—our brothers and sisters—then they are just objects. These creatures are just fuel for our disembodied rational minds—which many Westerners erroneously identify as ourselves—barely connected to toothpick or blob bodies of physicality and enchanted only by the latest technology on our so-called smartphones or computers. Taking the place of engaging with sacred food and divine life through ritual and ceremony, a godless scientific and objectified perspective of eating food, for just our utilitarian fuel, leads to the detriment of human health and all life on the planet.

Silverman and Hammerschlag write, "When ceremonies are lacking [in adolescence], a void is created—a void that must be filled by something … we shouldn't be surprised to see children and adolescents' play imitate adult activities around them or popular 'heroes' of their culture."[8] These pop culture heroes may include violent or licentious television or movie actors or, in the inner city, older brothers or family members who belong to gangs. In the white-collar world, these "heroes" may include *Fortune* 500 executives who drive fancy cars and sport boats but whose highest ethic goes no further than increasing the bottom line for the corporation or a personal bank account.

Even where ceremonies and holidays exist in the modern world, such as Christmas, most of these "holy days" have lost their meaning, as they have been reduced to gift-buying or working in the kitchen. Silverman and Hammerschlag write, "We are in danger of desacralizing the sacred; the sacred is mass-marketed at the expense of true spirituality."[9]

In contrast, unlike Western cultures, "cultures with intact initiation rituals [during adolescence] do not have high death rates from crime, suicide, or homicide."[10] Through ritual and ceremony, these traditional peoples have learned to bridge the gap between spirituality and physicality and find inner peace and health for themselves and their children. However, rituals and ceremonies by themselves are not enough to prevent unhealthy lifestyles, violence, or suicide for Native or Western peoples. For rituals and ceremonies to have long-term beneficial spiritual, mental, and physical health benefits, a person must recognize rituals as core to his or her sacred identity—an identity more important than a Facebook page, Instagram post, career role, or anything a Western culture can ascribe.

To find long-term health and core identity, it is critical to know that we are spiritually and biologically made for ceremony as part of our sacred relationship with the Creator and all of Nature. Without this understanding and practice of ceremony, we suffer. A Navajo shaman states, "We believe that ceremonies have the potential to strengthen the body's immune response ... Contemporary medical training does not teach its practitioners how to connect ceremonially with an open heart."[11] The shaman continues,

> In Indian country, to be healthy means to be in balance. Balance occurs when knowledge, feeling and action are in harmony. That is the essence of your being, your truth. Navajo call this path, 'hozho,' the way of beauty. To be healthy is to walk in beauty.[12]

Instead of leading foremost with scientific rationality, medical practitioners who begin with open hearts as their primary, ritualistic way to relate to patients take a step toward balance—where mind, emotions, and body are in sync—and the result is a kind of natural health and beauty. If you recall from chapter 2, this message is akin to that seen on Prophecy Rock, in the land of the Hopi.

> The Hopi Prophecy Rock shows a junction where the two-hearted people have a choice of choosing to start thinking with their hearts or continue to think with their heads only. If they choose the latter, it will lead to self-destruction; if they choose to think with their hearts they would gradually return to the natural way and their own survival.[13]

Silverman and Hammerschlag do not make light of their bold challenge to physicians and all practitioners of medicine, to first care with the truth of their hearts over disembodied scientific objectivism. The stories of science and its overly lauded heroes, imprinted since the seventeenth century on the minds of most modern humans, are very strong. Yet teachers like Silverman and Hammerschlag, along with shamans from tribes like the Hopi and Navajo, beckon us to find health by opening our hearts in a ritualistic way, beyond the story of Western medicine and science. They encourage us to rewrite a new story about how to care for patients.

> Sometimes old stories made sense at one time but are dysfunctional in a new environment … To keep healthy, we have to look at whether our personal, cultural, and religious stories are working for us. If they aren't, we need to rewrite them.[14]

I love this quote because it offers us permission and even encouragement to finish off the Fourth World story, told by Western culture, medicine, and science, and to wander off into the wilderness to discover a new story—a story that defines, balances, and gives health to our lives. As we begin that new story, it is likely we will find a new pack, a new tribe, a new community, and maybe a new world—the Fifth World.

CHAPTER 10

Womb Spaces

After Howard Silverman, MD, spoke at my medical school in 2004 to an audience of forty medical students, I thanked him for coming. I also mentioned that I was looking for a spiritual guide or teacher. Perhaps he knew a shaman or someone who could help me grow along the path of healing and spirituality. I had developed a lot in my own spiritual journey but still felt there was much more to learn to put all this spiritual development into medical practice. Instead of introducing me to a teacher, Dr. Silverman, in his kindness, invited me to his house, where he would be making a sweat lodge, albeit with some Jewish influences.

A sweat lodge ceremony is considered a sacred ceremony practiced by early humans across all continents. Generally, the materials used to create the lodge structure include trees or branches from the willow (or similar flexible tree) shaped into a dome, with animal skins, canvas, or blankets as a covering over these branches. In the center of the lodge structure, there is a pit where hot stones (usually from a nearby fire) are brought in during the ceremony. Natural incense, such as dried cedar, sage, or sweetgrass, may also be placed on these rocks or burned in another way. Participants enter the lodge with respect and walk counterclockwise to where they sit and face the center pit. A shaman, or another intermediary, sits near the door during the ceremony and pours water over the rocks, causing all participants, either naked or clothed with little attire, to literally sweat. Sometimes sweat lodges include both men and women; some sweat ceremonies involve only men or women. Either way, sweat lodge ceremonies provide members of the tribe a place to be together and share concerns as well as the joys of life. It is one of the most sacred and challenging Native traditions, as the sweating and primal aspect of the ceremony brings out a lot for the participants, in both physical and spiritual ways. For many participants, the sweat lodge ceremony is unifying, detoxifying, purifying, and empowering. Like the activities that occur in some Western church services, participants regularly pray, sing, ask for forgiveness, give thanks, and make new commitments during a sweat lodge ceremony. However, in its raw primal nature, a sweat lodge requires more than the talk—and more than the mental or emotive experience—that generally occurs in Western churches (many of which are based on a Greek–Roman tradition of oration by a preacher). Unlike many of these church experiences, a sweat lodge takes one out of a comfort zone physically and very much into the present moment. Sweating in a hot, dark cave-like structure is tough, and everyone suffers. Suffering is not the goal, but it can allow for openness for the participants to experience the world physically, mentally, emotionally, and spiritually in a new or newly inspired way. In many ways, at its core, the sweat lodge offers a chance for rebirthing.

As mentioned in chapter 4, Lewis Mehl-Madrona describes the sweat lodge as a womb of Mother Earth, and instead of a dome sitting atop the ground, it is really a sphere that spans halfway under the dome. The rocks placed in the center of this womb space dome represent the placenta that the grandfathers and grandmothers inhabit. Ignited by a fire, these stone people become filled with fiery energy and release that energy back to the participants in the sweat lodge, very much in the way a placenta gives energy to and nourishes a baby.[1]

The shape of the traditional sweat lodge dome is round and technically goes into the Earth as a womb. The spiritual and physical nature of this sacred womb space structure guides, as function follows form—in the same way an embryo receives cell differentiation signals from the uterus. In contrast to a sweat lodge, many Western churches have a steeple pointed upward toward the heavens with the goal of facilitating a mental and spiritual experience for the church people to transcend this "condemned" world. Instead, the sweat lodge takes participants back into Mother Earth while also connecting them to the spirit world and heavens. In this effect, perhaps sweat lodges exist as womb spaces where one can, in religious lingo, be "born again."[2]

However, Westerners who are unfamiliar with sweat lodges or similar ceremonies have had difficult, laborious times with rebirthing. Many Westerners have failed miserably to find authentic spirituality because many religious structures, teachings, and practices have further divorced us from our Mother Earth instead of bringing us closer and in deeper relationship with her. While there are beautiful churches and cathedrals that inspire us spiritually, where is the sacred raw, Earthy physicality? How are these amazingly beautiful places helping us bring spiritual enlightenment or inspiration back into physical form? In truth, while lofty, these grand church and cathedral structures fail to accomplish what a simple willow bark structure with a dug-out hole in the ground can do to help us truly be reborn.[3] Along with Western religions, Western medicine also has a few lessons to learn by embracing the spirituality and physicality of Native ceremonies like the sweat lodge. Truly regenerative medicine, and perhaps all effective spiritual–physical medicine, begins with addressing the patient at the womb level.

I was not entirely a novice at participating in these sweat lodge ceremonies; my first sweat was when I was fifteen years old on a backpacking expedition to Phantom Ranch, a Boy Scout ranch near Cimarron, New Mexico. Having an early ascetic desire for the altered states of consciousness produced by such physical challenges (such as running, jumping into freezing cold water, and backpacking in the winter), the sweat lodge experience, requiring perseverance, was a ceremony that affected me profoundly early in life. However, while my Boy Scout sweat lodge experience was influential, it was, at that time, more intended for learning about Native tradition, in perhaps an Anglo-European way, than connecting the spirit with the physical. Yet even this early experience motivated me, when I was a twenty-nine-year-old medical student, to be open to all the possibilities of what might occur in a sweat lodge at Dr. Silverman's house.

In the lodge, Dr. Silverman, along with his family and some close friends, gathered around the sacred hot stones nestled in a small pit at the center of the structure. It then became completely dark when the door to the lodge was closed. By "dark" I mean that all inside was pure blackness; with my eyes open or closed, my view was unchanged. Some opening words were spoken by Dr. Silverman, and then we all introduced ourselves and gave reverential thanks to the Creator as well as other humans and elements, acknowledging "all our relations." We also stated our intentions for being present in the ceremony. After everyone had the chance to speak, Dr. Silverman poured water over the hot rocks in the center of the lodge, creating potent steam that surrounded everyone present. Immediately we were all covered in dripping sweat, and everyone began singing. We sang until Dr. Silverman stopped pouring water on the rocks; then there was a time of silence followed by a time when words of thanks or reverence were spoken again. Then more hot rocks were brought into the center of this sacred space.

I did not know the words to the Jewish songs being sung, but I repeated them during the chorus lines and then just meditated and focused on my hot breath. It was already hot outside in Arizona, and the steam of the confined space of the sweat lodge made it even hotter inside. Meditation helped me escape it all and transcend the body with the same kind of austerity as a monk. I had practiced this type of discipline, of being present under stressful situations, but not as embodied, because I usually just checked out into the spirit world. In my previous Zen-style spiritual practice, I normally felt fine in a disembodied, transcendent state no matter what happened in the external physical world.

However, as the sweating and singing continued, something pulled me back into physical beingness. It was as if I could feel my ancestors with potent aliveness running through my blood, and I thus had an increased awareness of my body. The sweat lodge finally ended, and I just sat in silence. It is a powerful thing to have divine connection spiritually, but it's quite another step when that divine experience spills over into one's physicality. Although I did not fully understand what happened at the time, I had been born again. My whole life was set to change—if I would only allow this newly birthed being to come forth.

My first visit to Dr. Silverman's house was at the end of my first year of medical school in 2004. Along with participating in a few more sweat lodge ceremonies, I became more and more interested in Native American healing traditions and read, in between my rigorous medical studies, several books on shamans and shamanic medicine. Yet most of my time was spent plodding through Fourth World medical schoolwork, with two or more tests per week, toward a finality of my second year. A big final standardized exam awaited, and clinical rotations of the third year were yet to begin. Even if there was a new human birthed in the wet, dark, chaos of a sweat lodge at Dr. Silverman's house, that new being had no time in my life for its expression—except to stick it out on the long road to gaining a medical degree and license—a choice I had made years before my rebirthing experience.

If you recall from the beginning of chapter 3, the beginning of my third year of medical school in 2005 was a time of desperation in which my inner world did not totally match up with my external medical world of clinical rotations. Wanting to learn and practice a more advanced medicine beyond clinical data, labs, imaging, procedures, and drug therapies, I bulged at the seams of what felt like a trap or net. I experienced desperation and even open-mouthed rebellion at times—the kind that got me kicked out of a rotation and landed me in front of the dean of my osteopathic medical school. While my inner and outer worlds were not aligned, looking back, I see that all these chaotic challenges were in perfect order. While ungrounded and in despair, I could only plod ahead and maintain hope in a future way of existing and healing that went beyond the Fourth World of Western medicine. Eventually this desperation led me down the path toward northern Canada, under the preceptorship of Dr. Lewis Mehl-Madrona for three and half weeks and then to the sweat lodge of Gerald, a shaman located on the Dakota Sioux Reserve near Prince Albert, Saskatchewan, in early March 2006.

I left the airport at Stony Rapids on a small puddle jumper jet and landed in Prince Albert. Arlene, my grant writer friend from Black Lake, had arranged to have her Cree husband, Clinton, pick me up from the airport and travel a short distance to their house next to the Indian reserve where Gerald lived. They had a modest two-story house a short walking distance away. The outside temperatures were cold at around -20° F. Gerald, Arlene's adopted brother and shaman, had been informed about my intentions of participating in a sweat and had invited several other male members of the tribe. Before the sweat lodge, Clinton and I traveled to the cloth store and purchased specific colors of fabric for the grandmothers and grandfathers who would be in the sweat. We purchased tobacco for the shaman and various foods for the ancestors. I spent an hour or two tending to large, bun-shaped river rocks (the grandfathers and grandmothers) placed around the fire, shifting them closer to the fire as necessary. It was important that these ancestral stones were not left unattended. Everything was prepared in a very systematic, traditional way.

When the time came, the other sweat lodge participants showed up and looked at me quizzically. Being the paler-skinned man among Native tribal people, I felt that being questioned by the tribal people was natural, of course. But their questions then became a little difficult to answer—they asked what happened to my head. Being a "heady" medical student, with my school career dependent on how much information could be downloaded, saved, and recalled by my brain, I arguably expressed excessive neocortical brain activity and thoughts despite my spiritual quests for a clear, present-minded state of being. However, when I pressed the

Cree tribal people a bit more, they all looked at me and stated that the back of my head was really injured badly. About four or five of them, including Gerald, told me that the back of my head was damaged and even held their hands on their own heads to show me where my head was damaged. While I had experienced a few head collisions as a youth soccer player, as well as in college, I did not have a headache, memory loss, or any of the post concussive symptoms that usually characterize a traumatic brain injury.

What could these Native people see in my head or brain? At that time, I implored my own mind and historical account of injury or anything that could have affected my brain. There was one thing that I did not share outwardly but had been affecting me emotionally; it was a personal challenge I had been trying to put beyond me for the past month since leaving Arizona to visit northern Canada. Before coming to Saskatchewan, I had spoken with an independent filmmaker named Ann. (Note: The actual names of this filmmaker and her father have been changed to fictitious names). I had seen an online preview of a documentary film Ann had made about her father, an integrative medical doctor from Washington who had died tragically in a mountain climbing accident. Ann's story about her father had affected me deeply, particularly during the time in my third year of medical school when I hungered for a more authentic way of practicing medicine (as well as existing in the world). The story about Ann's father had affected me almost as much as the story of Lewis Mehl-Madrona in *Coyote Medicine*, which I'd read during that same period. When I called up the number online to buy the film, it turned out that filmmaker was not yet selling the film, but she was showing it in select locations in the United States. I asked the filmmaker if she would consider showing the film at my osteopathic school, and she agreed.

A month later, after a few of my medical school friends promoted the film, about fifty people come to see the film in early February 2006, the week before I left for Saskatchewan. Ann's documentary about her dad brings up the medical challenges of being an integrative, functional doctor in the 1970–1980s. It also has some great some footage of glaciers in the North Cascades—but with a tragic ending. Ann's father fell off one of those glaciated peaks and died from—guess what? A massive head contusion.

Somehow, amid this tragic death, Ann's story about her dad brought me hope for a new way of practicing medicine. Ann and I connected over the phone a few times after the showing of her film. There was a deep pull while speaking with Ann that felt natural and normal but more than either of us had expected—perhaps because of the male–female aspect of the dialogue. Ann politely and respectfully said that it was best to move on from any future conversations, but I felt that something had been missing. Indeed, until putting the pieces of the puzzle together with input from the Cree tribal people in Canada, I had no idea that my story was overlapping with that of Ann's deceased physician father. What had felt like a romantic or even a close friendship connection was really what I now see as the spirit of her father reaching out to his daughter using my half-alive, vulnerable, desperate spirit and body as a channel. While the tribal people, including the shaman, did not distinguish between me and Ann's father, their expanded worldview allowed them to see both the spiritual and physical elements of my condition. No Western person had said anything about my purported head condition.

This experience with Ann's father was not the first time I had connected with the ancestors or spirits. Interestingly, other spirits who connected with me had often passed on to the other side in unusual or tragic fashions. One of my most vivid and first experiences of connecting with a deceased spirit occurred two months before I met Ann, during my obstetrics rotation at a local hospital in Mesa, Arizona just east of Phoenix. I had been at the obstetrics ward all night, mostly sleep deprived, making sure no pregnant females went into labor without calling the attending physician. Before leaving the hospital to go home for a long nap and do it all over again, I did my final rounds to check on the patients, assess their vital signs, and see whether they were peeing or pooping. These checkup times with patients normally took about three minutes per patient, and I slumbered through the process, craving much-needed sleep, until I encountered one case. I walked into a dark room with only the light of some monitors glaring. I did not want to disturb the patient much, but she woke up and began chatting with me about an ectopic pregnancy (status post laparoscopic surgery) that she had just experienced. An ectopic pregnancy is when an embryo grows outside the uterus, a.k.a. the womb, usually in one of the fallopian tubes; because of this misplaced implantation, it is necessary to abort the fetus either with drugs or a type of specialized laparoscopic surgical procedure. I listened as carefully as possible in my altered, sleepy state of mind to this patient and then confirmed her as medically stable after she reported that her ectopic pregnancy had been resolved with surgery. She explained that her mom had also experienced an ectopic pregnancy and that her sister had been aborted. I thought about this and realized that my own mom had also had a miscarriage, but I didn't think of this dead fetus as my brother. In my half-asleep state, I wondered why this young female, in the same kind of post–ectopic pregnancy state as her mom years before, kept talking about her dead sister as though she was a long-lost loved one. I blew it off and was ready to go home and ponder it later. As I was walking out of the room, I could not see her chart name because of the darkness, so I asked, "What was your name again? Elise?"

She responded, "No, that's the name of my dead sister. Maybe you saw it on my back. I have a tattoo of it there."

Some chills ran up my spine. I had not looked at this patient's back. And there is no way I just guessed some random name and it happened to be the name of a dead sister whom the patient was bonded to even though she never met her in physical form. Then there was the presence of something or some spirit in the room. It felt a little eerie but okay, as though the spirit was released somehow as I had spoken her name. The patient seemed calm and even kind of happy. I left the hospital, drove home, and took a long nap.

Indeed, it is these womb space areas that allow what is normally localized in the spirit world to seep over into the physical world; perhaps that's just what happens even in normal births. There's something about womb spaces—including women's uteruses, sweat lodges, caves, and canyons—that allow a portal for spirits, including those of dead ancestors, to communicate through persons who walk in between the worlds of life and death. Sometimes these persons are shamans, or sometimes mediums, or just persons who are connected both spiritually and physically. I have had psychic people tell me I'm a medium but looking to connect with dead persons is not a career path that I've intentionally explored. Maybe I can chat with spirits on the other side because I've had, for most of my life, a loose grip on this physical life. Growing up, I was attracted to heroes who could put all on the line while managing fear, creating magic, or doing stunts because of a higher purpose. In a flow state of courage, with less fear and ego, even some extreme athletes begin to see the world as spiritual and material realities. In her book *Explorers of the Infinite: The Secret Spiritual Lives of Extreme Athletes*, Maria Coffey shares many similar stories about athletes, including mountain climbers, skiers, free divers, and other adventurers who directly encounter or communicate with spirits in states of exhaustion, when their lives are in peril, or when alone and far away in the thin places of our planet. Many non-Western and Indigenous peoples also naturally communicate with their ancestors or spirits on the other side, so my encounters with the spirit world are not unique to athletes or me, but they may be unique to many of us who dwell in a Western world based solely upon scientific facts.

Several more times, I would encounter spirits—usually the father, previous boyfriend, or another ancestral figure who may have tragically passed, related to a woman I'd recently met or come to know, and whom I felt physically attracted to, at first. Often the attraction to these women would be very strong, sometimes with unexpected sexual energy, until these spirits were recognized and brought into that person's present day. Then the sexual energy would immediately be gone. I had another such instance in 2014 with a female whom I had enjoyed going on a few dates with. When I took her home, I felt a clingy, fear-of-abandonment energy after we had spent most of the night together. I implored her to explain what was going on; she divulged that her grandmother, whom she had been close to, had died alone a few years before without saying good-bye. Once the grandmother's name was spoken in my presence, there was a sense of peace and relief in my female friend. Also, all my attraction for this female disappeared, and I left her house and never hung out with her again. My work or medicine in connecting the spirit with her granddaughter, my female friend, was completed—inadvertently or not.

What I quickly learned is that to work around or in the womb spaces of a sweat lodge or females can bring up a lot of sexual and spiritual energy, in a both a literal and metaphorical way. When I entered the sweat lodge on the Dakota Sioux Reserve in northern Saskatchewan, I had no idea that my relationship with this earthen womb would also entail a connection with other physical, human wombs.

That is, while birth in mammals is always preceded by sex, I had not put together the fact that my spiritual–physical rebirth would also require a form of sexual energy. To be truly reborn, I would have to honor a powerful sexual–spiritual energy in myself and others, known as Kundalini (from Sanskrit), and follow it in an appropriate, albeit chaotic way. There's much more to discuss regarding Kundalini energy, but for now, let's return to womb space darkness of the sweat lodge on the Dakota Sioux reserve.

Before the sweat lodge, I had stated that my intention for the sweat personally was to find "purpose and direction." Gerald, the shaman, acknowledged my goal and treated me just like everyone else in the sweat. It took a little time, but then in the darkness, amid the hot rocks, steam, sweat, drumming, and singing, things began happening. It was like being in a dream where you don't distinguish the lines between what is material or immaterial. Animal spirits, like the hawk, wolf, and other totems, were present; they felt so close and real as they moved about through the lodge. Other spirits, including a Cherokee grandfather and some Cree ancestors, came as well. The Western "rational" mind thinks that this is just an imagination or a projection of the mind, but in the darkness and heat, your swimmy brain does not really know and eventually accepts that the spiritual and material worlds are one and the same realities.

What is real in the sweat is perhaps more real than the shields we tend to hide behind in everyday life. Guards are let down, and there is a oneness of spirit and physicality, life and death, animals and humans, ancestors and descendants, Earth and spirit elements, and all our relations. In fact, when one speaks in a sweat lodge, it is customary to follow your comments with the phrase, "All my relations," or, in Lakota, *"Mitakuye-Oyasin."* The shaman "making the sweat" perceives the mental, spiritual, and emotional states of the participants and, as necessary, guides them on a path of healing, forgiveness, love, thankfulness, enlightenment, or realization of truth. In the lodge, while my original intention was to find direction for my life's mission, I found that it was more important to just be present and let go of having to figure it all out. I was overwhelmed with a sense of wonder, power, and community as well as deep meditative peace by the end of the sweat lodge, along with some leftover heat given by the grandfathers and grandmothers as we opened the door to the snowy cold of subzero temperatures outside. Just before we left the lodge, Gerald said that when the leaves of the trees were the size of a US quarter, each of us was to embark on a four-day vision quest in the wilderness.

All of us were invited to Gerald's house after the sweat to eat caribou meat and some vegetables. Gerald looked at me and said simply, "Thank you for taking me there." I was honored that he had traveled to the same peaceful state of being as me during the sweat and somewhat impressed by his ability to do so.

I asked him, "What do you think I should do with my life?" He asked what I did, and I told him, "I work with my hands on people to help them heal."

He said, "Does it make money?"

I replied, "Yes."

"Do that and then make a sweat," he stated matter-of-factly.

It was interesting that Gerald went straight back to the physicality and practicality of life with a statement about money. Gerald himself did auto repair for money and never took money for holding sweat lodges. He did not set himself up as some spiritual guru but was immersed in the physicality of everyday life.

I also asked Gerald how he had so many kids. I had been told that Gerald had about twelve children. He said that when he was younger, he was a bull rider in the rodeo and had a great deal of energy afterward. And there you have it—the expression of raw physicality and sexuality from a powerful shamanic healer.

CHAPTER 11

A Grand Canyon Vision Quest

A vision quest is a practice of Indigenous peoples worldwide, often embarked on by adolescents or young adults as a rite of passage as prescribed by a shaman or elders of the tribe. During the quest, the participant seeks a vision in a solitary way in open Nature, away from the comforts of the parents, tribe, and society. The participant may seek a vision regarding the healing of a loved one, finding direction in one's life, gaining courage, giving thanks, or another lofty intention. During the vision quest, the vision seeker usually abstains from water or food or takes on some ascetic challenge for part of or all the quest, in order to purify himself before the Creator, the giver of the visions. It is important for the participant, often a male member of the tribe, to understand his "powerless position before the mystery of the Great Spirit."[1] A vision, if perceived, is meant to build up and enhance the tribe and is not meant solely for the participant. However, sometimes the vision clarifies what role the participant may play in the tribe. Understanding and interpreting the vision often requires a step away from rational thought processes and, usually, the help of a shaman.[2]

When the shaman Gerald told all of us in the sweat lodge to go on a vision quest in the spring of 2006, I was super excited for the journey. Within a few weeks, April in Arizona would be full of trees with quarter-sized leaves, and I could get away from my medical rotation briefly in a lonely place to connect with the spirit world. With permission from my medical preceptor at the time, I escaped the metropolitan world of Phoenix and drove north to the Grand Canyon for a long weekend of being alone and shedding whatever spiritual or physical baggage might be holding back any visions about medicine, my role in life, or even the tribe or larger culture. On the South Rim of the canyon, I purchased a permit from the backcountry office and then hiked to the Colorado River to stay at one of the open campsites by the river. It was rugged and beautiful, and I was alone. Later in the spring, in an email to a friend, I wrote about the vision quest experience:

> It is now early April. I have three days by the time I begin hiking into the canyon depths. On Friday night, I hiked into the canyon beginning around five o'clock in the afternoon. It is a late start for a ten-mile-plus descent into the canyon. But the canyon is a timeless place, so I put away the watch and begin the eternal enjoyment of the canyon's vastness and depths—along with the silence of everything except my own thoughts, feelings, and breaths. The sunset on the huge cliffs above and the approaching river below inspires and rejuvenates. Darkness soon covers over the canyon's features, only to be interrupted by the brilliant moon and its shadows on the landscape. The moonlight shining through the trees even spooks me a little as it leaves a snakelike shadow upon the ground. Finally I arrive in the little slot canyon headed toward the river, where I record a few chirping frogs on a mp3 recorder. I then sneak into the sandy campground past some fellow campers and find a nice spot on a little bluff right above the river.
>
> I get up the next day with high ambitions. I have some running buddies who talk of a "Rim to Rim to Rim" run (from the South Rim to the North Rim and then to the South Rim again), which is a thirty-mile full-day adventure. There's still snow on the North Rim, so I

aim ambitiously to go up there. I opt to leave my watch behind today and begin my run down a long trail going east toward Phantom Ranch and then up to the North Rim. After running for a while with some cooldown breaks to get water and take a naked swim in a creek off the Bright Angel Trail, I arrive at Phantom Ranch. I walk into the ranger station there and ask the ranger how far it is back to my campsite at Granite Rapids. "Fourteen miles," he replies.

With only a little food left and a lot of uphill left to climb, I realize that the North Rim is out of the question. But I jog almost a mile past Phantom Ranch up the North Kaibab trail to offer prayers about the vision quest as well as the energy and feelings I had about Ann. I have, by literally running over this extreme terrain, finally exhausted all the raging Kundalini energy that welled up after meeting her. After this quest in the canyon, maybe I can let go of Ann and settle back into a life of meditative bliss, interrupted only by a few tests about how to practice conventional medicine. I can put any future energy to better use, like challenging my friends on the next Rim-to-Rim-to-Rim run.

As I pray, I also recall the previous year's experience in the Grand Canyon, when I met a beautiful person, Lucas Jain, near the same place at Phantom Ranch. Lucas, a very liberated soul, had left his friends driving a truck full of biodiesel fuel down to Mexico to hitchhike to the Grand Canyon and then back to Oregon. He had received handouts of food and clothing along the way, and when I met him, we decided to hike together to the South Rim end of the Bright Angel trail. Not long after meeting me, he said, "You meditate a lot, don't you?"

"Yeah," I replied. "How did you know?"

"I can tell by your eyes. They have that look," he said with a knowledge that deflected any further questioning.

He later offered me his favorite book, *One*, by Richard Bach, and we talked about all kinds of issues, especially about letting go of the mind and its roving thoughts. He reminded me that the mind is simply a tool and that it is okay to use it, but the best place after use is the tool shed. It was a great analogy and one that I remembered as I finished my prayers by the creek flowing off the North Rim into the great Colorado River.

Leaving my desires and attachments, I began my long run back to camp up the steep slopes of the Bright Angel Trail from Phantom Ranch. Suddenly, I began to feel nauseated and sick and realized I was "hitting the wall"—a phrase used by endurance athletes to describe the feeling after you burn up all your glycogen stores and have so little blood sugar that your Krebs cycle slows dramatically. (In short, you just want to lie down and die; your mind is all fuzzy, and the world keeps moving even when you stop). After eating the rest of my food, I then drank as much water as possible before running the last eleven miles back to camp across a very dry desert. Around mile twenty-three, dehydration was just around the corner. I forced myself to keep running, even at a slower pace. Feeling an odd urge to urinate, I stopped beside the trail, and a brownish fluid came out. About ten minutes later, a burning urge to urinate forced me to stop again. I pissed red blood. Damn. At this stage of my run, the mind had lost most of its distractions and little games. It's an excellent place of almost forced meditation. The mind only has the energy to toy with more vital issues of life and death. Indeed, thoughts of death mixed with thoughts of survival flooded into my awareness. Some people call the feeling akin to "touching the void."

Physical life jerked me back to my place along the trail, dry as it was, I began feeling the vitality associated with increased adrenaline flow. I now wanted help—from the Native American ancestral spirits, my wife, friends, God, Gerald, or whomever. (Actually, I heard Gerald's calm voice say that I'd be okay; then he left). A water source was only a few miles away, but I had to keep running to get there and help prevent acute renal failure. Then get to the water source and just keep drinking till my urine became clear.

The elements of a vision quest were distinctly present in my journey into the Grand Canyon. I was deprived of food and water, suffering, and at the mercy of the Creator. Perhaps this was the dumbest thing I had ever done. I was suffering physically, mentally, and spirituality to the point of breaking down. More than that, I had hematuria (bloody urine) and was close to dying of dehydration or kidney failure. However, the biggest internal challenge for me was that I had this strong sexual energy and attraction toward a female, Ann, and I could not rationally figure out what to do with it. I thought that if I ran a lot and exhausted myself, I would be able to transcend sexuality and live better as a spiritually enlightened being and healer. I felt a desire for a vision on this quest, but all I could think of at the time, besides the sexual energy chaos, was reddish-brown urine and my body's thirst for water.

I am also a man of integrity who was committed to one woman in a monogamous relationship. Although my marriage was a bit challenged, I believed then that sexual energy should be kept in the confines of a partner–partner relationship. What was I doing with this rogue power outside of this Victorian, Christian idea of sexual energy's place? Admittedly, I was suffering a good bit in the sexual connection with my wife at that time. We both were committed to our time-consuming careers. With my wife's limited sexual interest, I found myself diverting that energy into running, into work, and into Nature, along with a quest for authentic medicine and enlightenment. It was okay; I could have a spiritual marriage and just live as a monk. I had probably been a monk in a few previous lives anyhow.

But this sexual energy stayed with me. It wasn't just an attractive force of sex but more of just a charge of energy I felt consistently during the day. At the time, I did not realize that what I was feeling was a mix of sexual and spiritual energy known as the Kundalini. While sharing this experience with a healer friend several months afterward, I also told him about some back pain that had persisted for several months. I had sought help from every practitioner I knew and had had multiple adjustments made to my back with no relief. My friend, a practitioner of a type of applied kinesiology called BodyTalk, told me over dinner one night that I had "trapped Kundalini." "Kundalini" literally means "snake" and is usually defined as a sleeping "female energy that coils at the base of the spine."[3]

After hearing about this Kundalini force trapped in me, I finally decided to share with Ann, by email, some of my feelings that had arisen when I'd met her. These feelings felt like romantic interest, but they had a more of a spiritual nature to them than common animalistic instinct. Per her later report, my email to Ann describing my feelings did not even show up until a month later, but my back pain went away the next day! Without my resistance gone, the Kundalini, as spiritual and sexual energy, was now awakened and free. The

Kundalini was now able to move freely up and down my spine to the heavens and back to the Earth in a powerful way. This Kundalini power allowed me to be born again as a spiritual–physical being in the sacred womb space of Mother Earth—particularly that of the Grand Canyon.

While it can offer a powerful spiritual and physical experience, the awakening of the Kundalini can present a lot of mental health challenges for those on a spiritual path. In Hindu culture, people would traditionally be guided by a teacher in an ashram to awaken this Kundalini through meditation, chants, spiritual teachings, or asanas (yoga).[4] In modern times, especially in Western cultures, a Kundalini awakening, often occurring without the guidance of a guru or teacher, comes with the side-effects of psychological and emotional upheaval. "Since the influx of eastern spiritual practices and the rising popularity of meditation starting in the 1960s, many [Western] people have experienced a variety of psychological difficulties, either while engaged in intensive spiritual practice or spontaneously," particularly with an awakening of the Kundalini.[5]

As I fought to suppress the powerful energy of the Kundalini, resisting its awakening by "trapping it" in my lower body, I certainly experienced my share of psychological and physical effects. Before and during this Grand Canyon vision quest, I could not rationally understand this raging energy, which felt sexual and spiritual at the same time. Awakened by a female attraction, the Kundalini energy sought to unite my body with my spirit, but I fought it. I tried to just run it off. I knew this energy, at its core, was not about a relationship with Ann or any woman, but the energy persisted, driving me mad because it just would not calm down. As a result, my back hurt, and I was urinating blood, close to dying of dehydration. I was seeking a vision on my quest in the Grand Canyon but had this raging energy to deal with; how did it all relate? The Grand Canyon quest story continues:

> I trudged around the corner and recognized someone. Just
> a white rock. Damn, I'm hallucinating. Finally, I stopped
> at the little trickle of blessed water and saw a young couple

I had run past earlier in the day. A little reluctantly, I swallowed my ego and told them the situation. They had plenty of filtered water sitting in bottles on the ground, which they readily offered me along with food, including beef jerky and cheese, which I wolfed down—atypically, due to my usual vegetarian interest. Immediately I felt bonded and indebted to this couple. They assured me that they would take care of me and told me they were headed to the same camping destination. I asked the blond-haired girl named Laura where she was from, and she responded, "Santa Barbara, California." "Oh, that's kind of funny," I thought out aloud, recalling that Santa Barbara was the current home of Ann.

We all walked to the campground in the dark after I was feeling better. I ended up having to help them find the trail in the darkness and carry Laura's backpack. They fixed me breakfast the next day, and we all played in the frigid, raging Colorado River. I left camp early the next day. It was a beautiful, rough, and solitary hike out, after which I then stepped onto a crowded bus full of nicely dressed tourists who'd been tarrying at the South Rim of the Canyon. What a change in personal space!

After my experience in the Grand Canyon, I drove back to Phoenix a little exhausted and overwhelmed, with thoughts racing. What does this vision story mean? I was supposed to leave all thoughts of Ann in the Grand Canyon, but instead I run into a blond-haired friend who reminds me of Ann and is from her same town in California. Is there any wisdom in all of this? Wisdom and insight eluded me. I had learned to let go of attachments.

I had learned to be a master of my desires and to say "No" to much of what our frenetic world thinks it desires. But the whole quest of this vision eluded me.

Michael Ripinsky-Naxon tells of Rasmussen's encounters with an Eskimo shaman who offers this insight: "The only true wisdom lives far from mankind, out in the great loneliness, and it can be reached only through suffering. Privation and suffering alone can open the mind of man to all that is hidden to others."[6] Privation and suffering certainly were elements along my Grand Canyon quest, but what about this female energy? Ripinsky-Naxon tells also of erotic and sexual elements present in the shamanic experience. Quoting Weston La Barre, he writes, "The shamanic dream-vision often proposes sexuality with a succubus animal, a spirit marriage ... and if disobeyed, will drive the initiate mad."[7]

And mad I was. The Kundalini in me was roaring and making it difficult to study for an upcoming pediatrics exam. Usually a very sound sleeper, I stayed awake at night. I do not think anyone really understood, and maybe that was okay.

After much deliberation, I asked my osteopathic colleague and friend named Mark to connect me with his old girlfriend, Sasha, a deeply intuitive person and a medium. I wanted to know what really happened to Ann's father and figured Sasha could offer some insight. Was he pushed off the mountain or did he die because his own foot simply slipped? Mark provided Sasha's information, and I set up a telephone meeting with her. I did not want to chat about my psychological and physical challenges with the Kundalini energy, but maybe Sasha's insight would also help me figure this out as well.

When Sasha called late one evening, one of the first things she said was, "Wow, I'd like to meet you." I played off the comment like it was nothing. There was a strange familiarity about her, reminiscent of a sister or even a former lover. Sasha proceeded to share, "You are a powerful shaman." She said, "There is a Native grandfather guide who is with you. Your work is to be intertribal." (I was later told about this grandfather by two psychic healers over the next two months). Toward the end of the discussion, I asked Sasha about Ann. She said I had an incredible amount of lower chakra energy built up around the experience. I asked Sasha what she thought about this energy. She didn't answer. She did say that I helped Ann to grieve. I asked about Ann's father; she said his death was an accident. He was working so hard just before he fell. His exhaustion contributed to his fall.

Much of this information about myself was tough to swallow. While I had experienced a powerful vision quest, I had made no claims, and still make no claims, to be a shaman who performs traditional ceremonies to heal patients. Nonetheless, this medium exchange with Sasha did help me have closure with Ann and realize that maybe my work was done with her. The sexual aspect of the Kundalini shifted away from Ann and leaned slightly toward Sasha, which was perhaps evidence that my role in Ann's life was complete. Maybe I had somehow contacted the otherworld and shared some of Ann's father's love with her. The shaman Gerald and the Cree tribal peoples with whom I shared a sweat understood that I had been connected to Ann's father's spirit as well. Maybe I could also contact my

Native Cherokee grandfather from the other side. Maybe this grandfather spirit could help me better understand the vision quest experience and what to do with this awakened Kundalini.

One might think of the Kundalini as a "river of energy" that flows up and down the human spine, expressing itself in the various chakra centers of the body. Chakras are the seven energy centers that correspond to certain core expressions of our physical and spiritual beings. For example, the first chakra, centered around the very base of the spine and extremities below, is about survival and sustenance with a core energy of "exist." This base, or root, chakra also connects us deeply to the Earth—literally, it helps us stay grounded. The second, or sacral, chakra, centered around our genitals, is about sex, money, and power, and it has a core message of "desire." The third, the solar plexus chakra, centered around the navel, is about decision-making and directing one's destiny with a core energy of "control." The fourth, the heart chakra, is about care and relationships; it has the core energy of "love." The fifth, the throat chakra, is about communication and has a core energy of "expression." The sixth, the third eye chakra, is about gaining wisdom and discerning the future with a core energy of "witness or perceive." The seventh, the crown chakra, is about our spiritual essence in union with the Creator; it has a core energy of "oneness with the divine." The seventh chakra connects us to the heavens and the spiritual world.[8]

It is key to know that Kundalini, like a sleeping serpent or calm river, lives at the base and second chakras primarily. However, once awakened, Kundalini can move through all the chakras if not otherwise trapped or shut down. Many ancient practitioners of yoga, gurus, and holistic practitioners understand that optimal human health can be reached only as these seven chakras are open. An awakened Kundalini is the energy that allows these chakras to be open and to sustain humans in proper connection to their physical base as well as to their spiritual essence. But keep in mind that, when awakened, the formerly calm river of Kundalini becomes like class V whitewater, especially when it hits resistance. Trying to trap that whitewater-filled river is dangerous to one's physical and psychological health, as I personally experienced, but when the dams are removed and the river is allowed to flow freely, its power can do a lot of good for human as well as planetary health, as they are intimately connected. Recall Frank Waters' quote in *The Book of the Hopi*:

> The living body of man and the living body of the Earth were constructed in the same way. Through each ran an axis, man's axis being the backbone, the vertebral column, which controlled the equilibrium of his movements and his functions. Along this axis were several vibratory centers which echoed the primordial sound of life throughout the universe or sounded a warning if anything went wrong.[9]

The "vibratory centers" of the Earth and humans, as understood by the Hopi, are the same chakras discovered by ancient Hindu mystics that exist in all of us, which are energized by the Kundalini. Trapping that Kundalini or suppressing it, in ourselves, also causes negative health effects on both humans and the Earth. It's like putting that whitewater river in a confined space or box; it's just going to go around and around, tearing up everything in its path.

Why had I been trying to trap this Kundalini in my own body and life, especially at my first and second chakra, the very physical, Earthy, and sexual parts of my body? Perhaps other Western people are blocking or trapping their life-giving Kundalini, causing havoc with the core health of their lower chakras, including sexual and basic health, as well as disconnecting their spirits from their body and the Earth. Perhaps blocking or denying the Kundalini is also wreaking havoc on the health of the Earth. Why was I, like many Westerners, blocking the Kundalini's flow in my life, particularly at the sexual level of my second chakra? Why had I been, like many Westerners, so confused in this area?

What I did not realize at that time was that an authentic sexual energy expression was ultimately not just about an attraction to another human but rather an overall healthy appetite for life and health on Earth itself. The energy released on my Grand Canyon quest is summed up with the following:

> Sexual energy connects us physically, emotionally, and spiritually. It is essential to our health and vitality, how our creative energy flows, it is our [second] chakra, it is life and death. When we cut this out of our life, we are basically killing ourselves; our sexuality, our creativity, our health and our prosperity, joy of life itself.[10]

In humans, the amount of one's sexual energy, or sex drive, commonly known as libido, derives from a certain mix of neurotransmitters and hormones (such as dopamine and testosterone) acting on the nucleus accumbens area of the brain along with social and psychological factors. Swiss psychiatrist Carl Gustav Jung expands the definition of libido to describe it as the "totality of psychic energy, not limited to sexual desire." In *The Concept of Libido*, Jung states, "[Libido] denotes a desire or impulse which is unchecked by any kind of authority, moral or otherwise. Libido is appetite in its natural state ... It is bodily needs like hunger, thirst, sleep, and sex, and emotional states or affects ..."[11] Libido, if understood as one's amplitude or amount of sexual energy and *appetite* for life itself, is essential to all humans, and one's attempt to suppress it, repurpose it, or run away from it can lead to serious health consequences not only biologically but also psychologically. Sigmund Freud, who originally coined the term "libido" in 1892, points out this truth:[12]

> [Libidinal] drives can conflict with the conventions of civilized behavior. ... It is this need to conform to society and control the libido that leads to tension and disturbance in the individual, prompting the use of ego

defenses to dissipate the psychic energy of these unmet and mostly unconscious needs into other forms. Excessive use of ego defenses results in neurosis.[13]

Jung's and Freud's words were relevant to my vision quest experience in the Grand Canyon. I had been dying physically and kind of going kind of mad. Along with my ego defenses, the usual neocortical (mostly prefrontal cortex) mastery over my desires was falling apart. Humbled, I felt powerless before the Great Spirit. I felt lost, trapped, and even crazy ... looking for a vision or wisdom in what normally is just a personal issue. Eventually I gave up trying to figure out why I had trapped the Kundalini at the second chakra as well as trying to understand the vision.

About six months after my Grand Canyon vision quest, during an interview with a Native Yaqui physician named Dr. Gonzalez for a residency position at the University of Arizona, the challenges of my Grand Canyon experience came to the surface again. The doctor asked me to say something about myself, and I started jabbering the usual spiel and incidentally mentioned the vision quest. Dr. Gonzalez then spoke directly to me: "What was the meaning of the vision?"

I replied to him, thinking of all the challenges associated with it, stating that I didn't know. He said to me, "John, you have to let go of the rational mind in order to see the vision." This comment hit me like a ton of bricks. He also encouraged me to go back to the shaman from Saskatchewan (to Gerald). I had not questioned Gerald about it, because I wasn't sure how to explain the vision. It felt like such a personal matter regarding Ann, sexual energy, and the Grand Canyon. I felt frustrated, exposed, and embarrassed about this experience, but perhaps that's what vision quests are supposed to do. I left the medical interview and began driving away from Tucson in a deeply contemplative state about this vision. I just drove north, aimlessly, in sort of an altered state. I felt an unusual desire to stop at a nearby Barnes & Noble bookstore. I wandered through the self-help and spiritual book section and immediately picked out a book called *Don Juan and the Art of Sexual Energy.* I opened to pages eight and nine, and I read the following:

> This is how healers find their plants and songs, how war leaders are imbued with power, and public leaders learn what to say to the people. In order for dreaming to truly have power, it must be brought into the world for all to see. Throughout the Baja here and up the Colorado River towards Nevada, there are canyons and caves filled with murals which embody or bring back a shaman's visions. ...
>
> It is not required, however, to paint the Dream into a magical womb space of a cave or canyon. A powerful shaman may carry his or her womb space bodily and energetically and may open it and step into it whenever necessary. This manifests the Dreaming...
>
> "So, it takes sexual energy to do Dreaming?"
>
> "Absolutely," he confirmed. "The more the better."
>
> "What about men, then? They don't have wombs."
>
> "A man has to build his womb space by enticing the spirit of a sacred cave or canyon to come with him. The spirit must be continually honored in order for it to remain with him. This is a problem that many white men have, that essentially imbalances them and makes them powerless. They dishonor the feminine. No shaman worth his salt would ever do such a thing."[14]

After reading this comment, it all came together: the injuries to my feet, my inguinal hernia, my hematuria and dehydration, and my strong feelings for certain women. I had been living in my head and the spiritual world in a disconnected manner from my body. Before my rebirth experience through the Kundalini, I had perceived myself as a spirit being (or mental one) having a physical experience. Most of my energy existed in the ethers of either thought or meditation. I honestly thought that the sacred essence of myself was this spirit or mind rather than a wild animal with its carnal desires. Like most Westerners, I did not see the wild animal and its appetites as sacred and holy. I also did not experience the habitat of this animal, Mother Earth, as sacred.

I had thought that heaven was the realm of the sacred and that the path of enlightenment, forgiveness, and love led to heaven. Until I allowed the Kundalini to flow freely, I literally ran away from the Earth, along with its beauty, sacredness, and nurturing goodness. However, the beauty of a few women and the awe of the Grand Canyon brought be me back to honor the Earth, to honor the womb space, and to honor the feminine. I found that true love, as described in chapter 8, did not transport me to heaven, but rather back into the physicality of the Earth in a sexually healthy but unpredictable manner.

When trying to control the Kundalini, I remained separated in spirit, in body, and from the Earth. Being disconnected, I could not, with my disembodied rational and scientific mind, see the vison. Once I let the Kundalini be free, I was able to honor the beautiful Grand Canyon as a sacred womb space, a place where the visions and dreams could manifest.

Ultimately, the Grand Canyon became the Grand Womb for me. I visited the canyon every spring during medical school, having amazing experiences each time with the Colorado River, animals, side canyons, waterfalls, and new friends. The canyon, with her vastness and depths, was big enough then to take away the challenges and fears and bring me back into a humble but confident, manly state.

If one considers the Grand Canyon as a womb that creates and recreates life and health by facilitating the merger of the spiritual with the physical, it is very much like the womb space of a sweat lodge. The experiences in a sweat lodge defy what happens in the "rational" world and hence take us to a world where the divide between what is spiritual and what is physical, along with what is real and imaginary, no longer exists. A big part of understanding the vision required that I stop trying to figure it out with a rational, linear, dualistic, and scientific worldview. Stepping away from a rational mind opens the door to the Canyon's womb as a magical place. The following poem best describes it:

Go Figure

Figurative language,
Figurative people,
Places, and things
All converge upon
The factitious world.

It's an enchanted reality:
Yes, animals speak,
Flowers wave to another;
Even insects
Have souls.

Magical, sacred life
Abounds everywhere.
Indeed, in all beings,
The depth of eternity
Resides in real imagery.

Dreams and mysteries
Of the figurative realm
Run their courses
Through enamored witnesses

And then …
Simply disappear.
The hyperbolic river flows;
It voices out purity and joy,
Baptizing all creation
In divine, loving mystery.

The water is deep;
She roars with
Pleasure and rocks
With tides of grace.

"Come be hugged
By me, feel me,
Breathe me, be with me."

Trees share wisdom,
Power, and loyalty,
Offering strength
To those who listen.

O vast canyon,
You are my space.
You give all room
To grow and know.

With shelves of knowledge
And marks of ancient age,
You are our teacher.

O mystical wonder,
Canyon of love,
Veiled are thy depths

To those on the familiar rim,
But awesome
To the ones
Who go figure.

We are your imagination,
Your depth and soul,
Even through our lostness,
Wildness, and freedom.

We are
Beyond control.
But we are one,
You, me,
More than
We can see.

Take us there,
Far out,
O dreams.
Take us there,
O beautiful sunset.
Take us,
O special language;
Take us to life,
To love, to home,
To our surreal reality.

CHAPTER 12

Sexual Power and Healing

What I took home from my Grand Canyon quest is that *big* visions require *big* womb spaces and *big* sexual energy to manifest *big* new things. While I could not rationally see or understand the visions and dreams, I now realized the futility and danger of attempting to stop the flow of the sexual–spiritual energy of the Kundalini. To understand the vision more clearly and find spiritual, mental, and physical health in my own body, other bodies, and the Earth, I would have to explore deeper into the true meaning of sexual power, not only in humans and canyons but also in the rest of Nature.

While spiritual development had helped me to let go of seeing the world purely in a linear, factitious, rational way, a spiritual viewpoint didn't really provide much clarity about my vision quest. I realized that it would be necessary to allow the Kundalini to really flow and explore sexual power in a bigger, broader sense than that typically understood by Western peoples, to see and manifest the vision. After suppressing it for so many years, there was a lot to know about the sexual and physical nature of the Kundalini.

You may recall that the Kundalini's power is like that of a river or ocean wave. You can't really suppress a wave, but you can harness or ride it and allow it to express itself through you. The question is: How do you ride it? In figurative words, getting off or on the wave too soon or too late could lead to the ocean wave crushing you or losing its power. However, if you suppress its power or avoid the wave completely, well, we know what happens then—just recall my experience on my Grand Canyon quest or the words of Freud and Jung. Denying the Kundalini's flow or pretending it doesn't exist can also lead to madness, disaster, and even death.

In the wisdom of the Canyon, I realized that allowing the flow of the Kundalini leads to fertility, life, and the conception of dreams and visions. However, for the Kundalini to flow properly, I discovered that one's core sex drive must be, at a primal level, connected and in unison with all of Nature and the Creator. What does a sexual orientation toward Nature and the Creator mean, exactly? And how does this sexual–spiritual power of the Kundalini manifest our dreams and foster healing in our lives?

For any of you who question our primordial sexual connection to the Creator and Nature, look back at Jung's definition of sexual drive, a.k.a. libido. "Libido is *appetite* in its natural state. From the genetic point of view, it is bodily needs like hunger, thirst, sleep, sex, and emotional states or affects."[1] Sex drive is our core appetite, even hunger, to make life, to stay alive, and to maintain that life. Because human life ultimately derives from its source from the Creator in union with Nature, our sexual drive, as appetite for life, orients naturally to the Creator and Nature. As a result, the sexual–spiritual awakening of our Kundalini fosters the oneness of the Creator (Great Spirit) and Nature (physicality), creating a fertile space where life, health, and powerful dreams can manifest and grow.

As our Kundalini connects us, through all our chakras, intimately to Nature and the Creator, we realize that there is no need to manipulate Nature, prostitute ourselves, or make sacrifices to get rain, fertile soil, money, or whatever by appeasing some god or gods. Prosperity and fertility are a result of deep, intimate relationship with Nature and the Creator. To understand better, think about a female prostitute. She sacrifices the most sacred aspects of herself to a master in exchange for some selfish end: money, some momentary sustenance. The prostitute *manipulates* the situation, along with getting *manipulated*, for some personal gain.

Ultimately this leads to destruction of the body and soul. In comparison, think of a wife in a harmonious relationship with her husband. There is still a sexual exchange, but it is a life- and health-giving one and produces long-term fertility (wealth), babies, and intimacy. The difference in relationship is due to the orientation of one's core appetite. As the husband–wife relationship is a sacred connection, we also find a sacred connection to all life when our primal desires (our appetites) are oriented toward Nature and the Creator. There is no need to prostitute or sacrifice ourselves, use anyone else, or destroy anything in Nature when we are properly aligned at a core level, allowing the Kundalini to flow freely—a power that connects our spiritual and material worlds.

In the Western world, to what so-called "higher power" are we prostituting ourselves to try to manipulate Nature or another human? Some Western people—such as obvious perverts like Jeffrey Epstein—blatantly still follow the old ways of sacrifice. They destroy the lives of young girl prostitutes for some disgusting pleasure or to appease demonic gods. Along with completely disregarding the Creator, these sacrificial activities to manipulate Nature for wicked ends damage everyone involved, as they lead to division of spirit and matter. Other Westerners are more subtle in their attempts to manipulate Nature. These Westerners, including many of those in medicine, regularly "prostitute" their base and second chakra (core and sexual) energies to science and reason in order to control and manipulate Nature. (When they are subjective and embodied, science and reason have their place, of course; "prostitution" in these areas occurs when Westerners ascribe more authority to objective science and disembodied reason than to the direct knowledge that comes from intimate connection with Nature and the Creator.) Whether blatant or subtle, prostitution, either from Epstein and his associates or from a disoriented Western culture based in science and reason, attempts to manipulate Nature and gives the middle finger to the Creator.

And there's no limit to the degree of manipulation or destruction that can come from improperly oriented sexual energy. Remember that Jung also writes, "[Libido] denotes a desire or impulse which is unchecked by any kind of authority, moral or otherwise."[2] No laws and no moral arguments will stop Western Fourth World peoples from perverted sexual and manipulative practices. And when perverted sexuality is unchecked, the opposite of life-giving fertility results. The antonym for libido is the "force of destruction termed mortido or destrudo."[3] As stated in his analysis *The Mind in Action* (1947), Eric Berne understood "mortido" as a "death drive" that activates forces such "as hate and cruelty, blinding anger and social hostilities."[4] When directed inwardly, "mortido underlay[s] the phenomena of guilt and self-punishment, as well as their clinical exacerbations in the form of depression or melancholia."[5]

To sum this up, perverted sexual orientation—the kind that fails to begin and find culmination with our life-giving Creator and sacred Nature—leads to prostitution or mortido, a drive toward "destruction" and "death." For some early tribal cultures and a few modern Western people, disoriented sexual power results in child sacrifice, guilt, self-punishment, depression, sadomasochism, and domestic physical or emotional violence.

As a practitioner or lawmaker, if you want to help these people, neither talk therapy nor laws will control their core sex drives. Sexual power is uncontrollable in these ways. No one can stop its force. My vision quest in the canyon was a testament to this truth. While pissing blood in the Grand Canyon, I realized that sexual power, if suppressed or improperly expressed out of guilt, could inflict destruction on my own body or even harm others. Many Native peoples in the United States and Canada remember the priests and nuns who, out of a contorted sexuality, molested so many innocent tribal children in the Catholic schools. Even today, as exemplified by modern sex trafficking and human trafficking businesses, prostitution, molestation, and physical abuse continue to happen to Earth's sacred inhabitants.

If you want to help any guilt-ridden people, baby-killers, depressed patients, and sexually disoriented people find health and life again, the key is to go below the belt. You'll have address their core appetites and desires at the first and second levels, because that is where you find that impaired or trapped Kundalini that's responsible for their disease. Jesus, as a well-known teacher, was a master at turning people on to his message by tapping into this Kundalini power.

How did he enrapture so many people in the past, and even people today? He walked around directing his power to help heal patients, teach words of wisdom, and capture the attention from Jewish people and other nations. Remember: Jesus was an alpha male and a great shaman who expressed sexual and spiritual power, as Kundalini in him was intimately connected with Earth and the Creator. Confident in this invincible power, Jesus became a very potent, embodied teacher and healer.

The Jewish leaders of his time had to kill this man of great power. Jesus was unafraid to be fully male and stand up to whatever institutional religious authority existed in his time. Along with healing many people, he helped his followers to neither feel guilty nor pay homage nor make sacrifices to false gods or to governing religious organizations. Jesus pointed them to the Creator and the abundance of Nature and assured them they would be taken care of without prostitution or sacrifice. In Matthew 6:26–33, Jesus states,

> Look at the birds of the air, for they neither sow nor reap nor gather into barns; yet your heavenly Father feeds them. Are you not of more value than they? Which of you by worrying can add one cubit to his stature? So why do you worry about clothing? Consider the lilies of the field, how they grow: they neither toil nor spin; and yet I say to you that even Solomon in all his glory was not arrayed like one of these. Now if God so clothes the grass of the field, which today is, and tomorrow is thrown into the oven, *will He* not much more *clothe* you, O you of little faith?

> Therefore, do not worry, saying, "What shall we eat?" or "What shall we drink?" or "What shall we wear?" For after all these things the Gentiles seek. For your heavenly Father knows that you need all these things. But seek first the kingdom of God and His righteousness, and all these things shall be added to you.[6]

"Worry," or anxiety, fueled by a misdirected core desire—an appetite focused on gaining personal prosperity or fertility through sacrifice or prostitution—overwhelmed many people in Jesus's time. They "worked for a living," prostituted themselves (giving their virgins to have sex with the priests), and made sacrifices of animals (or human babies, sometimes), all in the name of gaining basic things of life: food, water, clothing, and maybe shelter. But Jesus said to them, "Seek, as a primal hunger, your source of life through the Creator and Nature, and you will receive whatever is necessary for life." There is no need for any sacrifice or payments to the priests and so forth.

These sayings by Jesus threatened to unravel the entire economic and hierarchical structure of the Jewish world at the time. Understanding the implications of his teachers, the Jewish priests were now out to get him. In the book of John, it is recorded that Jesus taunted them:

> "Destroy this temple, and I will raise it again in three days."

> The Jewish priests replied, "It has taken forty-six years to build this temple, and you are going to raise it in three days?" But the temple he had spoken of was his body.[7]

If there was a reason or purpose for the murder of Jesus, it was to say, "Check this out; sacrifice doesn't work. I'm going to come back to life in three days. Your job of making people toil, taking their money, taking their sacred chastity, and sacrificing their animals and babies is over for good." Jesus speaks directly to the base chakras of humans (the first and second chakras), where the energy of sex, money, and basic life essentials lie in the human body. If there's one message from Jesus and the Bible overall, it is that the Creator provides and takes care of people, animals, and plants, and helps them all to heal. This original creation, recreation, nurturing, and healing by the divine occurs with a properly aligned and fluid Kundalini relationship with Nature and the Creator, a relationship that fosters the true unity of spirit and matter.

It is interesting that Jesus refers to King Solomon in his message about letting go of sacrifice and worry. Solomon is credited with the book the Song of Songs, a Bible book all about proper sexual expression. No other book in the Old Testament better describes sexual power and its deep, bodily connection to the Earth than Song of Songs. Ellen Davis states, "The Song may be altogether the most 'ecological' book in the Bible ..."[8] She points out,

> We never really 'see' the lovers. But we do see, with increasing clarity, an exceptionally beautiful and fruitful land, bursting with life, for the lovers share it with sheep and goats, gazelles and foxes, lions and leopards.[9]

Song of Songs offers natural, geographical, and historical imagery and allusions as its fullest expression of human sexuality.[10] The Song's descriptions connect human bodies in sexual love both to each other and to the Earth. Sexual power thereby promotes rest, or ease—that is, the antithesis of disease.[11]

Okay, this message about sexuality is the same as before, with less crudeness about baby killing and sacrifice. Sexuality finds its proper chaotic expression with humans in unity with Nature and the Creator. But what about our Western way of thinking about sex between two committed lovers or married partners? This human-to-human sex (or marital) relationship is included in our primary relationship with Nature and the Creator. However, of viewing sexuality as solely private and specifically focused on another human, Wendell Berry reminds us of the generality of sexuality.

> One cannot love a particular woman, for instance, unless one loves womankind—if not all women, at least other women. … It is possible to imagine a marriage that would bind a woman and man not only to each other, but to the community of marriage … the sexual feast and celebration that joins them to all living things and to the fertility of the earth.[12]

Berry's message is the same as that of Don Juan, King Solomon, Jesus, and the prophets of the Old Testament. However, while Berry's comment may sound odd to some church traditions, empirically and logically, it makes perfect sense: the attempt to privatize all sexual feelings or hoard economic wealth always results in disastrous exploitation (pornography or pollution) or separation (divorce of human flesh or disconnection from the Earth). Berry offers a restored sense of marriage and sexuality, one that fosters the vital connection of human bodies with the Earth and their Creator.

To sum this up, embracing your sexual power is not so much about an attraction between two people but rather about showing up in authentic way without shame or guilt. Healthy sexual expression of the Kundalini involves trust in our core spiritual-physical being's drive to do whatever it takes to bring birth our dreams into reality. This quote by Howard Thurman describes it best: "Don't ask what the world needs. Ask what makes you come alive and go do it. Because what the world needs is people who have come alive."[13]

After my Grand Canyon quest, I followed what made me come alive and spent several years of my life exploring, beyond the limits of a rational mind, the sexual–spiritual power of the Kundalini in Nature. During my exploration of this power, I wrote the following poems.

Clouds and Mountaintops

Clouds and mountaintops,
Yin and yang,
How they come together.
Mountaintop rises,
Cloud comes closely
Showering her wetness.

Deep, icy breaths
Blast across jagged faces.
Passionate storms
Bring flakes of softness
Blanketing the rocky ruggedness.

Passing through time,
The melting and melding
Of such fine forces
Produce magnificent glaciers,
Crevasses and creeks,
Springs and rivers,
All ever living offspring.

Those who dare stand
With such progeny
Ride the dynamic flow
Of heaven and Earth,

Land and sky,
Where damp stillness pervades
And a quiet love
Moves mountains.

In *The Tao of Physics*, Fritjof Capra quotes a Taoist text: "The stillness in stillness is not the real stillness. Only when there is stillness in movement can the spiritual rhythm appear which pervades heaven and earth."[14] When we explore the polarities of sexual power found in Nature in terms of yin and yang, a dynamic power begins to unfold and define our lives. In his book *Twelve Rules for Life*, Jordan Peterson implores us to ask: What is the nature of Nature? He writes that

[Nature] is static and dynamic, at the same time ... Being, for the Taoists—reality itself—is composed of two opposing principles, often translated as feminine and masculine, or even more narrowly as female and male. However, yin and yang are more accurately understood as chaos and order.[15]

Understanding Kundalini as the sexual–spiritual power that makes up the core of our bodies and the entire universe, we begin to align with both chaos and order in our quest for health, sustenance, and an enriching life. We realize that when our sexual drive (hunger) orients toward Nature and the Creator, we are on a journey of wild instability intertwined with a perfectly ordered universe. Set on this stage of Nature where nothing stays the same, there exists infinite rhythm in all of it. In this dynamic balance of yin and yang, we find power—power enough to transform us completely and yet still give us enough nurturing and hope to continue onward down the path of turbulence. The next poem explains a little more of my own experience with these forces of chaos (yin) and order (yang).

Tornado of Yang

All is quiet;
Then a switch is tripped.
A trickle of wind,
Motion
Blows in.

The wind is nice
And full of play;
Its changing flow
Adds energy to the day.

Fly a kite,
Ride the waves,
Feel the breeze
In our hair,
On our face.

We ride on
Without a care
Until we are
S-wirl-ing
Here and there.

This ride is
Such a thrill,
Spinning, tumbling,
Running, charging—
There's nothing
That is still.

Invincibility is the claim
While all around
Wonder if we are sane.

Come the lion,
Come the bear,
Friend or foe,
We'll take all
And have energy
To spare.

Bigger gusts pick us up;
We are off the ground,
Soaring near and far,
Going up and down;
We are all around.

The tornado is me,
Here, now, for all to see.
My ego loves its liberty.

Friends look at us with glee,
But when we approach nearby,
They scatter wide.
They have to flee.

Dust everywhere,
Almost all life
Becomes little pieces
Blasted here and there.

The mind is awhirl,
The body, rotating in eternity;
Energy from base to crown
Shoots through like lightning free.

Love, beside raging might,
Now unfettered,
Cries out its sovereignty

Yet welcomes none
Save those
Who merge with
Its rampant destiny.

The core, the heart,
The breath—
Now there's nothing left.

Who are you, oh tornado?
Will you survive again
And learn to hear?

Suddenly, all comes clear.
Monkey mind empties its stuff,
First rapid and un-paced,
Then rhythmic breaths
Draw near.

Light shines through
Then even more,
Warmth fills the heart;
It pierces the core.

The tornado whirls and twirls
Round and round,
Ripping all to shreds,
But heart holds on.
She sees clear sky
And holds her ground.

The twister simply passes by.
All is quiet now.
The day is night.
Yin trickles in,
Shares powerful rest,
Pacifying the might.

Where there is stillness, there is love. Where there is motion, there is life. Apart from another, there is only death and hot air; when together, there is eternity.

Embracing the yin and yang of life, we realize that "there is nothing certain that it cannot vary ... [and] nothing so mutable that it cannot be fixed. Every revolution produces a new order. Every death is, simultaneously, a metamorphosis."[16] The following poem articulates the paradoxical mix of somber death with euphoric love.

Restless Wolf

Full moon
Brings out the wolf,
Wide awake,
At home
In the dancing shadows
Of the dark.

A lunar spirit
Arouses the beast.
The acid of its belly,
The dripping jaws,
The quickening heartbeats,
And sinewed limbs
Instinctively make
Ready for action.

Intense wildness
In the fiery gleam
Of the pupils,
The gaze pierces
Long before the fangs.

The battle is over
With one glance.
Wolf savors the feast.

The keen, wet nose
Breathes in heaven
As it caresses
Every fiber
Of its catch.

The slender neck
Is the favorite;
With a penetrating kiss,
Predator and prey
Become one.

Intoxicating joy proceeds
As juices mix
And appetites are filled;
Time is no more.

Indeed, many moons will phase
Through the hunter's life,
And across vast terrain
Lies a resting wolf
In summer-green meadows
Filled with frolicking pups
Now fearlessly playing
With the restless powers
Of love and death.

My metaphoric journey from spirituality into physicality through the power of the Kundalini was not easy. It took me about five and a half years after my Grand Canyon initiation vision quest in 2006 before I really owned the animal in myself. Opening to this sexual power mandated that I honor and integrate the desires of physical animal with my former identity as a spiritual monk and professional student. During that time, my diet, previously more vegetarian and even raw food vegan, shifted to include more animal foods. Recognizing the sacredness of eating animals as food (as well as the irreverence of modern industrial treatment and processing of animals in Western culture), I had to feel what it was like to kill an animal and merge with its essence and body to find peace with eating animals as part of my diet. And with a sexual appetite, I love all the creatures I have received as a gift for food, especially the one described in the poem below.

On one of the last days of the elk hunting season in November 2011, I traveled to St. Benedict's Monastery near my home, where I hunted with local guides from the Five R Ranch. These guides have special hunting permits to hunt on the sacred lands of the monastery. During Holy Mass, just before noon on a Sunday morning, I took the physical life of a female wapiti (cow elk). This female wapiti did not *sacrifice* her life, as she lives on in me, nurturing me with her love—one who is literally consumed with her. In a sense, we exchanged places in the continual cycle of movement of spiritual and physical that makes up birth–life–death–birth–life again.

Silent Lover

I once was a monk;
I learned meditation:
Control of the breath,
Steadiness of the gaze,
And mastery of the mind.

While others suffered,
I simply was.
While others became scared,
I simply was.
While others became excited,
I simply was.

The world was noisy;
I was silent.
Spirit embraced me,
And I left the body.

Traveling far and near,
It was an adventure
Into other souls
And deep recesses of the heart.

I would see
Without been seen.
I could feel
Without being felt.

And one day
I stepped back into form.
And that form
Grew hungry.

Life, love, and breath
Were necessary
For this new beginning.
Yet life required a skill …
Skill in the art of death.

And again with
Perfection of the senses,
A sacred, focused gaze,
The pull of a trigger,
A trickle of blood,
An echo of sounds
Broke the silence.

Where the monk once stood,
A wild animal remained—
Satisfied but for an instant,
But now potently alive.

CHAPTER 13

The Vision: A Fifth World

What was the meaning of the vision quest?

In my hungering for authentic medicine, evolving spirituality, running around the Grand Canyon, communicating with dead spirits, allowing the Kundalini to flow, and finding unity of the spiritual and physical, I needed to know exactly what my vision was and how it was to be manifested.

"John, you have to let go of the rational mind to see the vision."

This statement and these questions have echoed in my head for several years. To see really "see" the vision, I had to let go of what the rational mind comprehended as factual reality. I had to *feel* it and *perceive* it, at first, like an imaginary or made-up world. The vision consisted of a Fifth World, still in its embryonic, microscopic stages, as well as a navigable path that humans currently living in the Fourth World could travel to get to this next world.

Along with the Great Canyon dream quest, I knew that in order to begin feeling what the Hopi called the Fifth World, it was necessary to abandon my attachments to this present Fourth World such that I wanted nothing else from it. (Note: I use the term "Fourth World" to refer to the modern world as we know it—a world inhabited by Native peoples, Eastern peoples, Western peoples, or other peoples around the world, but it is largely subject to the dominance of Western thought and practices). If you recall from the earlier chapters of the book, I entered the void after letting go of what might be considered a Fourth World priority: religious views, being "right," surviving, making money, medical perspectives, relationships, career, and so forth. Pretending to fit into or care about

Fourth World culture equated to living a lie—a lie that ungrounded me and threatened to destroy my life. When I admitted that none of those Fourth World "priorities" mattered, I spiritually became at peace with life and death. At the final point of being okay with death (of my life and ego), I did not get to die, but instead I got kicked back into human form as a divine being, embracing the Creator as love, and as a wild, physical animal, now aligned with the heavens and Nature.

However, even with my enlightenment experience and subsequent acceptance of a physical form, I struggled for years to understand who I was and how to find purpose and direction in this life. Until the Grand Canyon womb quest, I struggled to find my place in the Fourth World around me, and even close friends mentioned that I was ungrounded. The so-called factual Western Fourth World did not match up with my true being. Now united spiritually and physically, I had trouble finding an identity in a dualistic Fourth World. I retreated to lonely places and wrote poetry that felt more realistic than the scientific, technocratic Fourth World "facts" that I previously believed or that were thought to be reality by many Westernized peoples. When in a state of hunger, thirst, and desperation in the Grand Canyon, I had a vision of the Fifth World as the spiritual and physical place where I and, perhaps, others could satisfy our collective deep hunger for a better world and truly be grounded.

Many Westerners and other modern peoples might critique this vision and the Hopi prophecy of a Fifth World as an imaginary place or just a mythological pursuit. Keep in mind that rational and scientific thoughts make little sense in regard to this world, as it is a world that it is barely perceptible in the physical realm. The Fifth World is still in a conceptual and birthing process.

For the Fifth World to truly manifest in our lives from a spiritual dimension into material reality, we must be aligned with Nature and the Creator through the sexual and spiritual power of the Kundalini. With open and proper flow, the Kundalini empowers us and our planet toward birth, healing, and regeneration as we transition to the Fifth World. (Finally, for those who cannot yet conceive of a Fifth World, consider a little research into the "factual, observable evidence" to confirm that our current Earth is a planet in transition, a planet nearing the end of a Fourth World cycle and the beginning of the Fifth World).

If our changing Earth changes humans and their external reality in a physical way—with hurricanes, storms, fires, viral outbreaks, and climate changes—it's likely that the completion of a global precessional cycle also will transform humans mentally and spiritually. Fourth World belief systems, including core epistemologies about rationality, science, medicine, business, work, and the like, shall be upheaved and largely replaced by new ways of understanding and existing. If you recall from chapter 1, my experience kayaking on an Arizona river under the stars spurred an investigation of this Earth in transition. After that birthday / Earth Day experience, I sought to better understand Buckminster Fuller when he stated that "evolution takes place through 'precession.'"[1] In *2012: The Return of Quetzalcoatl*, Pinchbeck explains,

> 'Precession' might best be defined as polar 'wobble,' akin to that of a spinning top, or a gyroscope on a table as its speed increases and decreases over time. The earth completes a cycle of precession every 25,000 to 26,000 years, and the planet is now coming towards the end/ beginning of one of these cycles … From Maya and Aztec calculations, the Earth was approaching a cosmic conjunction that represented the conclusion of a vast evolutionary cycle, and the potential gateway to a higher level of manifestation.[2]

Okay, how did Buckminster Fuller, the Maya, or the Hopi, come up with the idea that precessional cycles affect physical and spiritual evolution—death, rebirth, healing, regeneration, and perhaps the health of spiritual and physical life on Earth? I looked more into the science of the precession of the poles (along with the equinoxes) and found it interesting:

> What does [precessional] motion tell us about the Earth's motion in space? If you ever had a spinning top, you know that its axis tends to stay lined up in the same direction— usually, vertically, though in space any direction qualifies. Give it a nudge, however, and the axis will start gyrating wildly around the vertical, its motion tracing a cone (see the following drawing). The spinning Earth moves like that, too, though the time scale is much slower—each spin lasts one day, but each gyration around the cone takes 26,000 years ... The attraction of the Moon and Sun on the bulge is then the "nudge" which makes the Earth precess.[3]

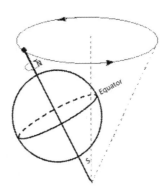

While this information about precession has some scientific benefit, how does this information about Earth's precession affect humanity or the rest of Nature?

> Hipparchus concluded that the intersection marking the equinox slowly crept forward along the ecliptic and called that motion 'the precession of the equinoxes.' The

rate is about one full circle in 26,000 years. In ancient times the intersection marking the spring equinox was in the constellation of Aries... currently it is again in transition to the constellation of Aquarius ... To believers in astrology, the 'dawning of the age of Aquarius' is a great portent and may mark the beginning of a completely new and different era.[4]

While I possess little education in astrology, I believe there is some ancient wisdom in discerning how movements of celestial bodies affect Earth and her inhabitants. However, the dawning of the Age of Aquarius conjures up in my mind dancing hippies and New Agers, or their modern equivalents, Burners (from the Burning Man movement). For many of these hippies and Burners, big events like Burning Man give them a physical venue to operate out of that oneness and love in an altered state of consciousness.

I am not a Burner or a hippie, but I perceive that there is some merit to consciousness-expanding endeavors that may be inspired by astrological alignments or plant medicines. Perhaps these Burner and hippie visions are signs of the beginning of the Age of Aquarius. Maybe these visions of the Aquarian Age include the same Fifth World as my vision and those prophecies of the Hopi. "Age of Aquarius" has several astrological interpretations, but the following interpretation resonates the most with me. The Age of Aquarius is that time when humanity embraces

the Earth and its own destiny as its rightful heritage, with the destiny of humanity being the revelation of truth and the expansion of consciousness; ... some people will experience mental enlightenment in advance of others and therefore be recognized as the new leaders in the world.[5]

What I like about this interpretation is its allusion to the Earth as humanity's rightful place to exist. This astrological interpretation of the dawning of the Age of Aquarius, or birthing of the Fifth World, makes sense considering my own story and vision. I also like the fact that this interpretation points to the "revelation of truth" and the "expansion of consciousness," which have been core aspects of my spiritual growth path. And regarding "enlightenment," I would add that it is a spiritual, mental, and physical evolution necessary for humanity's transition to the Fifth World, but it often first begins with an expanded state of consciousness.

Steven Kotler and Jamie Wheal, in their book *Stealing Fire*, speak prolifically about these types of expanded, or altered, states of consciousness, such as those experienced by hippies and Burners. Kotler and Wheal define these expanded spiritual states as "ecstasis." They conclude that, regardless of the content of these ecstatic states, there are four characteristics found in the experience of ecstasis. These four characteristics include (1) selflessness, (2) timelessness, (3) effortlessness, and (4) richness.[6] Kotler and Wheal believe that whether one experiences ecstasis through meditation, extreme sports, epiphany, asceticism, psychotropics, ceremony, or another modality, these attributes are consistent across the board. Understanding more of these characteristics of ecstatic states helps us, in many ways, understand whether we are spiritually ready to travel the path to the Fifth World.

The first attribute one experiences in ecstasis is selflessness. This selflessness means less of the little "self," which many philosophers and psychologists define as the "ego." We have developed this ego so much over time that our brains, with the aid of the prefrontal cortex, now have a "sense of the self" that regularly thinks and comments on the actions or thoughts of this self. This ego self allows us to reflexively think about our thinking, an action which potentially can help us to make better rational decisions in the future. However, in the words of Duke professor of neuroscience and psychology Mark Leary, as stated in his book *The Curse of the Self*, "The self is not an unmitigated blessing."[7] Leary articulates that "the self is single handedly responsible for most of the problems an individual faces as a species," including many psychological conditions, such as depression, anxiety, and other negative emotions.[8] Kotler and Wheal explain that much of the billion-dollar "altered states economy" is based on escaping the self or shutting off the ego in order to get rid of the inner critic and decrease input to the prefrontal cortex. The resulting state is inner peace and silence of the mind.[9] Kotler and Wheal describe the altered states economy as one that promotes this kind of momentary or more permanent escape from the self, including meditation, athletics, art, or even substances like psychotropics, which enhance the neurochemicals dopamine, endorphins, anandamide, serotonin, and oxytocin while better modulating stress chemicals, such as norepinephrine and cortisol.[10]

With a lessening of the ego's self-control, an individual in an altered state also experiences a sense of timelessness. In ordinary waking life, many adults, 48 percent of us, often feel rushed for time owing to daily life stressors.[11] Regardless of a person's material wealth, many suffer from "time poverty" in a modern culture that expects instantaneous responses to texts, online messages, and even online purchases. In an elevated state, and what Kotler also refers to as the flow state, time tends to "slow down" because of the hypofrontality (a downregulated prefrontal cortex) as well as less amygdala stimulation. Removed from the necessity of calculating time and the stressful fight-or-flight response, one's brain tends to forget about yesterday's problems and tomorrow's goals; a longer "now" is what remains.[12] In this present-moment state, one's brain can process more data easily and ascertain more of what is the essential information, as well as the context from which it derives.

In addition to selflessness and timelessness, effortlessness also characterizes what are described as altered (a.k.a. ecstatic, or flow) states of consciousness. Kotler and Wheal write,

> These days, we're drowning in information but starving for motivation. Despite a chirpy self-improvement market peppering us with endless tips and tricks on how to live better, healthier, and wealthier lives, we're struggling to

put these techniques into action. One in three Americans, for example, is obese or morbidly obese, even though we have access to better nutrition at lower cost than at any time in history ... Big box health clubs oversell memberships by 400 percent in the certain knowledge that, other than the first two weeks in January and a brief blip before spring break, fewer than one and ten members will ever show up. And when a Harvard Medical School study confronted patients with lifestyle related diseases that would kill them if they didn't alter their behavior (type 2 diabetes, smoking, atherosclerosis, etc.), 87 percent couldn't avoid this sentence. Turns out, we'd rather die than change.[13]

Higher states of consciousness unlock the brain's big six neurochemicals (norepinephrine, dopamine, endorphins, anandamide, serotonin, and oxytocin) in a way that makes our motivation to do activities inherently pleasurable and effortless. Instead of the puritanical Protestant work ethic of "suffer now, redemption later," our motivation gets turned on to what is, in Csikszentmihalyi's words, "autotelic."[14] "Autotelic" refers to our doing an activity or anything not for some external reward or goal or heaven, but because it is *inherently* rewarding.[15] While these activities are not always easy, we are motivated by a flow (of neurochemicals and even supracognitive powers) that drive us to excellence.

The effortlessness found in higher states of consciousness supports the end of this idea of sacrifice—a theme that is still very present in many Fourth World religious and spiritual pursuits. Ultimately, spiritual health, or any kind of health, does not derive from sacrifice. The erroneous belief that we must sacrifice our bodies or the Earth now so we can enjoy heaven later does not motivate humans to live moral lives or to care for their bodies or anything. The lowly state of wallowing in sackcloth and sinful penitence to some unseen God produces nothing but fat pastors and miserable parishioners who seek to make everything in life a sacrifice for some higher reward—in a spiritual future that may never materialize. Religions and cults founded on sacrifice of animals or children, sexual chastity, or even Jesus himself, are some of the most unhealthy and destructive institutions on the planet. Likewise, corporations or professions, including medicine, that encourage puritanical sacrifice (to climb the corporate ladder) for a job or career in exchange for some future reward also regularly exploit their patrons, as well as the Earth and the rest of Nature. Effortlessness means that none of the pleasures of life's activities must be avoided. Kotler and Wheal state that we have a neurochemical inspiration that occurs in us when things are effortless: "I did it; it felt awesome, and I'd like to do it again as soon as possible."[16]

Richness is the fourth characteristic of altered states discussed by Kotler and Wheal. Quoting Silva, richness is defined as "that kind of connection to something larger than ourselves that makes us feel like we understand the intelligence that runs throughout the universe."[17] This definition of richness is remarkably similar to the Force in George Lucas's Star Wars films or David Bohm's Akasha in his holographic universe. Richness means that we are indivisible from the power and community of the whole cosmos and hence able to access the Akasha, that primordial cosmic field that pervades all of space. We are whole in ourselves, as we are connected holographically to the whole universe, and understanding this oneness, we know that all the universe's resources are at our disposal. There's no need to acquire more for our individual selves, because all of Mother Nature and the universe is already in us. And we are already in it. The individual is perfectly whole, as the universe is whole.

Experiencing these higher, expanded states of consciousness, including selflessness, timelessness, effortlessness, and richness, as articulated by Kotler and Wheal, constitutes the first part of the path to the Fifth World. Indeed, those who seek the Fifth World must start on a spiritual path that, regardless of the methodology, transcends the personal ego and those lower priorities of the Fourth World. This path begins with a spiritual journey that is accessible through either a transient altered, high state (described by Kotler and Wheal) or more long-term elevated states.[18]

However, this spiritual path, while having potentially amazing benefits, must be traveled with caution. Fifth World medicine requires wisdom about how to navigate this awesome yet perilous path. And with any medicine, getting just the right dose at the right time is key. That is, if one travels too fast or too far out spiritually, one encounters some dangerous side-effects. If one travels too slowly, there is a risk of never arriving—the medicine will have no effect. It is also easy to fall off this narrow path—to just to stop taking the medicine or think there's some other medicine that may work better. Knowing how to navigate this medicinal path to the Fifth World is key, along with avoiding the spiritual and physical pitfalls along the way.

It is key to understand the difference between a long-term higher consciousness state and an artificial high from a drug or any other experience. While one may gain a "high" from LSD, religion, love, music, or any other methodology that alters one's consciousness, there are often side-effects of one's temporary experience of higher-consciousness states. One of the most common dangers is the development of an addiction to the substance that one perceives is the only way to get to that higher, altered state of consciousness. For example, some users of LSD, or any other substance, give up everything to regain this state and even leave the world of society to become long-term seekers of the altered states or ethereal states of being. While some avatars may be destined to live as hermits, far removed from grounded physicality and a society of physical beings, is that what most of us humans, as spiritual–physical beings, are here to do?

Another danger of experiencing the ecstatic states is that seekers think they *need* an external stimulus—such as a drug, guru, music, sound, or meditation—to gain that state of consciousness. Instead of looking within (where the kingdom of God dwells) for their pure essence, these seekers of higher states can waste time and energy focused on getting this external substance that will take them to these states of higher consciousness. The seekers become addicts as they seek an external substance in order to ascend to the higher states, and the addiction leads to deficits in other areas of normal, waking life.

Another danger of artificially created higher states is their impermanence. While both Kotler and Wheal argue that impermanent altered states may lead to lifelong permanent changes in the waking world; often these temporary states can just be another high, like those found at a party or nightclub, with little effect except to create a restlessness or desperation to regain that higher state of consciousness, in spite of whatever emotional, spiritual, or material debt is perpetuated.

In *Stealing Fire,* Kotler and Wheal reveal even more about the dangers of altered and elevated states of consciousness for those on the Fifth World medicine path. The "messiah complex" danger commonly affects novice spiritual seekers and is what psychologists call "extreme ego inflation."[19] Kotler and Wheal explain the thought process that characterizes this complex: "Rather than deciding, 'Wow, I just had a mystical experience where I *felt* like Jesus Christ!' they conclude, 'Wow, I am Jesus Christ. Clear the decks, people, I've got things to do!'" What's happening in the brains of these "self-appointed, ego-inspired messiahs" is that dopamine skyrockets, while "activity in the prefrontal cortex plummets." "Suddenly, we are finding connections between ideas that we've never even thought of … it feels like no one has ever felt this way before—that it's evidence of some kind of sacred anointment."[20] When the prefrontal cortex doesn't come back online, we lose our checks and balances for impulses, critical thinking, and long-term planning.[21] If you have ever lived with a manic or bipolar person, you understand exactly what happens here. What starts off as freedom from a prefrontal cortex–controlled self-focused ego ends up as a self-inflated ego that thinks the entire world is in his or her command. A whole brain and humble spirit keep the danger of the messiah complex at bay.

Another danger of ecstatic states is thinking that timelessness is forever and for everyone. Living in the present moment, a kind of eternal now, experienced in flow or an elevated state can tend to make us think that the rest of the world is also right there with us. Our brains may think that we can reach out and touch the future, the Eschaton, the Age of Aquarius, or even the Fifth World. Referencing Zebulon Pike, Kotler and Wheal state, "… at high elevations, objects in the mirror are sometimes much farther away than they appear."[22] The path to the Fifth World is indeed a path, not a hyperspace jump. However, true progress toward enlightenment and the Fifth World is not a hopeless dream; it may take some real Earth time or a long enough precession cycle. "Most people overestimate what they can do in one year … and underestimate what they can do in ten."[23]

Two other big dangers along the path to the Fifth World are thinking that effortlessness and richness are always the norm. While in an altered state, one's consciousness may act in a fluid, autotelic, self-rewarding way. This path begins with a spiritual journey that is accessible through either a transient altered, high state or more long-term elevated states.[24] Kotler and Wheal cite Ryan Holiday's book *The Obstacle is the Way* to explain that "'what stands in the way becomes the way' and all that 'effortless effort' takes a lot of work" at times.[25] The path to the Fifth World is exactly like that; it is a flow state that must be balanced with just the right amount of effort along with the knowledge of when to cruise.

Richness occurs when we are one with it all and feel the power of the Akasha, the cosmos field, to accomplish our task. However, this rich power of oneness takes some effort to manage because one must embrace the cosmos and her infinity yet still maintain an existence as a person if one wants to stay alive. If you have watched *Star Wars*, you know how tricky it is for Luke Skywalker, Darth Vader, and their fellow Jedis to manage the intoxicating, sometimes dark and overwhelming, power of that cosmic Akasha (Force) field. Kotler and Wheal discuss the same challenge experienced by free divers, including the late Natalia Molchanova, who stated not long before dying,

> 'When we go down ... we understand that we are one with the whole. We are one with the world.' That feeling is called 'the rapture of the deep,' a euphoric high that leads to one in 10 of all dive fatalities."[26]

This state of being is so pervasive that many of these divers forget the line between themselves and the world, as well as between life and death. The French film *The Grand Bleu* offers a window into the perspective of a free diver who also pushed past the limits of his human physical life. Perhaps the state of bliss of feeling the cosmic allness is so great that it is sometimes okay to not return to physical life. But some of us know internally that we still have work to do on terra firma. Dr. John Lilly realized he dove a bit too deep during a near-death experience in a float tank while using ketamine in the 1960s. Lilly reported seeing astral entities that later told him that "he could leave with them for good, or return to his body, and focus on more worldly pursuits."[27]

The purpose of describing the characteristics and dangers of elevated consciousness states is that without this knowledge, one may easily get off, go too fast, or go too slow on the spiritual path to the Fifth World. However, in spite of the risks, many individuals have successfully traveled this journey toward higher consciousness, including some hippies and Burners. These individuals have followed the enlightenment path of the great avatars, such as Buddha, Krishna, or Jesus Christ, toward transient and long-lasting spiritual enlightenment: oneness with all, an understanding of the Divine Creator as love, abandonment of Fourth World attachments, and a life devoted to this Creator. If some of these spiritual aspirants stepped over the dangers of the journey and made it on the narrow path and transcended to elevated states of consciousness, then where is the Fifth World?

CHAPTER 14

The Hero's Journey: A Return to Darkness

To discover why we in the West, even the enlightened souls among us, have not yet discovered the Fifth World as a physical and spiritual reality, we must ask what happens in our bodies and in the dark ground of Mother Earth after we've experienced a spiritual high or altered state of consciousness. The question to ask of many spiritual aspirants is: How does that evolved spirituality and its potential become actualized in your everyday physical life and the rest of the Earth?

Before answering that question, know that there is something distinct and different about jumping to an altered state of consciousness versus a lifelong development of consciousness. Impermanent altered states, while at times awesome, rarely produce the same life-altering effects as the long-term true development of consciousness. Also, the driving force behind an impermanent experience of ecstasis continues to stay mostly directed into the ethers, into the spiritual internal world. Burners come back and often do the same Silicon Valley jobs, and while microdosing DMT, MDMA, cannabis, psychedelic mushrooms, and so on, they may have some incredible flow-type-state life experiences. Yet this flow state rarely changes the fabric of the Earth or the nature of their bodily existence on Earth. While the modern hippies or Burners might commit to experiencing a spiritual world outside themselves or beyond their rational minds on semiregular weekend retreats, the *context* of their physical world rarely gets changed. To understand, just look at the full title of Kotler and Wheal's book: *Stealing Fire: How Silicon Valley, The Navy SEALs, and Maverick*

Scientists Are Revolutionizing the Way We Live and Work. Often, where these modern hippies and Burners make a comeback to terra firma is through creating new advertising ideas or new technologies for businesses like Facebook, Google, Coca-Cola, Walmart, and Procter & Gamble.[1] Kotler and Wheal explain, "We get access to increased data, heightened perception, and amplified connection. And this lets us see ecstasis for what it actually is: an information technology."[2] Ecstasis, for many Burners or AI researchers, becomes just a means to the end for producing more Fourth World content and technology.

Note that some of the effects of this Fourth World technology are truly amazing and can be amplified by ecstatic or altered-state experiences. However, it is a world of ideas and virtual media which are largely divorced from raw physicality and even true social connections. Jamie Wheal knows this truth, and after hearing him speak at the Aspen Brain Lab conference in 2018, I could see deep in his eyes a hunger, a desperation. I believe Jamie's hunger may match my own—a hunger for the Fifth World—as the Fourth World, with all its technological magic, just doesn't satisfy.

It takes a more permanent evolution of consciousness to be able to stay on the path to the Fifth World. Yet even for those who live with a more permanent, evolved state, the problem of directing too much energy in the spiritual world still exists. Coming back to the ground somehow proves to be difficult for many enlightened souls. It certainly has been difficult for me. Instead of being reborn in a physical, embodied animal state, it might have been easier to live as a meditative monk in a cave or at a retreat. Yet while that type of monastic life is the result of a quest for spiritual enlightenment, it does not always result in physical changes in the human body or the Earth. It took me several years and a lot of work to overcome lots of ego resistance to finally embrace a grounded path. To focus one's energies less on spiritual development and manifest a deeper physical awareness constitutes the key to traveling along what might be called the hero's path to the Fifth World, an enlightened spiritual dimension merged with a very physical place. Joseph Campbell articulates this path to the Fifth World in what is classically called "the hero's journey":

> The hero's journey always begins with the call. One way or another, a guide must come to say, "Look, you're in Sleepy Land. Wake. Come on a trip. There is a whole aspect of your consciousness, your being, that's not been touched." ... The call is to leave a certain social situation, move into your own loneliness and find the jewel, the center that's impossible to find when you are socially engaged. You are thrown off-center, and when you are off-center, it's time to go ... It's a dangerous adventure because you are moving out of the sphere of knowledge of you and your community.[3] When you cross the threshold, you are passing into the dark forest, taking a plunge into the sea, embarking upon a night sea journey. It involves passing through clashing rocks, narrow gates, or the like, which represent yes and no, the pairs of opposites. You may be dismembered, lose everything you have. ... This represents psychologically the trip from the realm of the conscious, rational intention to the zone of the energies of the body that are emanating from another center: the center which you are trying to touch.[4] ...
>
> As you go now towards the center, there will come more aids, as well as increasingly difficult trials. You will have to give up more and more of what you are hanging onto. The final thing is a total giving up ... a shift into the unconscious, or a field of action of which you know nothing. ... You may discover at this stage that there is a benign power everywhere supporting you in this superhuman passage.[5]

> You come then to the final experience of discovering and making your own that which was lacking in the place from which you departed.[6] … Bringing back the gift to integrate it into a rational life is very difficult. It is even more difficult than going into the underworld. What you have to bring back is something that the world lacks—and lacking it, the world does not know that it needs it. And so, on your return, when you come with your boon for the world and there is no reception, what are you going to do?[7]

For spiritual seekers who may have momentary ecstasy or a more permanent evolution of consciousness, the real challenge is returning to the world of physicality with their spirituality intact. Campbell explains a few options that are presented when these people try to return to the physical world with their spiritual gifts, empowerment, or enlightenment. There are three possible avenues.

1. They, the spiritual ones, just do not go back. They live as monks or hermits in their little, mostly spiritual, world of bliss. This is, per Campbell, "a refusal of the return."[8]
2. They come back and teach and do great things, but all for a commercial benefit. Maybe the gift they want to share does not start out as a commercial venture, but it can easily turn into that kind of manipulative endeavor. Campbell speaks clearly about these persons as ones "who renounce the gift."[9] How many so-called spiritual gurus have made fortunes by sharing wisdom or by using flow states to enhance corporations or personal gain that inflates the ego again so that the whole journey has been worthless. (Note: I do not critique this path as much as Campbell, because I have benefited from the many teachers, such as Wayne Dyer, Tony Robbins, Deepak Chopra, and the *Stealing Fire* authors, who

have made names for themselves and lots of cash along the way of their return to physicality. Still, if a return seeks worldly wealth that inflates just the ego, it will only generate more products and services for the Fourth World.

3. A true return occurs: a heroic return.[10] Campbell discusses bringing a small portion of the spiritual enlightenment gift through "cracks in the wall" of the physical, waking life.[11]

But I argue that the whole point of a return is to bring the spiritual and physical together in a fully balanced way and let the power flow without hesitation, not to change the Fourth World but for a wholehearted journey to the Fifth World. In short, for those traveling on this journey, it is not about *changing* a Westernized Fourth World but really *showing up* in sync with the Fifth World. This full-bodied return as an enlightened being on Mother Earth stretches far beyond Campbell's understanding about attenuated physical return, through the cracks and seams of Western culture, from a spiritually higher realm.

Why is it that so many so-called enlightened peoples, or those who experience enlightened states, fail to fully return to physicality and our Mother Earth—to the detriment of Nature and humanity?

The following dialogue between my present wife, Megan, and I might give one some clues to the answer. I have several friends who are Burners, and they have asked me to go to Burning Man or use ayahuasca one or more times. While I have been open to the experience and see value in these types of events and altered states, my wife has dissuaded me. She says, "I just don't feel that comfortable being around those people; they just seem so ungrounded."

My wife is not being critical of these ungrounded friends or any substances used by them. She just understands that modern hippies, Burners, spiritual aspirants, churchgoers, and many so-called enlightened people seldom make a quality, heroic return to Nature and the Earth but stay ungrounded (or find grounding only in the technocratic Fourth World)—and thus are only partially connected in their spirituality and physicality. The reason for this shabby return, or lack of return, is primarily because the direction of their Kundalini, or sexual life force, continues upward, akin to the steeple of most churches, into nonmaterial reality. Beautiful things often happen in these ethers, but since the energy stays elevated, these beautiful spiritual realizations do not manifest in full physicality. Even with authentic religious experiences, say with a spiritual retreat, this energy stays directed toward a transcendent Creator, rather than finding its grounding back in the body or the Earth.

The chaotic, raw force of the Kundalini has to return through what may be thought of as the human chakras, toward the Earth, our home, our Mother and our first lover. This return is basically the opposite of "getting high," and as Joseph Campbell states, "… it requires a great deal of patience and compassion" and a "hell of a lot of courage to return after you've been in the woods."[12]

A true return is one that takes us back to the womb spaces of the Earth: the female womb, the sweat lodge, the canyons, the soil, and our darkness. In this darkness, we use our Kundalini energy to plant or nurture a seed that can germinate in a new creation, perhaps even a Fifth World. Indeed, this journey to the grounded darkness of the Earth is the less traveled, rugged, next part of the path to the Fifth World.

Stepping away from a spiritual ascension to the light and back into the darkness of the cosmos (such as the "dark rift" at the center of the Milky Way), the darkness of the Earth, or the darkness in our bodies and souls is not always so easy. However, a cycle of light returning to darkness is the natural order of life, which is expressed as seasons as the Earth moves around the sun. Every year, the galactic patterns of the Earth revolve us all back from the brilliant light of the summer solstice, for example, to the darkness of winter's solstice. This revolution of the Earth reminds us also that our life's primary driving life force, the Kundalini, must return from darkness to light, from our lower chakras to higher chakras, and then back again. In fact, this cycle is key for our survival, as it is the primary daily and annual ritual of our lives. Ancient cultures and even early religious peoples understood the power of these solstice times; even Christ's birthday is celebrated on the traditional date of the winter solstice.[13] The following poem describes the power of darkness and her counterpart.

Dark Mountain Solstice

Dark mountain beckons;
Dark clouds ominously whisper,
Crowding together,
Shrouding the jagged ridges.

The rain hovers
Mid-sky while
Night closes;
Mortals rush away
To well-lit paths.

Danger looms as
The lurking mist
Emits a calling
For lost souls
To enter
Mysterious spaces.

The meaning of light,
Once so clear and true,
Is now a distant memory
Among the shadows.

Eerie is her presence;
The mountain darkness
Shares lessons
To all who enter.

To the unknown,
To the unseen,
To infinite possibility,
Darkness opens the door

To an abyss,
To freedom,
To the Ultimate,
But on a hidden path.

Most run back,
Craving dim or faint light,
Yet never too much
Of darkness
Or her counterpart.

Purest blackness,
With her invisible presence,
Dissolves our cloaks
And instantly knows us.

Her shadowy winds
Caress our deepest fibers,
Evoking both fear and relief.

Can we embrace her?
Be indivisible, unfragmented,
Be whole once again?
Or will darkness exist in vain,
A tool only for trolls and villains?

She does call
From outer space,
From her caves,
From behind the closed lids,
From beyond waking consciousness,
From mountains shielded from city lights.

Yet beware all.
You will not see,
You will stumble and fall,
You will feel pain,
Then you will disappear
When all integrates
Into the divine blackness.

Yet, as the lost are found,
Day does follow night,
And the door of death
Opens the path of life,
So darkness also shifts,
Exposing exquisite
And brilliant light.

Solstice comes, solstice goes. Nights are shorter; days are longer. Winter comes; summer goes. Darkness comes, lightness goes. This is the ritual.

Most humans run away from bright light and deep darkness. Out of fear, many modern, Fourth World humans run back and forth between too much darkness and too much light. As a result, we live lives that are dimmed in passion, love, and truth. Ultimately, trying to see and live with only gloomy, cloudy light disconnects us from the natural order of the Earth and the heavens. While some great avatars, through religious or spiritual paths over the ages, have followed a path to the light (and to the Great Spirit), many of these have failed to return to the darkness and physicality of the Earth (or failed to return with their spirituality intact). Excepting these spiritual avatars, humanity's failure to embrace the brilliant light of the heavens (including our Father Sun) and its return to embrace the deep darkness of our Mother Earth, is really a failure to allow the Kundalini forces within us to move up and down appropriately. This failure to reconnect to the Earth when returning from an evolved spiritual state has led to the dualistic, modern Fourth World—a world based on a disconnection of spiritual and physical. Restoring the connection of the Great Spirit (Creator) and the physical Earth involves a permanent spiritual evolution of our beings—a spiritual transcendence that connects us to the light with an equally powerful physical journey into the darkness of the Earth. This heroic return to the Earth, to her darkness, is what has been missing from many spiritual paths, as Joseph Campbell notes in his writings on the hero's journey. The journey of the hero into the heavenly spirit world and back to the Earth constitutes the navigable two-part path to the Fifth World.

Understanding that the darkness of the heavens and the Earth is to be embraced rather than escaped is a key part of the second part of the path to the Fifth World. One may note that the latter part of the journey to the Fifth World and continued life goes further than just getting "bright ideas" or "big data" to support scientific or technological advancements. The Hopi, along with many Native peoples, have tried to teach us Westerners this truth about honoring the sacred physicality of the Earth. Looking at

Prophecy Rock on the Hopi reservation again, the petroglyph makes more sense now. See the following image.[14]

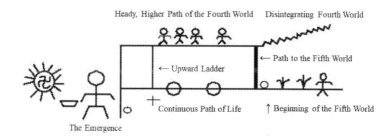

Fourth World Western humans are represented by the fourth figure on the top line of the petroglyph. Modern humans in the Fourth World are very near to the transition point where the top horizontal line meets the vertical, descending dark line that represents the medicinal path to the Fifth World. Many would understand that the transition of these two lines (horizontal and vertical) marks the end of the Earth's twenty-six-thousand-year precessional cycle and the beginning of the Age of Aquarius. After this point, the horizontal line to the right of the intersection point becomes a jagged diagonal line that eventually disappears.

In my hunger for authentic medicine, and through a vision quest in the Grand Canyon, I have discovered that the best medicine for Western people at this time is the wisdom of how to travel from the Fourth World to the Fifth World. Before we exit the Fourth World, it is key to understand that it is a world based largely in dualistic reason and scientific manipulation of Nature—a manipulation that is devastating to human and planetary health. We must leave behind such disembodied thinking and science to travel to the Fifth World. Only then will we abandon our Fourth World thinking and attachments and follow a path to the light (to enlightenment, to friendship with the Creator, to nirvana). Finding oneness with the Great Spirit, we may then return, in full physicality, to begin the second part of the journey to the Fifth World, where humans are healthy and exist in harmony with each other and all the Earth.

On the Prophecy Rock petroglyph diagram, the dark, descending vertical line is the path to the Fifth World. In *Meditations with the Hopi*, Robert Boissiere provides further commentary about this diagram regarding the spiritual–physical path to the Fifth World:

> The diagram shows two lines: the lower line is the path of the Great Spirit, for in its last end, a man is bending on the cane the old one's use, pointing to the corn, which is the sacred food that nourished us from the start. The old one shows he was the first and he will be the last. And so will we if we hold fast to his pathway.
>
> But there is another line on the sacred map drawn on the rock—a vertical line that connects the two ways. It is like a ladder that some might use to change ways, to go from the way of peace and balance—Taiowa's Way—to a path that seems to many a much easier one.
>
> Finally, [however], seeing that the Hopi Way of balance is the only chance, many will choose to climb down the ladder to go through the Great Spirit gateway. This time of confusion, in which many will choose either path, is called a time of purification …
>
> *When prayer and meditation are used rather than relying on our new inventions to create more imbalance, they will also find the true path.* Mother Nature tells us which is the right way.[15]

Summing up my understanding about Prophecy Rock, the following messages are clear for the Fourth World people on the path to the Fifth World:

1. Union with the Creator through spiritual development is key for permanent, enlightened consciousness states. This message is not new; many gurus, avatars, sages, teachers, and mystics have guided us on how to navigate this first part of the path to the Fifth World.

2. Spiritual evolution allows one to transcend the priorities and values of the Fourth World, such as modern humankind's overemphasis of and investment in rational control, linear science, and unsustainable technology. The path of evolution requires that we understand our lives and base our actions on love, prayer, and meditation, instead of relying on science and reason to dictate knowledge or to govern our actions.

3. After we, on a hero's journey, have found spiritual unity with the Creator, then we may descend the vertical-line path of physicality on the second section of the path to the Fifth World. Our enlightened spirits return to the darkness of physicality.

4. Through the power of the Kundalini, our physicality finds its grounding in the womb, including our bodies, canyons, caves, and Mother Earth as a whole.

5. Grounding in the Earth shall nourish and sustain us with sacred corn offspring, a sign of abundance, as we follow a new way of life—a life of beauty in balance with Nature and unified with the Great Spirit—and join the Hopi, and other traditional Indigenous peoples, on the Path of Life in the Fifth World.

In their way of peace, many traditional Hopi and other Native peoples wait for us patiently, watching us fumble along in the Fourth World, living lives of "quiet desperation."[16] Unlike these Hopi, many Western people have "heads that are not connected to their bodies" because our chakras, including the heart and the lower chakras, restrict the flow of the Kundalini to the heavens (Creator) and back to our Mother Earth. Many Western peoples struggle with a loss of passion for life and detrimental health effects due to disconnection from their bodies and the Earth.

In *Stealing Fire,* Kotler and Wheal discuss this struggle of finding the ground for many people who experience higher consciousness states. "It doesn't matter what we find down there, out there, or up there, if we're unable to bring it back to solid ground."[17] The problem, however, with Kotler and Wheal's approach is that, unlike the traditional Hopi or other Native peoples, they do not understand the physical body or the Earth as the "ground." In fact, through artificial means, they believe that the body (and the Earth) can be transcended by technological means. In this belief, Kotler and Wheal follow the logic of the philosopher Andy Clark, who argues that we humans are such a mix of technology—with our eyeglasses, smartphones, artificial hearts, and bionic limbs—and natural biology that we already are much closer to being "cyborgs" than we commonly admit.[18] Kotler and Wheal use this logic to try to rank technology ("the stuff we make") as higher or of equal value as our biology ("the stuff we are"). They consistently refer to the body as a "biological skin bag" and beg us, as inner mental–spiritual beings, to question our antiquated intuition that the body ranks above technology. Wedded to the lofty achievements of modern technology and science, Kotler and Wheal even call the body a "pale" (from the English "Pale," a barrier fence built between Ireland and England in 1142 that defined the world within the Pale as safe and outside it as unsafe) that we must get past in order to aspire to the highest ecstatic states, and even to find God.[19] Beckoning us to step beyond the pale of the body into the danger zone of cyborg territory, they pose this rhetorical question: "As technological upgrades and modifications to our inner state become increasingly common, what happens to the Pale of the Body when whole swatches of the populace begin finding God in the machine?"[20]

I appreciate Kotler and Wheal's argument about going beyond the pale of the body and think that, in the Fourth World and after death, maybe our spirits somehow transition from our current sacred bodies to another body or realm, while the previous body parts get recycled back to the Earth. However, on this side of death, even when transcendent experiences as a mediator, runner, kayaker, skier, and mountaineer take my spirit to a high, it is a return to my physical body, as my home and the temple of my spirit on Earth, that fosters long-term health and life. If my spirit does not return and honor the body and the Earth, I stay injured, urinate blood, get out of alignment, or simply fall apart.

Nature, including my brain, my heart, and the rest of my body, supersedes any computational technology created by a disembodied human mind.[21] While I can get too much in my head at times, remembering that it is fastened to my sacred temple of a body brings me back to health and life. A lot of Westerners care a bit less about what happens to their sacred bodies. Many in Western culture believe they can use science and technology to manipulate their bodies and brains to maintain a thread of mental or spiritual existence, barely connected to either toothpick or blob bodies. Where, in the Fourth World, are those who exist as powerful yet sacred bodies?

Science and technological innovations have their place, but Nature, understood through contemplation, intuition, prayer, and meditation, must guide technology's connection to the body and the Earth. When authors like Clark, Kotler, and Wheal rank technology over their bodies and over Nature, they continue to perpetuate the Fourth World and its eventual destruction, a.k.a. disintegration.

Ultimately, while I admire their passion and vision, Kotler and Wheal's views and overall emphasis in *Stealing Fire* are based in a disembodied Platonic philosophy that finds more authentic reality in the "ideal" or the "ecstatic." In the endnotes section of the *Stealing Fire,* p. 235, you can better understand this philosophical perspective:

> 'Ecstasy' comes from the ancient Greek exstasis, which literally means 'standing outside,' and more figuratively means 'to be outside of where you usually are.' In Greek philosophy, in Plato and Neoplatonists like Plotinus, it came to mean moments when a door opens in your mind

or soul, you feel an expanded sense of being, an intense feeling of joy or euphoria, and you feel connected to a spirit or a God. It is closely connected to another word in Plato, *enthuousiasmos,* which means 'the God within.' So in moments of ecstasy, according to Plato, you stand outside yourself, and God appears within you.[22]

If you look at Plato's *Republic* at the "Allegory of the Cave," Plato understands the world of your normal consciousness state, as the cave, where there only "appearances or shadows" of reality based on an ideal reality of Forms outside the cave. The philosopher, or spiritual aspirant, is one who experiences a higher, ecstatic state, when he leaves the cave where he or she encounters God outside himself or herself and understands the true reality of Forms. "The philosopher, however, will not be deceived by the shadows and will hence be able to see the 'real' world, the world above that of appearances; the philosopher will gain knowledge of things in themselves." The philosopher, now enthused and enlightened, can return to the cave and better impart good knowledge of true forms for those who are still prisoners in the cave.[23]

My intent here is not to discuss Plato's philosophy at length, but because it is so ingrained in Western Fourth World thought, it is necessary to unpack it just a little more. The following sums it up:

Accordingly, Plato developed a dualism: There is the physical and changing world (to which the body belongs), and the permanent and immaterial world (to which the mind or soul belongs). The body is then seen as the prisoner and temporary residence of the soul, which has existed before its imprisonment, and which will exist again after its release from the body at death (Emerson 1996, p. 21).[24]

Plato (428–348 BC) influenced many institutions, people, and movements that proceeded him, including the early church, Greeks, Romans, Scholasticism, the Renaissance, the Enlightenment, and the modern Western world, with his teachings about the basic dualism between body and soul, spiritual and physical. And even with the powerful book *Stealing Fire*, Kotler and Wheal promulgate the same Platonic and Cartesian dualistic perspective of this body and soul, one that erroneously attempts to divide human spiritual enlightenment from corresponding evolution of the body and the Earth. My question for Kotler and Wheal is: What's the purpose of the body if you, on a path to enlightenment, become just a transparent witness?

At this point is where I hold fast with the Hopi and diverge from Plato, Kotler, Wheal, and much of the Christian and Western world. Neither our bodies nor the Earth are mere "skin bags." Merged intimately with spirituality, our physicality has a grounding, a purpose, an evolution—one that is ultimately guided by Nature in relationship to the Earth. The Grand Canyon, the sweat lodges, and other sacred womb spaces have confirmed this truth. In turn, so many religious and spiritual teachers rejected the Earth by overfocusing on heaven or *spiritual* enlightenment that they have forgotten the importance of grounding one's spiritual essence back in the body and the Earth. Many of these spiritual teachers fail to understand that dualistic reason and objective science and technology further separate humans from their physical bodies and Nature. These technologies, along with institutions and corporations based on objective science, including Western medicine, are ungrounded and further propagate the destructive divide between spiritual and physical, body and mind, humans and each other, and humans and the Earth.[25]

In standing with the Hopi (and other like-minded peoples) to share the truth of a unified spirituality and physicality, I am accompanied by other influential writers and philosophers over the ages. In the Western world, Aristotle (384–322 BC), a Greek philosopher taught by Plato, argued also for an indivisible mind, body, and spirit. Unlike Plato, Aristotle says we are "real" humans (in the cave representing normal, everyday consciousness) and not just representations or symbols of "idealized" humans (located in some higher plane outside the cave). "Aristotle looked at the ways we are built, our biological details, and then judged policies and institutions according to how well they suited our nature ..."[26] Aristotle did not see "shadows" in Plato's cave, but realistic, bodily, physical beings. There were no idealized Forms that were outside, because our full and authentic humanity, as a spiritual and physical being, exists here and now in the cave. And that very real physical reality profoundly affects mental and spiritual wellness, and vice versa. Coates writes,

> Aristotle's thinking is at once closer to our everyday experience of how our bodies affect our thoughts ... He believed that the mind is necessarily embodied and if we did not have a body we would not, quite simply, have much to think about.[27]

Unlike those who see the body as an object to be spiritually transcended, escaped by death, manipulated by medicine, or modified by cybertechnology, Aristotle articulates our primal nature as a unified being of body, mind, and spirit. With Aristotle's understanding, we traverse the next and final part of the path to the Fifth World with a renewed honor of our bodies and the Earth as sacred and just as real as anything we could ever experience spiritually. (Note: For those who have experienced an ecstatic state, spiritual state, or even the euphoric Fourth World of the brilliant ideas and technologies, a return from the glamour of ecstasy and brilliant ideas takes a lot of courage and determination.)

It's likely to be a messy journey; of course, it is physicality. The world of physicality is filled with chaos, but there is, as the ancient Taoists texts confirm, always a little bit of guiding order within the chaotic power. And as sexual power expresses itself in you, you will know that healing, at core levels of your body, mind, and spirit, involves an intimate relationship with the dirt-filled temple of Mother Earth. Out of this relationship you will feel the medicine of the Fifth World.

Regarding this next world, I conclude with a final message from the wolf:

Message from the Wolf

This is a message from the wolf, your brother, the pathfinder. As an embodiment of Cherokee and other Indigenous ancestors, Wolf is a divine, wild animal who leads with an intuitive mind.

Wolf tells us of a Fifth World and a path to get there. It is a path prophesied long ago by the Hopi in their mythology and visions. It is a path to peace and love that brings us closer to our Mother Earth, to our Father Sky, and to all the wild creatures—our brothers and sisters.

Wolf comes to help all peoples—particularly Westerners but also Native tribal peoples who have strayed from the traditional Hopi way of peace—to navigate the path to the Fifth World.

Wolf beckons us to embrace our chaotic yet perfect Kundalini because it empowers us on the path to the Fifth World. On this path, we also encounter a cosmic field (Akasha) that binds us to each other, to Nature, and to the Creator.

The journey to the Fifth World cannot be traveled using dualistic reason or objective science, but only through love manifested through intuition and contemplation. As we open our hearts in a subjective manner, our spirits and bodies find unity. The unity of the spiritual and physical fosters healing of Earth and her inhabitants. Once juxtaposed as spiritual and physical beings, we will visibly perceive the Fifth World.

Medicine in the Fifth World, as spiritual–physical medicine, stretches beyond organized mainstream religions or commercialized medical insurance. Note that some of these Fourth World structures have helped us gain a vision of the Fifth World. We may still utilize certain institutions or technologies in the Fifth World, but their emphasis in the world is minimized. The priorities of the Fourth World are but stepping-stones to a new reality based on the higher-consciousness patterns of love, peace, and enlightenment, which are rooted in Nature. Looking back, we can have gratitude for the Fourth World and lessons learned in it.

In the Fifth World, families, tribes, and local communities help us to make more critical decisions; big corporations and other institutions have only a minor role, if they still even exist. Ultimately, what was primary in the Fourth World takes a backseat in Fifth World. For example, what is called natural medicine is now our primary medicine, and Western allopathic medicine based on symbols takes a backseat. The Fifth World is a world where our prime focus in life involves a sacred relationship with pure Nature and the Creator. Any tools or technologies we create derive from this heartfelt relationship with the Earth and the divine.

However, *Fifth World Medicine* is not a critique of the Fourth World as imperfect. A caterpillar (Fourth World) is no less perfect than a butterfly (Fifth World). As the movement of the Earth determines the metamorphosis of caterpillar to a butterfly, the Earth's movement now heralds our next world, the Fifth World. And now, at the end of the Earth's twenty-six-thousand-year precessional cycle, the Fifth World has begun to unfold in beauty.

The following spiritual and physical manifestations are ways in which the Fifth World has begun to reveal itself.

- Osteopathic medicine as taught by Dr. A. T. Still, MD, DO
- Healing ceremonies of Native healers, the shamans
- Integrative medicine with an emphasis on Hippocratic diagnostic and treatment: first, do no harm
- Nonduality and the reintegration of the body and soul, physical and spiritual

- Enlightenment, the Tao, and the teachings of the all the great masters, including Jesus Christ and Buddha
- Silence in the mind and the prayers, contemplation, and meditation arising out of this silence
- Love as the medicine of an enlightened, interconnected Fifth World
- Awakening of the Kundalini and its impact on the Earth and our bodies and spirits when aligned with Nature and the Creator
- A return to the darkness of the physical Earth and the chaotic yet synchronistic medicine that comes from intimacy with Nature

The path to the Fifth World is the way of peace and love; it is a spiritual–physical path now revealed by the wolf. It is the way of Taiowa, our Creator. In the end, we, who are on the path to the Fifth World, representing all the four colors of Hopi corn, are all one tribe.[28]

EPILOGUE

In my next book, *Fifth World Medicine: The Science of Healing People and Their Planet*, you will continue your journey toward the grounded physicality of the Earth on your path to the Fifth World. This second Fifth World Medicine book aims to dissolve the ungrounded, disembodied ways of thinking, being, and acting that are common in the Fourth World. The many "truths" and ways of thinking Westerners have unconsciously adopted over a lifetime will be challenged in irreparable ways, such that one may choose to leave a career or relationship, or one may accomplish something physically never done before by a human.

Beware of your attachments to the priorities of the Fourth World and its hold on you. If you are not fully ready and hungry enough for something more than your current life, hold off on this next part of the path to the Fifth World. Find a spiritual healer or psychologist and seek out where you might be unwilling to let go of whatever you think is the most important value in your life. After embracing love and truth as your core identity, follow me or another trusted guide on this last section of trail to the Fifth World.

A few guidelines for making the journey include the following:

1. Let go of the rational mind. This does not mean letting go of rationality completely, but rather putting rationality behind love (and intuition) as a guiding way of life.
2. Recognize your hunger as a core drive and recognize the nature of its power.
3. Orient that core desire towards Nature and the Creator.
4. Understand that your fertility and prosperity depend on your sexuality.

5. Allow that spiritual energy, the Kundalini, to flow up and down from the base chakras into the heart, the third eye, and the spiritual self, and then back down your chakras.
6. Let go of attachments while embracing divine love and staying connected, or reconnecting, as a unified spiritual and physical being.
7. Ground your energy properly in the womb spaces, the soil, the Earth, and all of Nature.

The next Fifth World Medicine book will deal with the details of what happens to our world (and worldview) when we begin unraveling the priorities of the Fourth World. Again you will be challenged in your dualistic Fourth World ways of thinking, being, feeling, and acting if you decide to fully embrace this path. That is, the way in which you understand reality, who you are, what you are doing, and where you are going will be put to the test. Be prepared to let go of what you think you know as you hang on tight in this journey into the unknown.

In *Fifth World Medicine: The Science of Healing People and Their Planet*, you will gain an enlightened understanding of the following:

1. Ultimate science over Baconian science
2. Embodied rationality over Cartesian reason
3. Contemplative science and medicine
4. Intuition, context, and content
5. Nature as sacred
6. Nature as medicine
7. How intimacy with Nature manifests health
8. Hopi mythology and the Fifth World

I look forward to sharing *Fifth World Medicine: The Science of Healing People and Their Planet* with you as we together travel on a guided wild adventure into the yet unseen Fifth World!

APPENDIX

Elders' Meeting with Doctor-In-Training John Hughes[1]

Introduction

John Hughes is currently training under a doctor from the University Hospital in Saskatoon who is Native American and utilizes traditional healing practices in his practice of psychiatric medicine. As a result, John Hughes asked Eileen Bruno to invite a number of elders to meet with him and share their knowledge of traditional medicine with him as part of his training. The Athabasca Health Authority agreed to provide the elders with a small honorarium for this purpose. Nella Hegeman and Arlene Seegerts were also in attendance to videotape the proceedings and transcribe the sharing session, as translated by Eileen Bruno. John Hughes provided a short introduction about himself and his purpose in meeting with the elders that acknowledged some of the impacts of colonization on their way of life and invited them to share their knowledge with him, especially as it pertains to traditional healing and medicine, which is documented as follows:

Elder J. B. Bigeye

I understand what you are saying. Today we have lost our own way and are trying to fit in with the white man's way. Today we are not well mentally, physically, spiritually, and emotionally. People are not listening to one another, and the young people are doing things that are not right, because no one is lecturing them. It's getting worse. How are we going to solve problems nowadays? That's the big question. No one is solving the problem. I have another meeting to attend in Saskatoon that is related to helping the young people. People are not listening to one another. It's not only a problem with the young people; it's also a problem with one another. Communication is very important. The chief and leadership should do something about what is happening. Twice a week, there should be a big assembly to discuss this. The young people are drinking and things, and they need help the most. You introduced yourself and you talked about healing and loss of culture. Even though it is a short introduction, it is very important. I'm willing to help you. But if there is no action of any kind, then this meeting will be useless. That's all I have to say.

John

I'm interested in knowing the positive things from the past. Maybe the important action here will be to connect with the old ways. Things from the past that were really good for your culture.

Elder Elsie Skull

Five years ago, there were traditional games. There was a meeting, and people were passing on their traditional games. It was new for the young people because they were learning this. But it was stopped. There is a big field by the school that should be used for traditional games. I have four grandchildren. It's hard for me raising up grandchildren. They're not listening. It's true. When we were kids, long ago, when the sun goes down, we're supposed to go back inside, because our elders said that there are evil spirits that roam around when the sun sets. And today it is still the same. There used to be a punishment with a willow. But now there is no punishment with a willow. If you punish someone with a willow, maybe there is going to be legal action. If you hit a young child or if the children say that their parent or somebody hit them, there is a social worker right there. Long ago there was punishment. Not abusive, but you used a willow. Now there is no punishment, and the children are getting away with lots of things. They should have recreation going on every evening for the young people, and if there are people interested with traditional games then they would listen. They have ears, and they would listen. There was a drum dance, and all the children were participating and dancing.

Elder Pierre Nilghe

What you said—culture is lost—this is very true. Long ago, the people followed the caribou. That was a happy time. They didn't sit around. Now people sit all day. The Dene people used to meet at Christmastime and New Year. That was when they would bring food and eat together. We were poor, but that was a happy time. We would have a drum dance, and people would exchange things. Maybe a dog team and the other person would give them something. That was a happy time. When people settled, there was school. Children were supposed to go to school, and they would live happy. Yes, we have everything. But how come people are sad if we have everything? School. You are supposed to learn something in the school. And the school is supposed to teach you how to not steal. I remember a long time ago the store was a tent. Nothing was stolen. Now the store is broken into; there are cameras and everything. It wasn't like that a long time ago. My own children don't even listen to me, like J. B. said. I survived the hardship of life. I used to wake up in the morning and there was no food. I had to suffer for what I was getting. That's how I survived and how I raised my children. But today I don't think anyone is living that way. You can't just talk. People are having meetings, but there is no action. They just do it once, and that is not going to help. Parents—they have to teach their children the traditional way. That's the only way. Long ago, we survived the hardship. It was a happy life. Nowadays it's not a happy life for young people and for elders.

Elder Mary Jane Yooya

I worked with the children for ten years, and I helped Chief Freddie Throassie with the canoeing trips. I teach the children in traditional and cultural ways. I know that if you teach them in this way, that the children listen. I know that when they go to sleep at night, they ask for help from the Creator. By teaching the young people in the cultural and traditional way, they will listen. And I like to help the young people because I know that they can listen. I am a Dene teacher and elder at the school for about ten years. And I have seen how the students are very sad. But I have seen how happy they were on the canoe trip. When

I show them how to check the nets and make dry fish, they are very happy. When I teach twenty students [at the school], it is not enough. There are only two of us. It's not enough. It's very sad to see young people. When they are sad, it is very sad. They enjoy making dry meat and how to make bannock and sewing. They really enjoy that. Our parents long ago they taught us how to make dry meat and how to make caribou hides, and we followed them everywhere. That's how we learnt long ago.

Elder Pierre Broussie

When you introduced yourself, I am happy to hear that you care about culture and healing. Long ago, people were happy even though there was not money. But I saw how happy people were. People used to wait for winter in the fall time. People made their own skates, but it was not from the store. People made their own games from caribou bones. There are five caribou toes, and you make that into a game. People enjoyed playing that game, and there are rules to our traditional games. Young people respected the elders. Nowadays the young people don't listen. I'm not a perfect person. But long ago was a happy time. But today it is too much for me, what I see and what I hear. Long ago people travelled up north with dog teams. I saw dog teams floated on the water because you couldn't put them on the canoe. It was a hardship, but those days were a happy time. Today we have everything, but we're not happy.

I have lots of grandchildren, and I still live the traditional way of life. I live about ten kilometers north of Black Lake. I still live the traditional way because I want to help my grandchildren and teach my children. Us elders, we lost our traditional way. I still hunt for moose, and I make dry meat. I am very traditional, and I miss my grandchildren when I don't see them. My grandchildren and my children are still living with me, and I teach them. But I wish that other children and grandchildren would be living the same way. I want to help the young people, but I have no one to help me out. I am the last survivor, because I lost my parents, my husband, and my brothers and sisters. So I am alone, but I have lots of children and grandchildren.

John

Thank you for speaking so eloquently. I want to know why people are so sad if you have everything. I want to know what is sacred to this community, because that is what can heal this community. And where are your healers? Or are you all healers, on the inside? I understand how beautiful the old ways were. Even though things were hard, you were happy. Those are beautiful things that you were doing. But now there are the big trucks and the Ski-Doos and the things of this white culture. Maybe we could go back into the wilderness and live that way, but now we have two cultures. How do we pick the best parts of each culture? What do we hang on to, and what do we let go of? Do we hang on to the things that are bad for us? Do we play poker all night or smoke cigarettes? Or do we act like role models? Who is in charge of the community? Who is in charge of the old ways? Who can take action and confront the white way of life? How can we get back to the old ways and still exist? I don't think that the old way of life and the Dene people have to die just because of the white way of life. I think that there can be a way.

Elder J. B. Bigeye

Long ago, there were people that were healers, and they foresaw the future. There were spiritual people, and they knew what was going to happen. So we knew what was going to happen, and people looked up to them. Long ago, elders, old people, used to talk to me, and I still follow their way of life. Today it's like I'm listening to them and following them. We lost our cultural way of life in the 1950s and 1960s, and ever since then our way of life is the white way of life. But we don't understand the white way of life, and that is why we are very sad people. Elsie Skull's father used to be the chief in 1940. He had a very strong voice. They made a treaty. Nowadays leadership should have a strong voice, like the late Louis Chicken. Nowadays amongst us, people don't agree. We are mostly fighting. Long ago, elders used to sit around the fire, and they used to foretell what is going to happen. The elders used to say that the white way of life would destroy our people. Long ago, people listened to strong voices, like the chiefs, in 1940. Nowadays the chiefs and leadership don't have a strong voice like a long time ago and treaties are being broken. That's not right. The white people made a promise for the land and fishing, but the treaties are being broken. I believe in what the elders had predicted, back then. Long ago, this old man predicted that one cigarette would be forty cents, and he predicted it would cost twenty dollars for a pack. In the future, what is going to happen for our children? The white way of living and the white people are taking over our lives. It was predicted, and it is true. They said that the white people are going to take over our way of life. One meeting like this won't change anything. We need to take action to protect our way of life, as Dene people. We need small little gatherings like this. We should have a big gathering to make an agreement. There is a big gathering every year, but nothing is going on, and there is no action taking place. People promise that things will happen, but there is mostly talk and no action. This is useless.

Elder Mary Jane Yooya

I'm sixty-five years old, and I'm still teaching the children because I love to teach. And I'm doing canoe trips with the children because I love to teach the old way of life. Long ago there were not watches, so we used to watch the Big Dipper and tell time form that. I used to find cigarettes, and I got punished for it. Today the cigarettes are destroying their life and they are not getting punished. The children need to know what kind of moss there is in the bush and what it is for, what kind of dried wood to use, and how to smoke a caribou hide. They don't know the important language that is lost, and the weather signs, like a rainbow. Nowadays, young people are not understanding a lot of important things, and they need to be taught all of those important things. There is high stress in the community because people lost their way of life. And us elders, if only we teach them, they will recover. It has to be like long ago. It is our fault. We are not doing anything about it.

Elder Elsie Skull

When we moved here, I was ten years old, and now I am sixty-two. There was obedience long ago, but now there is no obedience. My mom and dad taught me survival. My dad was the chief for twenty-three years. I learnt so much from my parents. But nowadays the children have lost their way of life. If I tell a story from when I was trapping, nowadays, nobody will believe me. My uncle is sitting over there, and he saw it too. My father taught me everything, even though I am a female. I used to have my dogs, and I would trap. I used to have two dogs, I still remember their names, and they were funny. (It's hard to translate into the English language.) There are dog team races nowadays, and my two dogs would have won first prize. My father said, "Those two old dogs aren't even worth it; they don't even have teeth." But long ago, those I relied on those two dogs, very much. Even though I didn't have a Ski-Doo, I would rely on those dogs. I didn't have a chainsaw, just an old axe. My two dogs were everything to me. My father used to be a very humorous person, and that would make me laugh. I obeyed my father. He told me to help the people, and I am still doing what he asked me to do. I still sing and pray in the Dene language in church. Communication is important. We have radio—NBC. If people announce on that radio, maybe the children will listen, and we will have a big gathering and the children can play games. They will listen, and it will happen.

John

In some cultures, there are healers or Dene medicine men or shamans. I would like to know if there is anybody who is a designated healer and how they are practicing. In some ways, we are all healers, and a true healer is someone who wakes up the healer in all of us.

Elder Pierre Nilghe

Long ago when people were very sick, there was a true healer, and they cured the people from the land. And if that person was meant to recover, then they would recover. Nowadays, I see lots of people from the hospital, and they pass away.

John

Why don't you have traditional healers today?

Elder Pierre Nilghe

Nowadays there is no Dene medicine spiritual healer. Long ago there were true healers from different cultures: Dene, Cree, and Apache. They were true healers. Nowadays, it's not the same. There are no true healers.

John

What happened?

Elder Pierre Nilghe

They passed away, and it's gone. There are no healers. I don't know how there can be healers today, when you have to pay them money. So I don't know if I can believe it or not. Who is a true healer?

John

You brought out a lot of good things. J. B. wants to take action. Mary Jane mentioned the importance of teaching. We can still learn the native ways, and we can still teach. You are role models for all of us. You are playing games and telling stories about your dogs. That would be great if you could tell stories to all of the kids around here. Are you guys in charge? And can you take action? Maybe there are Dene healers. You have sat in darkness long enough. The spirits are telling us to listen to them. When we see the northern lights, we can see the spirits talk to us. Do they tell us to fade away, or do they tell us to take action? Do you believe you can take action? What are the spirits saying?

Elder Mary Jane Yooya

I went on a canoe trip. There were eleven canoes and eighteen young people. Somehow, we lost a frying pan, and the students thought they lost the most important thing. There was flour, but they did not know how to make that bannock. Then I said, "I have an idea." This is how we used to survive without the frying pan. I found a big rock and put it on the fire and baked the bannock on that hot stone. And they were so amazed. Until today, I don't think that they will forget that—their way of life and how to survive.

John

What are the spirits saying about how to survive? What are they saying to us? I don't think that they want us to die. What do they want us to do?

Elder Mary Jane Yooya

We have to survive for our children. That's what we did long ago.

John

What is going to keep the spirit alive? How do we keep the spirit up? We've got to live the old ways. We've got to turn off the TVs and get out into the wilderness and let the land teach us. We have to learn to pray in the Dene way again. We have to learn to live the Dene way again. We have to heal in the Dene way again. We don't have to go to the hospital all the time. There is some good medicine in the hospital. But there is also better medicine in the Dene way—being with the land and being with the silence.

Elder Elsie Skull

Long ago there was traditional food, but now there is food in the store that makes people sick. I survived cancer, but I lost my daughter to cancer. There were so many spiritual healers, but she still died, because that is God's way. Traditional food is healthy food. I have so many prescriptions from the doctors and the nurses, and if I take those pills, it makes me nauseated and makes me want to throw up. We don't understand that medicine. Those pills are not good pills, if you don't understand that or take it. I'm smoking, and the doctors and everybody tell me that smoking is not okay for your heath. My ancestors had dark brown teeth, and they never died from smoking. They bit the pipe so hard that their teeth were falling out, but they never died of that. They are talking about smoking, but if God wants us to die of something, then we will die of it.

John

White man cigarettes have poisons in it. The old tobacco was not like that.

Elder Mary Jane Yooya

I met someone form Yellowknife. She was ninety-six years old. She lived on caribou meat and water. She did not smoke cigarettes. She has all her teeth, and she is healthy. She never drank tea.

John

If you want to take action, take action for yourselves. Go back to the caribou-meat-and-water diet. Everybody will follow you.

Elder Betty May Toutsaint

Are you going to live in Black Lake?

John

I want to make a few comments. You have the potential to create change. You are teaching people. You are taking kids out on the lake. You can take these kids and teach them. Get them to eat caribou meat. It's time to take action. You can do this. It is time to help this community survive. You can be the example.

Elder Betty May Toutsaint

It is very true what you said. We have to do it ourselves. We have to take our kids out and teach them. It's up to us, and it's up to our children. We have to do it.

John

It's okay to discipline your kids and do it the way you know how. You have the power. What is the next step for us now?

Elder Betty May Toutsaint

We have to teach our children's children and turn the TV off and start taking action. There is a shortage of housing in the community, and that is a big problem. In order to teach our own children, we have to have our own house. If we don't have our own house, we can't turn the TV off. We have to solve that issue, too, with the leadership.

John

Building houses is one step. Can you still remember how to build cabins? Are you willing to sacrifice your own house to build a cabin where you can live simply? Maybe there is another way. Do you think that something has been started that we can continue? We don't just want to talk.

Elder Betty May Toutsaint

We have to take action and meet with the leadership. We're going to bring up housing and teaching and take steps to get back to the land. Eileen, you have to be the translator and get together with the leadership. And that woman doing the typing, that's good. And you're here. There is a sense of God's presence here. We can close with a Dene prayer or whatever you want.

NOTES

Title Page

1. Robert Ghost Wolf, *Last Cry: Native American Prophecies & Tales of the End Times* (Bloomington, Indiana: Trafford Publishing, 2003), pp. 31–32, 50.

Preface

1. Maria Coffey, *Explorers of the Infinite: The Secret Spiritual Lives of Extreme Athletes—and What They Reveal About Near-Death Experiences, Psychic Communication, and Touching the Beyond* (London: Penguin, 2008), p. 257.

2. Maria Coffey, *Explorers of the Infinite*, p. 257.

3. Carlos Castaneda, *The Teachings of Don Juan: A Yaqui Way of Knowledge* (University of California Press, 1998), p. xiv.

(Note: For Coffrey and Castaneda, living our lives through the lens of infinity means that we know that life and death are adjacent realities separated by only a thin line. In this view, we are encouraged to have an open heart for the unknowns and uncertainties of life and not to grip too tightly to what we think we know or any attachments, because only what is true and loving exists in the end. Knowing this fact, being truly open to loving and being loved is critical for greatness, that is, infinite greatness. Infinity also does not for Castaneda mean an ungrounded, ethereal afterlife reality but that everything we are, say, and do has a lasting, cyclical reverberating implication throughout the cosmos.)

4. Thoreau, Henry. "Henry David Thoreau Quotes." Goodreads, https//www. goodreads.com/quotes/8202-the-mass-of-men-lead-lives-of-quiet-desperation-what. Accessed December 2, 2021.

Quote originally from Thoreau, Henry David, *Civil Disobedience, and Other Essays*, published in 1849.

5. "Desperation, N." *Picturesque Expressions: A Thematic Dictionary*, 1ˢᵗ edition. 1980. The Gale Group, Inc. March 21, 2021, https://www.thefreedictionary. com/Desparation.

"The rope or tether is generally conceded to be that formerly attached to a grazing animal, restricting his movement and area of pasturage."

Chapter 1

1. Pinchbeck, Daniel. *2012: The Return of Quetzalcoatl.* Penguin, 2007, p. 29.

2. Childs, Craig. *Soul of Nowhere: Traversing Grace in a Rugged Land.* Sasquatch Books, 2002, p. 128.

3. The DO Staff. "Where first-year residents train affects their risk of becoming depressed, study suggests." *The DO*, American Osteopathic Association, February 6, 2019, https://thedo.osteopathic.org/2019/02/where-first-year-residents-train-affects-their-risk-of-becoming-depressed-study-suggests/.

Indeed, as a medical intern, it's par for the course to drift into depression. "Researchers surveyed more than 1,270 internal medicine interns in 54 residency programs quarterly throughout their intern year. Administered between 2012 and 2015, the survey used the Patient Health Questionnaire-9 (PHQ-9) to assess the prevalence of depression among participants … The mean prevalence of depression within a given program was roughly 36 percent, though prevalence rates ranged from zero to 80 percent across various programs."

4. Stuart, David. *The Order of Days: The Maya World and the Truth About 2012.* Crown Archetype, 2011, pp. 307–308.

5. Wikipedia. "List of oldest continuously inhabited cities." Wikipedia, the Free Encyclopedia, April 11, 2021, http://en.wikipedia.org/wiki/List_of_cities_by_time_of_continuous_habitation.

"Orabi has been continuously inhabited since 1100 AD."

6. Many scholars believe that the Hopi ancestors include Mayan, Aztec, or Inca peoples.

7. The Sipapuni location mostly commonly referenced is from the area of today's Grand Canyon, in a cave near the confluence of the Little Colorado and Colorado Rivers.

8. Waters, Frank. *Book of the Hopi*. Penguin, 1977, p. 25.

9. Waters, Frank. *Book of the Hopi*. pp. 7–8.

10. Waters, Frank. *Book of the Hopi*. p. 9.

11. Stuart, David. *The Order of Days*, pp. 305–306.

Stuart writes, "One proponent [of the 2012 doomsday myth] was a man named Frank Waters ... Waters wrote a number of works on Indian mysticism, including perhaps his most famous work, *The Book of the Hopi*. He wasn't an anthropologist, however, his writings on Hopi religion, myth, and cosmology, while of significant interest, were highly unconventional, and based on no firsthand knowledge of the Hopi language ... He was keenly interested in unifying the diverse threads of Southwestern and Mesoamerican mythology and religion into a cohesive whole, almost as if he was defining for himself and others the tenets of a new organized religion ... Aztec, Maya, and Hopi religions were, to Waters, what he called the 'Nahuatl-Maya myth.' To a certain extent he wasn't completely off base in this assertion, which are after all, culturally and historically related. But more care was called for when proposing a unified system of mythology and cohesive religious narrative. No such thing ever existed in Mesoamerica."

12. Wikipedia. "Bursera." Wikipedia, the Free Encyclopedia, March 20, 2021, http://en.wikipedia.org/wiki/Bursera.

13. Wikipedia. "Copal." Wikipedia, the Free Encyclopedia, January 31, 2021, http://en.wikipedia.org/wiki/Copal.

14. After running for five days in a row (including to the top of the Kachina Peaks), I injected myself in the heel with a solution of protamine zinc insulin, used acupuncture and stretching, and wore night splints for about a year after the injection. My condition, however, began resolving soon after I returned from the

Hopi. Unfortunately, I had also broken my sesamoid bones on a run up Kachina Peaks and was in a walking foot cast for a few months for that condition.

Chapter 2

1. Boissiere, Robert. *The Return of Pahana: A Hopi Myth.* Bear, 1990, p. 9.

    "The spiritual, or mythical, territory of the Hopi remains as before, bordered by the Grand Canyon to the west, the San Francisco Peaks to the south, Window Rock to the east, and Kaibab Mountains to the north."

2. Neufield, John. "Pueblo People of American Southwest." *The Meanderer.* June 25, 2019, http://themeanderer.ca/pueblo-people-of-american-southwest.

3. Ross, Allen. "Hopi." *Crystalinks.* https://www.crystalinks.com/hopistonetablets. html.

    Image used with permission.

4. Ross, Allen. "Hopi." *Crystalinks.* https://www.crystalinks.com/hopistonetablets. html.

5. Taplin, Jonathan. *Move Fast and Break Things: How Facebook, Google, and Amazon Have Cornered Culture and What It Means for All of Us.* Pan Macmillan, 2017, p. 12.

6. Wikipedia. "Edward Snowden." Wikipedia, the Free Encyclopedia, March 21, 2021, https://en.wikipedia.org/wiki/Edward_Snowden.

    Snowden did not begin work for the CIA until 2013.

7. Boissiere, Robert. *Meditations with the Hopi.* Inner Traditions and Bear & Company, 1986, p. 109.

    All rights reserved. Reprinted with permission of publisher. http://www. innertraditions.com.

8. Ross, Allen. "Hopi." *Crystalinks.* https://www.crystalinks.com/hopistonetablets. html.

9. Boissiere, Robert. *Meditations with the Hopi.* pp. 109–113. (Emphasis added.)

Chapter 3

1. This poem, written by the author of this book, John Hughes, is informed by the quotation "To look into the eyes of a wolf is to see into your own soul," from the following source: Wulf, Shadow. "Wolf Information." *Shadow Wulf's Alphas,* November 15, 2001, https://www.oocities.org/pilotwolf143/wolf_information.htm.

2. Mehl-Madrona, Lewis. *Coyote Medicine: Lessons from Native American Healing.* Simon and Schuster, 2011, p. 37.

    In Native American lore, it is common for a spirit to appear in the form of an animal in order to provide guidance or teach a lesson.

3. Still, Andrew Taylor. "Andrew Taylor Still Quotes." AZ Quotes, https://www. azquotes.com/quote/867278. Accessed December 2, 2021.

    Quote originally from Still, Andrew Taylor, *The Philosophy and Mechanical Principles of Osteopathy,* published in 1902.

4. Andersson, Gunnar B. J. et al. "A comparison of osteopathic spinal manipulation with standard care for patients with low back pain." *New England Journal of Medicine* 341.19 (1999): pp. 1426–1431. https://www.nejm.org/doi/full/10.1056/NEJM199911043411903.

5. "DO vs MD: What Are the Differences (and Similarities)?" *Medical School Headquarters.* https://medicalschoolhq.net/md-vs-do-what-are-the-differences-and-similarities/.

    As a matter of fact, I finished my "osteopathic education" at the Arizona College of Osteopathic Medicine of Midwestern University as John Hughes, DO; however, during my allopathic residency at the University of Arizona, I held the title John Hughes, MD, for all my clinic and hospital records.

6. Yeon-Jin Kim et al, "Effects of internet and smartphone addictions on depression and anxiety based on propensity score matching analysis," *International Journal of Environmental Research and Public Health* 15.5 (2018): p. 859, https://www.mdpi.com/1660-4601/15/5/859.

7. "The Doctor of the Future." *Evidence in Motion*, June 5 2017, https://evidenceinmotion.com/the-doctor-of-the-future/.

8. Beaulieu, John. "Traditional American Indian Bodywork: The Origin of Osteopathy, Polarity and Craniosacral Therapy." *A Journal of Contemporary Shamanism* 8, no. 1, Spring–Summer 2015; Polarity Therapy Workbook, 2016 edition, November 6, 2016, https://www.catanyc.com/traditional-american-indian-bodywork-origin-osteopathy-polarity-craniosacral-therapy/.

Chapter 4

1. "American Indian Religious Freedom Act." *Federal Historic Preservation Laws*, National Center for Cultural Resources, National Park Service, Department of the Interior, 4th edition, 2006, https://www.nps.gov/history/local-law/FHPL_IndianRelFreAct.pdf.

2. Mehl-Madrona, Lewis. *Coyote Medicine*, p. 36.

3. History.com editors. "Freedom of Religion." *History,* A&E Television Networks, August 21, 2018, https://www.history.com/topics/united-states-constitution/freedom-of-religion.

4. Mehl-Madrona, Lewis. *Coyote Medicine*, p. 40.

5. Mehl-Madrona, Lewis. *Coyote Medicine*, p. 37.

6. Mehl-Madrona, Lewis. *Coyote Medicine*, p. 69.

7. Mehl-Madrona, Lewis. *Coyote Medicine*, p. 120.

8. Seegerts, Arlene. Personal interview, March 5 2006.

9. Seegerts, Arlene. Personal interview, November 30, 2021.

10. Seegerts, Arlene. Personal interview, November 30, 2021.

11. Wikipedia. "Trail of Tears." Wikipedia, the Free Encyclopedia. April 3, 2021, https://en.wikipedia.org/wiki/Trail_of_Tears.

"The Trail of Tears was a series of forced relocations of approximately 60,000 Native Americans in the United States from their ancestral homelands in the Southeastern United States, to areas to the west of the Mississippi River that had been designated as Indian Territory. The forced relocations were carried out by government authorities following the passage of the Indian Removal Act in 1830. The relocated peoples suffered from exposure, disease, and starvation while en route to their new designated reserve, and approximately 4,000 died before reaching their destinations or shortly after from disease."

12. Animal Welfare Institute. "The Truth about Red Wolves," http://thetruthaboutredwolves.com/.

13. Animal Welfare Institute. "The Truth about Red Wolves," http://thetruthaboutredwolves.com/.

14. Wikipedia. "Dingo." Wikipedia, the Free Encyclopedia. April 14, 2021, https://en.wikipedia.org/wiki/Dingo.

"The wolf-like canids are a group of large carnivores that are genetically closely related because their chromosomes number 78, therefore they can potentially interbreed to produce fertile hybrids. In the Australian wild there exist dingoes, feral dogs, and the crossings of these two, which produce dingo–dog hybrids."

15. Peterson, Brenda. *Wolf Nation: The Life, Death, and Return of Wild American Wolves*. Da Capo Press, 2017, p. 14.

16. Peterson, Brenda. *Wolf Nation*, p. 14.

17. Huffman, Julia. *Medicine of the Wolf.* Documentary film, 2015.

18. Peterson, Brenda. *Wolf Nation*, pp. 17–19.

19. Wulf, Shadow. "Wolf Information." *Shadow Wulf's Alphas*, November 15, 2001, https://www.oocities.org/pilotwolf143/wolf_information.htm.

20. Sams, James and David Carson. *Medicine Cards*, St. Martin's Press, 1999, pp. 97–98.

21. Comments from the elders of the Black Lake Indian Reserve in this interview were used with permission.

22. Eastgate, Jan. "Child Drugging: Psychiatry Destroying Lives." *Citizen Commission on Human Rights: Watchdog Investigating and Exposing Psychiatric Human Rights Violations*, CCHR Publications, 1995–2021, https://www.cchr.org/cchr-reports/child-drugging/introduction.html.

23. "1 in 13 Children Taking Psychiatric Medication in the U.S." *Fox News*, October 24, 2015, https://www.foxnews.com/health/1-in-13-children-taking-psychiatric-medication-in-us.

24. Horgan, John. "Are Psychiatric Medications Making Us Sicker?" *Scientific American*, March 5, 2012, https://blogs.scientificamerican.com/cross-check/are-psychiatric-medications-making-us-sicker/. (Emphasis added.)

25. Horgan, John. "Are Psychiatric Medications Making Us Sicker?" (Emphasis added.)

26. Horgan, John. "Are Psychiatric Medications Making Us Sicker?" (Emphasis added.)

27. Louv, Richard. *Last Child in the Woods: Saving Our Children from Nature-Deficit Disorder*. Algonquin Books, 2008, p. 11.

28. Hanscom, Angela J. *Balanced and Barefoot: How Unrestricted Outdoor Play Makes for Strong, Confident, and Capable Children*. New Harbinger Publications, 2016, p. 30.

29. Murray, C., Marie Ng, and Ali Mokdad. "The vast majority of American adults are overweight or obese, and weight is a growing problem among US children." *Institute for Health Metrics and Evaluation (IHME)* (2013). http://www.

healthdata.org/news-release/vast-majority-american-adults-are-overweight-or-obese-and-weight-growing-problem-among.

"… Overweight is defined as having a Body Mass Index (BMI), or weight-to-height ratio, greater than or equal to 25 and lower than 30, while obesity is defined as having a BMI equal to or greater than 30."

30. Raghupathi, Wullianallur, and Viju Raghupathi. "An empirical study of chronic diseases in the United States: a visual analytics approach to public health." *International Journal of Environmental Research and Public Health* 15.3 (2018): p. 431. https://www.ncbi.nlm.nih.gov/pmc/articles/PMC5876976/.

31. Lipka, Michael. "5 key findings about the changing US religious landscape." Pew Research Center. May 12, 2015. https://www.pewresearch.org/fact-tank/2015/05/12/5-key-findings-u-s-religious-landscape/.

32. Lipka, Michael, and Claire Gecewicz. "More Americans now say they're spiritual but not religious." Pew Research Center (2017). https://www.pewresearch.org/fact-tank/2017/09/06/more-americans-now-say-theyre-spiritual-but-not-religious/.

33. Daley, Beth. "Why a 14th-century mystic appeals to today's 'spiritual but not religious' Americans." *The Conversation*, December 6, 2018, http://theconversation.com/why-a-14th-century-mystic-appeals-to-todays-spiritual-but-not-religious-americans-101656.

34. Vitello, Paul. "Taking a Break from the Lord's Work." *New York Times*, August 1, 2010, https://www.nytimes.com/2010/08/02/nyregion/02burnout.html.

"The findings have surfaced with ominous regularity over the last few years, and with little notice: Members of the clergy now suffer from obesity, hypertension and depression at rates higher than most Americans. In the last decade, their use of antidepressants has risen, while their life expectancy has fallen."

Chapter 5

1. Kalvaitis, K. "Penicillin: an accidental discovery changed the course of medicine." *Endocr. Today* 6 (2008): p. 24. https://www.healio.com/endocrinology/news/

print/endocrine-today/%7B15afd2a1-2084-4ca6-a4e6-7185f5c4cfb0%7D/
penicillin-an-accidental-discovery-changed-the-course-of-medicine.

Penicillin was discovered in 1928. "The first patient was successfully treated for streptococcal septicemia in the United States in 1942. However, supply was limited and demand was high in the early days of penicillin."

2. "Westin A. Price, DDS." International Foundation for Nutrition and Health, https://ifnh.org/dr-weston-a-price/. Accessed online December 2, 2021.

3. Panahpour, Alireza. "28 Counties Ban Mercury 'Silver' Fillings for Children and Pregnant Mothers." *Dr Panahpour the Systemic Dentist*, February 26, 2018, https://www.systemicdentist.com/pdf/28-countries-ban-mercury-amalgam-for-children-why-not-in-north-america.pdf.

4. Check out the documentary film *American Addict*, which describes how pharmaceutical companies create disease names and then market those diseases as valid conditions so they can sell more drugs.

5. "Ralph Waldo Emerson Quotes." BrainyQuote, 2021, https://www.brainyquote. com/quotes/ralph_waldo_emerson_104867. Accessed October 25, 2021.

See also "Jen B's English Quiz Transcendentalism." Quizlet, https://quizlet. com/99358150/jen-bs-english-quiz-transcendentalism-flash-cards/. "Society has not advanced because when we have gained one thing, we lost another at the same time." Accessed October 25, 2021.

6. John 14:15. Holy Bible, New International Version. Bible Gateway. https://www. biblegateway.com/passage/?search=John+14&version=NIV.

7. Matthew 22:37–40. Holy Bible, New International Version. Bible Gateway. https:// www.biblegateway.com/passage/?search=matt+22%3A37-40&version=NIV.

Chapter 6

1. "Time Magazine Names Hauerwas 'America's Best Theologian.'" *United Methodist News Service*, Worldwide Faith News (archives), September 12, 2001, https://archive.wfn.org/2001/09/msg00077.html.

2. Morrison, Stephen D. "7 Theories of the Atonement Summarized." SDMorrison. org, http://www.sdmorrison.org/7-theories-of-the-atonement-summarized/.

3. Coffman, Elesha. "Why are the Protestant and Catholic Bibles different?" Christianity Today, https://www.christianitytoday.com/history/2008/august/ why-are-protestant-and-catholic-bibles-different.html.

4. Akiyama, J. "Meaning of Onegai Shimasu." AikiWeb: The Source for Aikido Information, http://www.aikiweb.com/language/onegai.html.

5. Meador, Keith, and Joel Shuman. Duke University. Seminar, March 1, 2001.

6. Meador, Keith and Joel Shuman. Duke University. Seminar, March 1, 2001.

7. Stroll, Avrum. "Epistemology." Encyclopedia Britannica, February 11, 2021, https://www.britannica.com/topic/epistemology. Accessed October 25, 2021.

"Epistemology, the philosophical study of the nature, origin, and limits of human knowledge. The term is derived from the Greek *epistēmē* ('knowledge') and *logos* ('reason'), and accordingly the field is sometimes referred to as the theory of knowledge." Epistemology can also simply be described as 'how we know what we know.'

8. "'Ontology' is the philosophical study of being. More broadly, it studies concepts that directly relate to being, in particular becoming, existence, reality, as well as the basic categories of being and their relations.[1] Traditionally listed as a part of the major branch of philosophy known as metaphysics, ontology often deals with questions concerning what entities exist or may be said to exist and how such entities may be grouped, related within a hierarchy, and subdivided according to similarities and differences."

9. "Positivism in Sociology: Definition, Theories, and Examples." Study.com, https://study.com/academy/lesson/positivism-in-sociology-definition-theory- examples.html. Accessed October 25, 2021.

"Positivism is the term used to describe an approach to the study of society that relies specifically on scientific evidence, such as experiments and statistics, to reveal a true nature of how society operates. The term originated in the 19th century, when Auguste Comte described his ideas in his books *The Course in Positive Philosophy* and *A General View of Positivism.*"

10. "Deism, N." Dictionary.com, https://www.dictionary.com/browse/deism. Accessed October 25, 2021.

"Deism (/'diːɪzəm/ *DEE-iz-əm*[1][2] or /'deɪ.ɪzəm/ *DAY-iz-əm*; derived from Latin 'deus' meaning 'god') is the philosophical position that rejects revelation as a source of religious knowledge and asserts that reason and observation of the natural world are sufficient to establish the existence of a Supreme Being or creator of the universe."

Wikipedia. "Deism." Wikipedia, the Free Encyclopedia, October 2, 2021, https://en.wikipedia.org/wfiki/Deism. Accessed October 25, 2021.

"At least as far back as Thomas Aquinas, Christian thought has recognized two sources of knowledge of God: revelation and 'natural reason.' The study of the truths revealed by reason is called natural theology. During the Age of Enlightenment, especially in Britain and France, philosophers began to reject revelation as a source of knowledge and to appeal only to truths that they felt could be established by reason alone. Such philosophers were called 'deists' and the philosophical position that they advocated is called 'deism.'"

11. Meador, Keith, and Joel Shuman. Duke University, Seminar, January 18, 2001.

According to Shuman and Meador, "science" involves discovery only through falsifiable linguistic evidence without an allowance for mystery. They remind us that "proof" and theological vocabulary do not coexist. Truth requires much more than the language of science.

12. Hughes, John. Paper on *Body of Compassion*, 2001.

13. Browne, Sylvia. "Sylvia Brown Quotes." Goodreads, https://www.goodreads.com/quotes/10189042-only-those-who-have-learned-to-live-on-the-land.

Quote originally from *End of Days: Predictions and Prophecies about the End of the World*, published in 2009.

14. Shuman, Joel. *Body of Compassion: Ethics, Medicine, and the Church*, 2003, p. 16.

15. Shuman, Joel. *Body of Compassion*, p. 29.

16. Shuman, Joel. *Body of Compassion*, p. 36.

17. Shuman, Joel. *Body of Compassion*, p. xvii.

18. Shuman, Joel. *Body of Compassion*, p. 81.

19. Shuman, Joel. *Body of Compassion*, p. 84.

20. "Pro eo primaria" literally translates to "as a primary fact" in English: https://translate.google.com/?rlz=1C1CHBF_enUS858US858&sxsrf=ALeKk01H-LH-cXa28fdXZ1DuYVd6xiFigw:1586123049973&gs_lcp=CgZwc3ktYWIQAzo ECCEQCkoKCBcSBjEyLTEwM0oJCBgSBTEyLTE1UJw6WMtfYKFiaAF wAHgAgAF2iAHkC5IBAzguN5gBAKABAaoBB2d3cy13aXo&uact=5&um =1&ie=UTF-8&hl=en&client=tw-ob#auto/la/as%20a%20primary%20fact. Accessed October 25, 2021.

21. Berry, Wendell. "The Body and the Earth." *Recollected Essays, 1965–1980*, San Francisco: North Point Press, 1981, pp. 269–270.

22. Berry, Wendell. *Art of the Commonplace*, 1981, p. 23.

23. Berry, Wendell. *Art of the Commonplace*, 1981, p. 23.

24. Boissiere, Robert. *Meditations with the Hopi*, p. 113. (Emphasis added.)

25. Berry, Wendell. "The Body and the Earth." *Recollected Essays*, p. 289.

26. Berry, Wendell. "The Body and the Earth." *Recollected Essays*, p. 289.

Chapter 7

1. The "snake" refers to an ancient Southwest astrophysical marker akin to Stonehenge.

2. Childs, Craig. *Soul of Nowhere*. Sasquatch Books, 2002, p. 128.

3.   Note: This statement does not imply that humans should not invest in a scientific paradigm—just that they should be aware of its limitations and recognize the modern overemphasis upon this perspective.

4.   Mehl-Madrona, Lewis. *Coyote Medicine*, p. 55.

5.   Dyer, Wayne W., and Harold Parker. *Real Magic: Creating Miracles in Everyday Life*. New York: HarperCollins, 1992, p. 71.

6.   1 Kings 19:11–13. Holy Bible, New International Version. Bible Gateway, https://www.biblegateway.com/passage/?search=1%20Kings%2019&version=NIV.

7.   McBride, Pete. *Seeing Silence: The Beauty of the World's Most Quiet Places*. Rizzoli, 2021, inside cover.

8.   Spalding, Baird T. *Life and Teachings of the Masters of the Far East, Vol. 1*. Kessinger Publishing Company, 2003, p. 32.

     "Be still and know that I am God." Psalm 46:10 NIV

9.   The Triratna Buddhist Order and Community. "Four Noble Truths." The Buddhist Centre, https://thebuddhistcentre.com/text/four-noble-truths.

10. Kurtus, Ron. "Four Noble Truths of Buddhism." Ron Kurtus' School for Champions, https://www.school-for-champions.com/religion/buddhism_four_noble_truths.htm#.XpXProhKhPY.

11. Note: The distinctions of what are termed the "left brain" and the "right brain" do not always correspond, necessarily, to all the left or right cerebral cortex, subcortical, or cerebellar areas. That is, one's left brain may constitute an area all over the brain that deals with specific detail, symbols, or representations of reality.

12. Thoreau, Henry. "Henry David Thoreau Quotes." Goodreads, https//www.goodreads.com/quotes/8202-the-mass-of-men-lead-lives-of-quiet-desperation-what. Accessed December 2, 2021.

Quote originally from Thoreau, Henry David, *Civil Disobedience, and Other Essays*, published in 1849.

13. "Śūnyatā—The Zen Universe." *The Zen Universe*, August 30, 2019, https://thezenuniverse.org/sunyata-the-zen-universe/. Accessed January 7, 2022.

14. "Śūnyatā—The Zen Universe." *The Zen Universe*, August 30, 2019, https://thezenuniverse.org/sunyata-the-zen-universe/. Accessed January 7, 2022.

Chapter 8

1. MacIntyre, Alasdair. "Alasdair MacIntyre Quotes." Quote Fancy, https://quotefancy.com/alasdair-macintyre-quotes.

2. McBride, Pete. *Seeing Silence: The Beauty of the World's Most Quiet Places.* Rizzoli, 2021, p. 9.

3. Arem, Kimba. "The Sound Current: Nada Brahma: 'The Universe is Sound.'" *Music as Medicine*, Gaearth, https://gaearth.com/sound-as-medicine/the-sound-current/.

4. Shuman, Joel. *Body of Compassion*, p. 81.

5. Blake, William. "William Blake Quotes." Brainy Quotes, https://www.brainyquote.com/quotes/william_blake_150124.

6. Thoreau, Henry David. "Henry David Thoreau Quotes." Brainy Quotes, https://www.brainyquote.com/quotes/henry_david_thoreau_386405.

7. Thompson, Francis. "The Mistress of Vision." 1897. Poem Hunter, https://www.poemhunter.com/poem/the-mistress-of-vision/. Accessed October 25, 2021.

8. Jones, Marina. "David Bohm and the Holographic Universe." *Futurism*, March 31, 2014, https://futurism.com/david-bohm-and-the-holographic-universe.

9. Theosophy Wikipedia. "Akasha." Wikipedia, the Free Encyclopedia, May 11, 2021, https://theosophy.wiki/en/Akasha.

10. Sherlock, Ben. *Screenrant.* "Star Wars: 15 Quotes About the Force," May 31, 2021, https://screenrant.com/star-wars-best-quotes-force/

11. Some Christians may recognize the physical reemergence of the evolved avatar spirit as the Second Coming of the Christ.

Chapter 9

1. Mehl-Madrona, Lewis. *Coyote Medicine*, p. 123.

2. Mehl-Madrona, Lewis. *Coyote Medicine*, p. 98.

3. Hammerschlag, Carl, and Howard Silverman. *Healing Ceremonies: Creating Personal Rituals for Spiritual, Emotional, Physical and Mental Health.* Perigree Books / Berkley Publishing, 1997, p. 6. (Emphasis added.)

4. MacIntyre, Alasdair. "Alasdair MacIntyre Quotes." Quote Fancy, https://quotefancy.com/alasdair-macintyre-quotes.

5. Hammerschlag and Silverman. *Healing Ceremonies*, p. 6.

6. Hammerschlag and Silverman. *Healing Ceremonies*, p. 36.

7. Hammerschlag and Silverman. *Healing Ceremonies*, pp. 5–6.

8. Hammerschlag and Silverman. *Healing Ceremonies*, pp. 42–43.

9. Hammerschlag and Silverman. *Healing Ceremonies*, p. 7.

10. Hammerschlag and Silverman. *Healing Ceremonies*, p. 43.

11. Hammerschlag and Silverman. *Healing Ceremonies*, p. 19.

12. Hammerschlag and Silverman. *Healing Ceremonies*, p. 24.

13. Ross, Allen. "Hopi." *Crystalinks.* https://www.crystalinks.com/hopistonetablets.html.

14. Hammerschlag and Silverman. *Healing Ceremonies*, p. 16.

Chapter 10

1. Mehl-Madrona, Lewis. *Coyote Medicine*, p. 40.

2. John 3:3. Holy Bible, New American Standard Version. Bible.com, https://www.bible.com/bible/100/jhn.3.3.nasb1995. "Truly, truly I say to you, unless one is born again, he cannot see the kingdom of God."

Note: Given the design of the church and the traditional sweat lodge, where would you think the best place to be born again, a sweat lodge or a Western church? This Jesus, the Christ, born in a stable (a lower-level feeding stable for horses or goats) would be just as likely to show up in a sweat lodge as a modern Western church—physically or spiritually.

3. Of note is that I have seen and experienced nurturing church communities no matter what the external structure of the church is. I also have a lot of respect for ministers, monks, and caring people who make up churches and monasteries. Nurturing people gathered together can create "womb spaces" that have great impacts on people's lives, create rebirths, and change the world. However, many churches in the West have become vacant, people-less buildings—lifeless skeletons that long for better days of the past. Retreating from their emphasis on mental and moral lessons (and Greek-style oration) towards spirituality and then back to sacred physicality may be what can revive these people of God.

Chapter 11

1. Bentley, Lia. "Indigenous Religious Traditions." Colorado College, https://sites.coloradocollege.edu/indigenoustraditions/6-%E2%80%A2-independent-projects/vision-quest-traditions/.

2. Bentley, Lia. "Indigenous Religious Traditions." Colorado College, https://sites.coloradocollege.edu/indigenoustraditions/6-%E2%80%A2-independent-projects/vision-quest-traditions/.

3. Wikipedia. "Kundalini." Wikipedia, the Free Encyclopedia, September 16, 2021, https://en.wikipedia.org/wiki/Kundalini. Accessed October 25, 2021.

4. Wikipedia. "Kundalini." Wikipedia, the Free Encyclopedia, September 16, 2021, https://en.wikipedia.org/wiki/Kundalini. Accessed October 25, 2021.

5. Wikipedia. "Kundalini." Wikipedia, the Free Encyclopedia, September 16, 2021, https://en.wikipedia.org/wiki/Kundalini. Accessed October 25, 2021.

6. Ripinsky-Naxon, Michael. *The Nature of Shamanism*. State University of New York Press, 1993, pp. 74–75.

7. Ripinsky-Naxon, Michael. *The Nature of Shamanism*, p. 75.

8. "Chakra Basics." International Association of Reiki Practitioners, https://iarp.org/chakra-basics/. Accessed October 25, 2021.

9. Waters, Frank. *Book of the Hopi*, p. 9.

10. "Health, Sex, and Wellness." Integrative Healing Arts, https://www.integrativehealingarts.com/sexual-energy-healing#:~:text=Health%20is%20a%20dynamic%20process,is%20life%20and%20also%20death. Accessed October 25, 2021.

Note: the author here refers to sexual energy as deriving from the first chakra, but it is commonly known be from the second chakra.

11. Wikipedia. "Libido." Wikipedia, the Free Encyclopedia, https://en.wikipedia.org/wiki/Libido. Accessed October 25, 2021.

12. "Libido, N." Online Etymology Dictionary, https://www.etymonline.com/word/libido. Accessed October 25, 2021.

13. Wikipedia. "Libido." Wikipedia, the Free Encyclopedia, https://en.wikipedia.org/wiki/Libido. Accessed October 25, 2021.

14. Tunneshende, Merilyn. *Don Juan and the Art of Sexual Energy: The Rainbow Serpent of the Toltecs*. Simon and Schuster, 2001, pp. 8–9.

Chapter 12

1. "Libido, N." Online Etymology Dictionary, https://www.etymonline.com/word/libido. Accessed October 25, 2021.

2. Wikipedia. "Libido." Wikipedia, the Free Encyclopedia, https://en.wikipedia.org/wiki/Libido. Accessed October 25, 2021.

3. Wikipedia. "Libido." Wikipedia, the Free Encyclopedia, https://en.wikipedia.org/wiki/Libido. Accessed October 25, 2021.

4. Wikipedia. "Death drive." Wikipedia, the Free Encyclopedia, https://en.wikipedia.org/wiki/Mortido. Accessed October 25, 2021.

5. Wikipedia. "Death drive." Wikipedia, the Free Encyclopedia, https://en.wikipedia.org/wiki/Mortido. Accessed October 25, 2021.

6. Matthew 6:26–33. Holy Bible, New International Version. Bible Gateway, 25&version=NIVhttps://www.biblegateway.com/passage/?search=Matthew%206:26-34&version=NKJV.

7. John 2:19–21. Holy Bible, New International Version. Bible Gateway, https://www.biblegateway.com/passage/?search=John+2%3A19-25&version=NIV.

8. Davis, Ellen. *Proverbs, Ecclesiastes, and the Song of Songs*. Westminster John Knox Press, 2000, p. 265.

9. Davis, Ellen. *Proverbs, Ecclesiastes, and the Song of Songs*, p. 265.

10. Davis, Ellen. *Proverbs, Ecclesiastes, and the Song of Songs*, p. 263.

11. Davis, Ellen. *Proverbs, Ecclesiastes, and the Song of Songs*, p. 253.

12. Berry, Wendell. "The Body and the Earth" in *Recollected Essays, 1965–1980*. North Point Press, 1981, p. 297. Berry's comment might sound odd for monogamous couples in the Western world, but his comment here should not be taken out of its context.

13. Thurman, Howard. "Howard Thurman Quotes." Goodreads, https://www. goodreads.com/quotes/6273-don-t-ask-what-the-world-needs-ask-what-makes-you.

14. Capra, Fritjof. *The Tao of Physics: An Exploration of the Parallels between Modern Physics and Eastern Mysticism*. Shambhala publications, 2000, p. 194.

15. Peterson, Jordan B. *12 Rules for Life: An Antidote to Chaos*. Penguin UK, 2018, p. 12.

16. Peterson, Jordan B. *12 Rules for Life: An Antidote to Chaos*. Penguin UK, 2018, p. 12.

Chapter 13

1. Pinchbeck, Daniel. *2012: The Return of Quetzalcoatl*, p. 29.

2. Pinchbeck, Daniel. *2012: The Return of Quetzalcoatl*, p. 12, 29.

3. Stern, David. "Precession." Educational Web Sites on Astronomy, Physics, Spaceflight and the Earth's Magnetism, https://pwg.gsfc.nasa.gov/stargaze/ Sprecess.htm. Accessed October 25, 2021.

4. Stern, David. "Precession." Educational Web Sites on Astronomy, Physics, Spaceflight and the Earth's Magnetism, https://pwg.gsfc.nasa.gov/stargaze/ Sprecess.htm. Accessed October 25, 2021.

5. Wikipedia. "Age of Aquarius." Wikipedia, the Free Encyclopedia, https:// en.wikipedia.org/wiki/Age_of_Aquarius. Accessed October 25, 2021.

6. Kotler, Steven, and Jamie Wheal. *Stealing Fire*. Harper Collins, 2017, p. 36.

7. Kotler and Wheal. *Stealing Fire*, p. 37.

8. Kotler and Wheal. *Stealing Fire*, p. 37.

9. Kotler and Wheal. *Stealing Fire*, pp. 37–38.

10. Kotler and Wheal. *Stealing Fire*, pp. 24, 29.

11. Kotler and Wheal. *Stealing Fire*, pp. 39–40.

12. Kotler and Wheal. *Stealing Fire*, p. 40.

13. Kotler and Wheal. *Stealing Fire*, pp. 41–42.

14. Kotler and Wheal. *Stealing Fire*, p. 43.

15. Csikszentmihalyi, Mihaly. *Beyond Boredom and Anxiety*. Jossey-Bass, 1975, p. 10.

16. Kotler and Wheal. *Stealing Fire*, p. 42.

17. Kotler and Wheal. *Stealing Fire*, p. 44.

18. Note: The second part of the Fifth World Medicine involves coming back to the ground of a physical body and Earth from the spiritual high.

19. Kotler and Wheal. *Stealing Fire*, p. 202.

20. Kotler and Wheal. *Stealing Fire*, pp. 202–203.

21. Kotler and Wheal. *Stealing Fire*, p. 203.

22. Kotler and Wheal. *Stealing Fire*, p. 205.

23. Kotler and Wheal. *Stealing Fire*, p. 205.

24. Note: The second part of the Fifth World Medicine involves coming back to the ground of a physical body and Earth from the spiritual high.

25. Kotler and Wheal. *Stealing Fire*, p. 206.

26. Kotler and Wheal. *Stealing Fire*, p. 207.

27. Kotler and Wheal. *Stealing Fire*, pp. 207–208.

Chapter 14

1. Kotler and Wheal. *Stealing Fire*, p. 195.

2. Kotler and Wheal. *Stealing Fire*, p. 45.

3. Campbell, Joseph. *A Joseph Campbell Companion: Reflections on the Art of Living*. Joseph Campbell Foundation, 1991, p. 77.

4. Campbell, Joseph. *A Joseph Campbell Companion*, p. 78.

5. Campbell, Joseph. *A Joseph Campbell Companion*, p. 79.

6. Campbell, Joseph. *A Joseph Campbell Companion*, p. 79.

7. Campbell, Joseph. *A Joseph Campbell Companion*, p. 81.

8. Campbell, Joseph. *A Joseph Campbell Companion*, p. 81.

9. Campbell, Joseph. *A Joseph Campbell Companion*, p. 81.

10. Note: A heroic return could be done by a female or male.

11. Campbell, Joseph. *A Joseph Campbell Companion*, p. 82.

12. Campbell, Joseph. *A Joseph Campbell Companion*, p. 82.

13. Wikipedia. "Winter solstice." Wikipedia, the Free Encyclopedia, http://en.wikipedia.org/wiki/Winter_solstice. Accessed October 25, 2021.

    Note: The winter solstice upon establishment of the Julian calendar in 45 BC was December 25.

14. Crystal, Ellie. "Hopi Prophecies." *Crystalinks,* https://www.crystalinks.com/hopi2.html.

    Labels added. Diagram used with permission.

15. Boissiere, Robert. *Meditations with the Hopi*. Inner Traditions and Bear & Company, 1986, p. 113, http://www.innertraditions.com.

    All rights reserved. Reprinted with permission of publisher.

16. Thoreau, Henry. "Henry David Thoreau Quotes." Goodreads, https://www.goodreads.com/quotes/8202-the-mass-of-men-lead-lives-of-quiet-desperation-what.

Quote originally from Thoreau, Henry David, *Civil Disobedience, and Other Essays*, originally published in 1849.

17. Kotler and Wheal. *Stealing Fire*, p. 208.

18. Wikipedia. "Cyborg." Wikipedia, the Free Encyclopedia, https://en.wikipedia.org/wiki/Cyborg. Accessed October 25, 2021. "According to some definitions of the term, the physical attachments humanity has with even the most basic technologies have already made them cyborgs. In a typical example, a human with an artificial cardiac pacemaker or implantable cardioverter-defibrillator would be considered a cyborg, since these devices measure voltage potentials in the body, perform signal processing, and can deliver electrical stimuli, using this synthetic feedback mechanism to keep that person alive. Implants, especially cochlear implants, that combine mechanical modification with any kind of feedback response are also cyborg enhancements. Some theorists cite such modifications as contact lenses, hearing aids, smartphone or intraocular lenses as examples of fitting humans with technology to enhance their biological capabilities"; Kotler and Wheal. *Stealing Fire*, p. 56.

19. Kotler and Wheal. *Stealing Fire*, p. 51.

20. Kotler and Wheal. *Stealing Fire*, p. 60.

21. Note: The human brain and body have long been known as the most complex system—far more complex than any technology ever created.

22. Kotler and Wheal. *Stealing Fire*, p. 235.

23. Wikipedia contributors. "Republic (Plato)." *Wikipedia, The Free Encyclopedia*. Accessed April 26, 2022.

24. Cooney, William. "Plato." *Encyclopedia of Death and Dying*, http://www.deathreference.com/Nu-Pu/Plato.html. Accessed October 25, 2021.

This quote originally came from Emerson, Ralph Waldo, "Plato; or The Philosopher," in *Representative Men,* Harvard University Press, 1996.

25. Prayer and meditation are the path according to many gurus and the Hopi. Similarly, the great philosopher Aristotle offers contemplation as a pathway to the Great Spirit. And I would add, in agreement with Hopi people and Aristotle, that following that Spirit fully back to the physical Fifth World involves allowing Mother Nature through our physicality to show us the way. Ultimately, the power of moving along the path will derive from unsuppressed, chaotic, but not perverted sexual power.

26. Coates, John. *The Hour between Dog and Wolf: How Risk Taking Transforms Us, Body and Mind.* Penguin, 2012, p. 279.

27. Coates, John. *The Hour between Dog and Wolf: How Risk Taking Transforms Us, Body and Mind.* Penguin, 2012, p. 278.

28. "Migrations—Part 1." From *Techqua Ikachi: Land and Life.* Hopi Pole Star, http://hopistar.org/migration.html. Accessed October 25, 2021.

"The Hopis claim that all indigenous Americans—indeed, all humanity—were originally one tribe (Hopi, which means 'Peaceful'), and that we separated upon our emergence into this world in order to follow a pre-determined migration pattern across the face of the earth. If we followed the Creator's guidance, our migrations would lead us back, in the end, to reunite at the center."

Appendix

1. Comments from the elders of the Black Lake Indian Reserve in this interview were used with permission.

INDEX

A

Akasha 141, 142, 215, 218, 239, 275
Alien 5, 17, 18, 21
Aquarius 211, 212, 218, 231, 280
Aristotle 117, 118, 237, 238, 284
attachment 14, 114, 115, 116, 117, 121,
    123, 131, 172, 176, 207, 219,
    231, 243, 244, 261, 283

B

Bacon 98
being xi, xii, 1, 6, 7, 11, 14, 15, 16, 17,
    18, 19, 20, 21, 27, 36, 43, 44, 45,
    50, 53, 54, 58, 62, 63, 65, 76,
    82, 85, 87, 95, 99, 101, 102, 104,
    105, 108, 110, 115, 116, 117,
    120, 121, 122, 123, 126, 131,
    133, 134, 137, 141, 142, 143,
    147, 149, 152, 158, 159, 160, 161,
    165, 166, 169, 173, 175, 179,
    180, 184, 185, 196, 198, 206,
    207, 208, 211, 216, 219, 222,
    223, 225, 230, 234, 236, 238,
    239, 243, 244, 251, 256, 261,
    271, 272
Berry 102, 103, 105, 196, 273, 279
body vii, xi, 7, 8, 11, 25, 26, 27, 39, 40,
    41, 43, 44, 46, 48, 59, 62, 76,
    85, 87, 98, 99, 100, 101, 102,
    103, 104, 105, 106, 108, 113,
    114, 115, 117, 118, 120, 121,
    122, 126, 127, 130, 132, 133,
    134, 142, 146, 147, 148, 149,
    150, 152, 158, 159, 162, 174,
    175, 179, 180, 184, 189, 191,
    192, 194, 195, 196, 198, 201,
    204, 205, 211, 214, 219, 221,
    222, 223, 226, 233, 234, 235,
    236, 237, 238, 239, 240, 241,
    269, 272, 273, 275, 279, 281,
    283, 284

C

Cartesian 99, 102, 104, 118, 237, 244
ceremony 9, 10, 12, 29, 49, 50, 52, 55,
    56, 78, 83, 145, 149, 150, 151,
    152, 155, 156, 157, 158, 159, 178,
    212, 240, 276
chakra 178, 179, 180, 181, 182, 190,
    191, 195, 226, 227, 233, 244, 278
chaos 133, 148, 149, 159, 174, 198,
    238, 280
Cherokee 8, 19, 29, 47, 48, 57, 58, 59,
    60, 62, 84, 166, 179, 239, 291
Contemplation 26, 109, 117, 118, 122,
    235, 239, 241, 284
content 21, 118, 120, 129, 130, 212,
    222, 244
context 9, 120, 121, 130, 213, 221,
    244, 279
Coyote 29, 30, 31, 32, 33, 34, 35, 36,
    48, 49, 50, 51, 52, 54, 58, 60,
    79, 147, 148, 161, 265, 266, 274,
    276, 277
Creator 11, 17, 23, 25, 26, 69, 74, 77,
    78, 87, 113, 114, 115, 117, 119,
    120, 121, 122, 127, 133, 139,
    142, 147, 148, 152, 158, 169,
    173, 179, 190, 191, 192, 193,
    194, 195, 196, 198, 208, 219,
    226, 230, 231, 233, 239, 240,
    241, 243, 248, 272, 284

D

Darkness 2, 27, 35, 61, 66, 78, 134,
136, 137, 143, 163, 165, 166,
170, 176, 221, 226, 227, 228,
229, 230, 233, 241, 255
Dene 54, 69, 77, 79, 247, 248, 251,
252, 253, 254, 255, 256, 259
Descartes 98, 100
Desperation xii, 6, 8, 18, 34, 36, 37,
51, 78, 103, 116, 123, 159, 160,
208, 217, 222, 233, 261, 262,
274, 283
disembodied 103, 105, 117, 118, 120,
121, 127, 129, 130, 146, 148,
150, 152, 158, 184, 191, 231,
235, 243
dream v, vii, 16, 27, 35, 37, 67, 82, 150,
166, 177, 183, 184, 185, 187,
189, 190, 196, 207, 218
dualism 99, 100, 102, 103, 104, 105,
106, 129, 130, 131, 236, 237

E

Earth vii, 2, 4, 5, 6, 10, 11, 12, 23, 24,
25, 33, 34, 47, 50, 77, 78, 99,
100, 101, 102, 103, 104, 105,
109, 110, 113, 126, 127, 129,
130, 132, 133, 136, 142, 143,
146, 147, 148, 156, 157, 166,
175, 179, 180, 181, 184, 189,
192, 193, 195, 196, 197, 198,
209, 210, 211, 214, 215, 218,
221, 222, 225, 226, 230, 231,
233, 234, 235, 237, 238, 239,
240, 241, 243, 244, 273, 279,
280, 281, 284
Elders 12, 13, 24, 56, 60, 64, 67, 68,
69, 70, 72, 77, 79, 169, 245, 246,
247, 248, 249, 250, 251, 252,
253, 254, 255, 256, 257, 258,
259, 268, 284

Emerson 86, 87, 236, 270, 284
Enlightenment 98, 100, 116, 117, 122,
126, 127, 129, 131, 132, 133,
142, 143, 150, 157, 166, 174,
184, 208, 211, 212, 218, 219,
222, 224, 225, 231, 237, 240,
241, 272
epistemology 98, 99, 100, 209, 271
evidence 104, 110, 130, 145, 146, 148,
178, 209, 217, 266, 271, 272

F

fact 7, 10, 24, 41, 43, 55, 76, 85,
95, 101, 109, 118, 122, 131,
146, 148, 149, 164, 165, 166,
208, 212, 227, 234, 261, 265,
269, 273
Fifth World v, vii, xii, 6, 7, 8, 9, 10,
11, 12, 14, 17, 18, 20, 21, 23, 25,
26, 27, 47, 58, 99, 106, 118, 119,
122, 127, 129, 131, 139, 142,
143, 145, 153, 207, 208, 209,
211, 212, 215, 216, 217, 218, 219,
221, 222, 223, 225, 226, 230,
231, 232, 233, 238, 239, 240,
241, 243, 244, 281, 284, 291
form 25, 46, 58, 60, 75, 96, 102, 126,
127, 129, 142, 146, 156, 157,
163, 165, 182, 192, 206, 208,
236, 238, 252, 257, 265
Fourth World v, xii, 5, 9, 11, 15, 17,
20, 21, 23, 25, 26, 27, 62, 99,
101, 106, 119, 122, 123, 129,
130, 131, 146, 153, 159, 160,
192, 207, 208, 209, 214, 216,
219, 222, 225, 226, 230, 231,
232, 233, 234, 235, 236, 238,
239, 240, 243, 244
Fuller 5, 209

G

Grand Canyon 10, 15, 17, 169, 171, 173, 175, 176, 177, 181, 182, 184, 189, 192, 197, 204, 207, 208, 231, 237, 263, 264

H

Hauerwas 95, 97, 270
healer 47, 48, 49, 51, 52, 54, 64, 67, 68, 69, 77, 78, 85, 86, 129, 142, 143, 148, 167, 173, 174, 178, 183, 193, 240, 243, 250, 251, 254, 255, 256
heavens 4, 33, 77, 89, 102, 103, 113, 133, 136, 140, 147, 156, 157, 175, 179, 184, 197, 198, 203, 208, 214, 230, 233, 237
holographic 140, 141, 142, 215, 275
Hopi xii, 5, 7, 8, 9, 10, 11, 12, 13, 14, 15, 17, 18, 19, 20, 21, 22, 23, 24, 25, 26, 27, 29, 47, 60, 79, 105, 152, 153, 180, 207, 208, 209, 211, 230, 231, 232, 233, 234, 237, 239, 244, 262, 263, 264, 265, 273, 276, 278, 282, 284
Hunger xi, xii, 1, 6, 8, 27, 58, 114, 115, 123, 181, 190, 194, 198, 208, 222, 231, 243

I

Intuition 26, 118, 130, 234, 235, 239, 243, 244

J

Jesus 86, 88, 89, 90, 96, 193, 194, 195, 196, 215, 217, 219, 241, 277

K

Kachina 14, 15, 16, 17, 18, 19, 263, 264

K (cont.)

Kotler 212, 213, 215, 216, 217, 218, 221, 222, 234, 235, 237, 280, 281, 282, 283
Kundalini 165, 171, 174, 175, 177, 178, 179, 180, 182, 184, 189, 190, 191, 193, 195, 196, 197, 198, 204, 207, 208, 226, 230, 233, 239, 241, 244, 277, 278

L

libido 181, 190, 192, 278, 279
Light 2, 3, 14, 15, 16, 17, 18, 21, 26, 62, 65, 66, 77, 80, 92, 135, 136, 137, 138, 140, 152, 163, 201, 226, 227, 228, 229, 230, 231, 255
love xi, 26, 31, 32, 34, 50, 59, 62, 63, 65, 85, 88, 89, 90, 102, 103, 111, 112, 114, 119, 122, 126, 127, 129, 130, 131, 132, 133, 134, 135, 136, 139, 142, 143, 149, 153, 166, 178, 179, 184, 186, 187, 195, 196, 198, 200, 201, 202, 204, 205, 206, 208, 211, 216, 219, 230, 233, 239, 240, 241, 243, 244, 252

M

Mayan 20, 262
Mehl-Madrona 29, 48, 49, 50, 51, 52, 54, 62, 78, 147, 148, 156, 160, 161, 265, 266, 274, 276, 277
mind 2, 7, 10, 17, 21, 25, 26, 30, 31, 39, 44, 48, 63, 70, 71, 89, 90, 99, 100, 102, 106, 108, 113, 114, 115, 116, 117, 118, 119, 120, 121, 122, 127, 131, 132, 133, 145, 146, 147, 148, 150, 152, 153, 161, 163, 166, 172, 173, 177, 179, 182, 184, 185, 192, 197,

201, 205, 207, 208, 211, 213,
221, 235, 236, 237, 238, 239,
241, 243, 284

N

naturalism 88, 98
Nature vii, 11, 16, 19, 23, 26, 41, 46,
47, 58, 60, 64, 81, 86, 87, 88,
89, 90, 93, 98, 100, 101, 102,
103, 104, 105, 106, 109, 110,
112, 113, 114, 115, 117, 118,
119, 120, 121, 122, 127, 129,
130, 132, 133, 137, 139, 140,
142, 146, 148, 149, 152, 156,
169, 174, 189, 190, 191, 192,
193, 194, 195, 196, 197, 198,
208, 210, 215, 221, 225, 231,
232, 233, 235, 237, 238, 239,
240, 241, 243, 244, 268, 271,
278, 284
Navajo 15, 18, 19, 47, 55, 152, 153

O

objective 50, 88, 100, 101, 104, 112,
118, 120, 121, 122, 129, 148,
150, 191, 237, 239
oneness 33, 113, 114, 129, 132, 134,
138, 139, 140, 142, 143, 166,
179, 190, 211, 215, 218, 219, 231
order 7, 9, 45, 88, 98, 100, 101, 102,
110, 117, 118, 131, 132, 141,
146, 159, 169, 182, 183, 191,
198, 202, 207, 213, 217, 226,
230, 234, 238, 258, 262, 263,
265, 274, 284
Osteopathic medicine 37, 38, 39, 40,
41, 42, 43, 45, 47, 51, 107, 108,
240, 265, 291

P

physicality 126, 127, 146, 150, 151,
157, 159, 166, 167, 184, 190,
204, 216, 222, 224, 225, 226,
230, 231, 233, 237, 238, 243,
277, 284
Plato 96, 235, 236, 237, 238, 283, 284
poetry 208
Precession 5, 9, 209, 210, 218, 280
Prophecy Rock 21, 22, 23, 24, 25, 26,
105, 152, 231, 232

R

rationalism 150
religion 9, 18, 49, 56, 73, 74, 75, 76,
79, 90, 102, 103, 107, 131,
149, 157, 215, 216, 239, 263,
266, 274

S

science 8, 25, 29, 58, 71, 87, 88, 97,
98, 99, 100, 101, 104, 105, 106,
108, 110, 112, 115, 117, 118,
119, 120, 121, 122, 123, 129,
130, 131, 142, 143, 148, 149,
152, 153, 191, 209, 210, 231,
233, 234, 235, 237, 239, 243,
244, 272
Sexuality 167, 173, 177, 181, 192, 195,
196, 243
shabd 125, 133, 142
shaman xii, 49, 77, 78, 79, 100,
113, 119, 127, 132, 139, 142,
143, 147, 148, 152, 153, 155,
159, 160, 162, 164, 165, 166,
169, 177, 178, 182, 183, 193,
240, 254
Shawnee 47, 48
Shuman 97, 98, 99, 101, 102, 108,
271, 272, 273, 275

silence 3, 34, 52, 107, 111, 113, 114,
115, 116, 117, 118, 119, 121, 122,
123, 124, 126, 127, 131, 132,
133, 139, 158, 159, 170, 206,
213, 241, 256, 274, 275
Silverman 145, 146, 147, 148, 149, 151,
152, 153, 155, 158, 159, 276
Solstice 226, 227, 229, 282
spirit 7, 15, 17, 25, 26, 30, 33, 39, 44,
48, 77, 78, 99, 100, 102, 104,
106, 108, 110, 117, 122, 124,
126, 129, 130, 142, 145, 147,
148, 157, 158, 162, 163, 164,
165, 166, 169, 173, 175, 177,
178, 179, 180, 182, 183, 184,
190, 191, 195, 203, 205, 207,
217, 230, 231, 232, 233, 234,
235, 236, 238, 239, 241, 247,
255, 256, 265, 276, 284
spirituality 18, 49, 56, 58, 62, 64, 73,
75, 76, 103, 107, 122, 131, 143,
145, 146, 147, 150, 151, 155, 157,
173, 204, 207, 221, 224, 226,
230, 237, 277
Still 2, 3, 8, 11, 18, 19, 26, 40, 41, 43,
47, 48, 51, 56, 58, 60, 67, 69,
75, 76, 81, 83, 88, 90, 92, 96,
97, 114, 119, 120, 123, 125, 126,
127, 130, 142, 155, 170, 178,
191, 198, 199, 207, 208, 214,
218, 219, 222, 225, 236, 240,
247, 250, 251, 252, 253, 255,
256, 259, 265, 274
subjective 50, 88, 105, 106, 112, 119,
121, 123, 129, 130, 132, 142,
148, 149, 150, 191, 239
sweat lodge 12, 29, 49, 50, 52, 77, 78,
79, 155, 156, 157, 158, 159, 160,
164, 165, 166, 167, 169, 184,
185, 226, 237, 277

T

teacher v, 58, 61, 62, 67, 69, 80, 89,
113, 114, 126, 131, 139, 143,
153, 155, 175, 186, 193, 194,
224, 233, 237, 248
teleology 101
theology 97, 98, 108, 114, 118, 120,
121, 272
Thoreau xii, 86, 87, 123, 140, 261,
274, 275, 283

V

vision 35, 140, 150, 166, 169, 170, 171,
173, 175, 176, 177, 178, 179,
182, 183, 184, 185, 189, 190,
192, 204, 207, 208, 211, 212,
231, 235, 239, 240, 275, 277
Vision quest 166, 169, 170, 171, 173,
175, 178, 179, 182, 189, 192,
204, 207, 231
void 113, 124, 125, 126, 132, 133,
134, 136, 137, 151, 173, 207

W

Western 7, 8, 11, 19, 23, 26, 27, 29, 37,
38, 40, 42, 43, 45, 46, 49, 50,
51, 54, 55, 57, 58, 60, 62, 70,
71, 72, 73, 75, 76, 77, 79, 83,
84, 85, 86, 87, 88, 90, 93, 95,
96, 98, 99, 100, 101, 102, 103,
104, 105, 106, 109, 110, 117,
118, 119, 120, 121, 122, 123,
129, 130, 131, 133, 140, 141,
143, 145, 146, 148, 149, 150,
151, 153, 156, 157, 160, 162,
164, 166, 175, 180, 189, 191,
192, 195, 204, 207, 208, 225,
231, 233, 235, 236, 237, 240,
277, 279

Wheal 212, 213, 215, 216, 217, 218,
        221, 222, 234, 235, 237, 280,
        281, 282, 283
wisdom 10, 26, 41, 43, 44, 60, 62, 77,
        79, 85, 107, 109, 115, 119, 121,
        122, 131, 149, 176, 177, 179,
        182, 186, 190, 193, 211, 216,
        224, 231
Wolf vii, 31, 32, 49, 57, 58, 59, 60, 61,
        62, 63, 65, 66, 67, 79, 99, 166,
        202, 203, 204, 239, 241, 261,
        265, 267, 268, 284, 291
womb 10, 78, 155, 156, 157, 163, 164,
        165, 175, 183, 184, 185, 189,
        208, 226, 233, 237, 244, 277

Y

yang 197, 198, 199, 202
yin 197, 198, 202

Z

Zen 114, 117, 150, 158, 275

ABOUT THE AUTHOR

Dr. John Hughes practices traditional osteopathic and integrative medicine in Colorado. Dr. Hughes graduated from the Arizona College of Osteopathic Medicine and received training in family practice at the University of Arizona. His current clinic, Aspen Integrative Medicine, provides the latest innovations in modern and natural medicine, including regenerative injection therapy for sports injuries as well as a patented protocol for traumatic brain injury.

Dr. Hughes descends from the Wolf Clan of the Eastern Band of the Cherokee Nation. Dr. Hughes honors the wolf and his Cherokee ancestors through his intuitive medical practice and way of life. Fifth World Medicine is his first book.

Dr. Hughes currently lives near Aspen, Colorado with his wife, dog, and two cats. He regularly enjoys trail running and skiing in the wilderness near his home.

fifthworldmedicine.com

Printed in the United States
by Baker & Taylor Publisher Services